The Address Book

THE ADDRESS BOOK

How to Reach Anyone Who's Anyone

Michael Levine

A Perigee Book

Perigee Books
are published by
The Putnam Publishing Group
200 Madison Avenue
New York, New York 10016

Library of Congress Cataloging in Publication Data

Levine, Michael.
The address book.

Rev. ed. of: How to reach anyone who's anyone. 1980.
1. United States—Directories.   2. United States—
Social registers.   I. Levine, Michael. How to reach any-
one who's anyone.   II. Title.
E154.5.L48   1984   973'.025   83-24980
ISBN 0-399-50988-7

First Perigee printing, 1984
Printed in the United States of America
1 2 3 4 5 6 7 8 9

ACKNOWLEDGMENTS

Each person listed here has been so helpful that "thank you" doesn't seem sufficient. So, to each—my love:

My agents Bart Andrews and Sherry Robb; editor Judy Linden and her Putnam comrades, Karla Olson, Sam Mitnick and Ron Green; my friends, Sandy Charon, Arthur and Marilyn Levine, and Julie Nathanson.

The following people helped me track down the heretofore inaccessible notables contained in this book: Jennifer Rose, Barbara Spector, Dionne Bennett, Shonte' Clayton, Andrew Stein, and Diana Fung.

(To the dozens and dozens of people who, along the way, said this book would never work—eat your heart out!)

It's been four years since the first edition of *The Address Book* (originally titled *How to Reach Anyone Who's Anyone*) was published. It was dedicated, with love, to my wife, Darlene. This second edition also is dedicated, with love, to my wife, Darlene. It's nice that some things don't change.

Introduction

The biggest question regarding writing to notables is, "How can I make sure the notable receives my letter?" Well, the number one reason why mail to notables is left unanswered is that it is addressed improperly and never reaches its intended destination. A letter simply addressed to "Barbra Streisand, Hollywood, California" will find its way only to the dead-letter file of the post office. And so, here's this book: complete, accurate addresses that will get your mail to the homes, offices, agents, studios, or managers of the addressees.

The following are other commonly asked questions:

Q. Will the notable personally read my letter?
A. I have been unable to find even one notable, no matter how busy or important—ranging right up to the President of the United States—who doesn't personally read some of his mail. That doesn't mean notables read and answer every single piece, but it should offer encouragement to people who write to them. Amazing things have been accomplished with letters as long as they have the proper mailing addresses.

Q. Are there any professional tricks you can reveal that might improve the chances of having my letter read and answered?
A. Yes! Here are several important things to remember. . . .
 1. Always include a self-addressed envelope. This is the single most important bit of advice I can offer to people writing to notables. Because of the unusually high volume of mail they receive, *anything* you can do to make it easier for them to respond is going to work in your favor.
 2. Keep your letters short and to the point. Notables are usually extremely busy people, and long letters tend to be set aside for "future" consideration. For instance, if you want an autographed picture of your favorite TV personality, don't write three pages of prose to explain your request.
 3. Make your letter as easy to read as possible. This means type it or, at the very least, handwrite it *very neatly*. Avoid crayons, markers and even pencils. And don't forget to leave some margins on the paper.
 4. Be sure to include your name and address (even on all materials that you include with your letter, in the event the materials are

9

separated from your letter). You would be amazed how many people write letters without return addresses and then wonder why they never heard from the person to whom they wrote!

Q. What are the don'ts in writing to notables?
A. Actually, there are very few don'ts but here are some good general rules to follow.
1. Don't send food to notables. Due to spoilage and other security matters, it cannot be eaten anyway. (Would *you* eat a box of homemade brownies given to you by a total stranger??)
2. Don't send—or ask for—money.
3. Don't wrap gifts in large boxes with yards of paper, string, and tape around them. In other words, not everyone is fortunate enough to have a crowbar on hand. And—again—don't forget to include your name and address on all material you send.

Q. Do corporation heads pay attention to mail from a single individual?
A. Wow, do they! Most corporation heads rose to their lofty positions because they were better problem-solvers than their company peers. Good corporation heads are zealous about finding solutions to written complaints (especially if you have sent copies of your complaint letters to appropriate consumer organizations). A recent survey of corporations showed that 88 percent of all letters of complaint were resolved. Therefore, the old adage, "When you have a problem, go to the top," appears to be accurate. Likewise, corporation executives greatly appreciate hearing good news (satisfaction, extra service, helpful employees, and so forth). For a sample complaint letter and additional tips, see page 13.

Q. What about politicians? Are they really interested in what I have to say?
A. You better believe it! Politicians have a standard rule of thumb: For every letter they receive, they estimate that 100 people who didn't take the time to write are thinking the same thought as the letter expresses. So you can calculate the effect of your single letter by multiplying it by 100!

Q. Do celebrities consider mail important?
A. Second only to money! All notables—especially entertainment figures—keep a very close watch on their mail. It is a real indication of what people are thinking and feeling. Often the notable is surrounded by a small group of close associates who tend to isolate the star from the public. Your letter helps break down this barrier.

Q. Why have you included infamous people in your book?
A. Where is it written that mail should only be filled with praise and congratulations? I thought people would enjoy shaking their fist at their favorite villain. So, go get 'em!

Q. What do most people say in their letters?
A. Usually people are very kind and sincere, writing what they would say or ask if they had the opportunity to do so in person. This is especially true

of children who are *extremely* honest. On the other hand, infamous people and others who are out of favor with the public predictably receive hostile and angry letters.

Q. What if my letter is returned to me?

A. Most of the people listed in *The Address Book* are movers and shakers, and, thus, highly transient, changing their addresses far more often than the average person. Their mail is usually forwarded to them, but occasionally a letter may be returned to the sender. If this should happen to your letter, first check to make sure that you have copied the address correctly. If you wish to locate another address for the person to whom you are writing, begin your search by writing to him/her in care of the company or association with which they have been most recently associated. For example, if a musician or singer has last recorded an album with a specific record company, write in care of that company; a sports figure might be contacted through the last team he/she was associated with; an author through his/her most recent publisher; and so forth.

Again, I cannot emphasize enough how many truly amazing things have happened as a result of a single letter. Remember eleven-year-old Samantha Smith of Maine? She wrote an emotional letter to Soviet Premier Yuri Andropov, urging world peace. Before too long she was off to Russia where she spent two weeks as an unofficial diplomat. World peace as the result of a letter? Why not?

Michael Levine

Tips for Writing an Effective Complaint Letter

1. Include your name, address, and home and work phone numbers.
2. Type your letter, if possible. If it is handwritten, be sure it is neat and legible.
3. Make it brief and to the point. Include all pertinent facts (i.e., date of transaction, item involved, store, and so forth) and what you believe would be a fair and just settlement of the problem. Attach documentation to support your case; send copies, not originals.
4. Remember, the person reading your letter is not personally responsible for your problem, but may be responsible for solving it. Therefore, avoid writing a sarcastic, threatening, or angry letter. It may lessen your chances of getting the complaint resolved.
5. Send copies of your letter to a lawyer, the Better Business Bureau, Chamber of Commerce, consumer advocates, and so forth. This technique carries a lot of weight and shows that you mean business.
6. Keep copies of your letter and all related documents and information.

Sample Complaint Letter

Your Address
City, State, Zip Code
Date

Appropriate Person
Company Name
Street Address
City, State, Zip Code

Dear *(Appropriate Name)*:

Specific background information___ On *(date)*, I purchased a *(name of product with serial or model number)*. Upon taking it home and following the enclosed instructions for

13

State problem clearly and concisely————————————————

its use, I discovered that your product does not perform satisfactorily. Specifically, it does not *(describe function)* as I expected it would based on the advertising and packaging.

Ask for satisfaction————————

Enclose copies, not originals————

State time parameter——————

Include phone numbers—————

I would appreciate your *(state the action you want)*. Enclosed you will find copies of my records *(receipt, warranty, guarantee, canceled check, etc.)* to verify the purchase. I look forward to your reply within *(reasonable period of time)* before seeking third-party assistance. You may contact me at the above address or by phone at *(home and office numbers)*.

Thank you for your prompt resolution of this problem.

Sincerely,

Your Name

Send copies of letter to all appropriate persons and organizations————————————

cc: Chamber of Commerce
    Related Associations
    Dealer Through Whom Product Was Purchased
    Local Media or Consumer Advocate

How to Use This Book

Most of the entries in this book are names of persons notable in some field. You also will find many companies, agencies, and institutions. These are listed under the name of the organization. This is done so that you can find the address of IBM, for example, without knowing the name of its president. The entry will then give you the address *and* the president's name.

The Address Book is compiled alphabetically for easy reference. There are, however, two exceptions:

—All of the telephone companies are listed alphabetically in a separate group labeled "Telephone Companies" under the letter *T*.
—All of the state utility commissions are listed alphabetically in a separate group labeled "Utility Companies" under the letter *U*.

This has been done to make it easier to find the address and person you need to contact.

Are *YOU* Anybody?

The Address Book is updated regularly and you can play an active role in this procedure. If you are notable in any field, or know someone who is, send the name, mailing address, and some documentation of the notability (newspaper clippings are effective) for possible inclusion in our next edition.

Also, we are very interested in learning of any success stories that may have resulted from *The Address Book*.

Thank you.

> Michael Levine, Author
> *The Address Book*
> 967 N. LaCienega Blvd.
> Los Angeles, CA 90069

A

Aach, Herbert
404 E. 14th St.
New York, NY 10009
Painter

Aamco Transmissions, Inc.
408 E. 4th St.
Bridgeport, PA 19405
Robert Morgan, Chairman

Aaron, Henry
1611 Adams Dr., SW
Atlanta, GA 30311
*Former baseball player, holds record
for most total career home runs*

ABBA
Box 26072 S-100 41
Stockholm, Sweden
Rock group

Abbe, Elfriede Martha
Manchester Applewood
Center, VT 05255
Sculptor; graphic artist

Abbott, Berenice
% Horizon Press
156 Fifth Ave.
New York, NY 10010
Photographer

Abbott, George
1270 Avenue of the Americas
New York, NY 10020
Playwright; producer

Abbott, Preston Sargent
801 N. Pitt St.
Alexandria, VA 22314
Psychologist

Abdul-Aziz Al Saud, Fahd ibn
Office of the Prime Minister
Riyadh, Saudi Arabia
*King & Prime Minister, Saudi
Arabia—since 1982*

Abel, Robert, Jr.
1300 Harrison St.
Wilmington, DE 19806
Ophthalmologist

Abell, George Ogden
Department of Astronomy
UCLA
Los Angeles, CA 90024
Educator; astronomer

Abell, Murray Richardson
American Board of Pathology
112 Lincoln Center
5401 W. Kennedy Blvd.
Tampa, FL 33623
Pathologist

Abelson, Alan
22 Cortlandt St.
New York, NY 10007
Editor; columnist

Aberastain, Jose Manuel
Dance Division
Southern Methodist University
Dallas, TX 75275
Ballet master

Abernathy, Ralph David
1040 Gordon St., SW
Atlanta, GA 30310
Clergyman; civil rights activist

Abourezk, James G.
1129 20th St., NW, Suite 500
Washington, DC 20036
*Lawyer; former U.S. Senator (D),
South Dakota, 1973–1978*

Abrahamsen, Samuel
Department of Judaic Studies
Brooklyn College
Brooklyn, NY 11210
Foremost Jewish educator

Abrams, Herbert Leroy
Harvard Medical School
Boston, MA 02115
Radiologist; educator

Abrams, Martin B.
41 Madison Ave.
New York, NY 10010
*Toy manufacturing company
executive (Mego Corp.)*

Abzug, Bella
76 Beaver St.
New York, NY 10005
*Feminist; former U.S.
Congresswoman (D), New York,
1971–1977*

**Academy of Motion Picture Arts &
Sciences**
8949 Wilshire Blvd.
Beverly Hills, CA 90211
*James M. Roberts, Executive
Director*

Accuracy in Media
1341 G St., Suite 312
Washington, DC 20008
Reed Irvine, Editor

Acker, Joseph Edington, Jr.
1928 Alcoa Hwy.
Knoxville, TN 37920
Cardiologist

Ackerman, Forrest
(Mr. Science Fiction)
2495 Glendower Ave.
Hollywood, CA 90027
*Collector of monster memorabilia
and science fiction*

Ackerman, Harry S.
1438 N. Gower St.
Hollywood, CA 90028
Motion picture company executive

Ackerman, Helen Page
405 Hilgard Ave.
Los Angeles, CA 90024
*University of California, Berkeley,
librarian*

**Action for Children's Television
(ACT)**
46 Austin St.
Newtonville, MA 02160
Peggy Charren, President

Acuff, Roy Claxton
2510 Franklin Rd.
Nashville, TN 37204
Country and western entertainer

Aczel, Janos Dezso
Centre for Information Theory
Faculty of Mathematics
University of Waterloo
Waterloo, ON N2L 3G1
Canada
Mathematician

Adabuse
% Jeffrey L. Black
81-13 Broadway
Elmhurst, NY 11373
Jerry L. Blask, President—
organization of businessmen in New
York who protested the splitting of
the Manhattan Yellow Pages into
two volumes

Adair, Red
8705 Katy Fwy., #302
Houston, TX 77024
Fire fighter

Adam, Helen
223 E. 82d St.
New York, NY 10028
Poet

Adam and Eve
1008 White Oak
Arlington Heights, IL 60005
Emil Benitez, Secretary—interested
in divorce reform

Adam and The Ants
CBS
51 W. 52d St.
New York, NY 10019
Rock group

Adams, Alvin
Phoenix Suns
Fink's Greyhound Bldg.
2910 N. Central
Phoenix, AZ 85012
Prof. basketball player

Adams, Ansel
Rte. 1, Box 181
Carmel, CA 93923
Photographer

Adams, Cindy
1050 Fifth Ave.
New York, NY 10028
Syndicated entertainment columnist

Adams, Don
David Licht
9171 Wilshire Blvd.
Beverly Hills, CA 90210
Actor

Adams, Edie
3633 Crownridge Dr.
Sherman Oaks, CA 91403
Actress

Adams, Harriet Stratemeyer
(Carolyn Keene)
Stratemeyer Syndicate
197 Maplewood Ave.
Maplewood, NJ 07040
Author

Adams, James Luther
60 Francis Ave.
Cambridge, MA 02138
Theologian

Adams, Joey
1050 Fifth Ave.
New York, NY 10028
Entertainer

Adams, Larry
969 Park Circle
Boone, IA 50036
Blank check collector

Adams, Maud
151 El Camino
Beverly Hills, CA 90212
Actress

Adams, Park, III (Pepper Adams)
8715 Avenue B
Brooklyn, NY 11236
Musician

Adams, Richard Newbold
Department of Anthropology
University of Texas at Austin
Austin, TX 78712
Anthropologist; educator

Adams, Sherman
Pollard Rd.
Lincoln, NH 03251
Former Governor of New
Hampshire (R), 1949–1953; former
adviser to President Eisenhower,
1953–1958

Adams, Stanley
ASCAP
1 Lincoln Plaza
New York, NY 10023
Lyricist

Adams, William Roger
Box 1987
St. Augustine, FL 32084
University historian

Adamson, John William
Division of Hematology
Department of Medicine
University of Washington
Seattle, WA 98195
Hematologist

Addams, Charles Samuel
% *The New Yorker* magazine
25 W. 43d St.
New York, NY 10036
Cartoonist

Adelman, Kenneth L.
Arms Control & Disarmament
Agency
Department of State Building
Washington, DC 20451
Director, 1983–present

Adisman, I. Kenneth
100 Central Park South
New York, NY 10019
Dentist

Adler, Freda Schaffer
(Mrs. G. O. W. Mueller)
School of Criminal Justice
Rutgers University
15 Washington St.
Newark, NJ 07109
Criminologist; educator

Adler, Louis Kootz
1630 Bank of Southwest Bldg.
Houston, TX 77002
Investor

Adler, Richard
8 E. 83d St.
New York, NY 10028
Composer; lyricist

Adolfo, Sardina
Adolfo Inc.
538 Madison Ave.
New York, NY 10022
Fashion designer

Adrenal Metabolic Research Society
of the Hypoglycemia Foundation
153 Pawling Ave.
Troy, NY 12180
*Marilyn H. Light, Executive
Director*

Adriani, John
Charity Hospital
New Orleans, LA 70140
Physician, anesthesiologist

Aerosmith
% Leber-Krebs
65 W. 55th St.
New York, NY 10019
Rock group

Aetna Life & Casualty Co.
151 Farmington Ave.
Hartford, CT 06156
John H. Filer, Chairman

Agent Orange Victims International
27 Washington Square North
New York, NY 10003
Frank McCarthy, President

Aghayan, Ray (Raymond G.)
51 W. 52d St.
New York, NY 10019
Costume designer; TV producer

Agnew, James Kemper
McCann-Erickson Inc.
485 Lexington Ave.
New York, NY 10017
Advertising agency executive

Agnew, Spiro
1517 Ritchie Hwy., #207
Arnold, MD 21012
*Former U.S. Vice President,
1969–1973*

Agosta, Karin Engstrom
40 Guernsey St.
Stamford, CT 06904
Book club director

Ahmanson, William Hayden
3731 Wilshire Blvd
Los Angeles, CA 90010
Savings & loan & insurance holding company executive

Ailey, Alvin
Alvin Ailey American Dance Theater
1515 Broadway
New York, NY 10036
Choreographer

Ainge, Danny
Boston Celtics
Boston Gardens
North Station
Boston, MA 02114
Prof. basketball player

Ainsworth-Land, George Thomas
6950 Washington Ave.
S. Eden Prairie, MN 55344
Philosopher; author

Air Supply
Jet Management
9959 Beverly
Beverly Hills, CA 90210
Rock group

Aitay, Victor
Chicago Symphony Assn.
220 S. Michigan Ave.
Chicago, IL 60604
Violinist

Aitken, Webster
128 Christopher St.
New York, NY 10014
Pianist

Akins, Claude
151 El Camino
Beverly Hills, CA 90212
Actor

Aks, Frank P.
954 Armfield Circle
Norfolk, VA 23505
Titanic survivor

Alabama
% D. Morris
816 19th Avenue South
Nashville, TN 37203
Rock group

Aladjem, Silvio
2160 S. First Ave.
Maywood, IL 60153
Educator; obstetrician & gynecologist

Al-Anon Family Group Headquarters
One Park Ave.
New York, NY 10016
Susan Handley, Public Information Coordinator

al-Assad, Hafez
Office of the President
Damascus, Syria
President, Syria—since 1971

Albee, Edward Franklin
14 Harrison St.
New York, NY 10013
Author; playwright

Alberghetti, Anna Maria
2337 Benedict Canyon Dr.
Beverly Hills, CA 90210
Singer; actress

Albert, Eddie
ICM
8899 Beverly Blvd.
Los Angeles, CA 90048
Actor

Alberto-Culver Co.
2525 Armitage Ave.
Melrose Park, IL 60160
Leonard H. Lavin, Chairman

Albrecht, Ronald Frank
Department of Anesthesiology
Michael Reese Medical Center
Chicago, IL 60616
Anesthesiologist

Albright, Jack Lawrence
Purdue University
West Lafayette, IN 47907
Animal scientist

23

Alcoholics Anonymous
P.O. Box 459, Grand Central
Station
New York, NY 10017
Robert Pearson, President

Alcott, Amy Strum
Little Women Enterprises, Inc.
P.O. Box 956
Pacific Palisades, CA 90272
Prof. golfer

Alda, Alan
Warner Bros.
4000 Warner Blvd.
Burbank, CA 91505
Actor

Aldrin, Edwin (Buzz)
400 Maryland Ave., SW
Washington, DC 20546
Former astronaut

Alexander, Denise
1888 Century Park East, #1400
Los Angeles, CA 90067
*Actress; photojournalist;
writer*

Alexander, Jane
RR 2
Gordon Rd.
Carmel, NY 10512
Actress

Alexander, Shana
444 Madison Ave.
New York, NY 10022
Journalist; author; lecturer

**Alexander Graham Bell Assn. for
the Deaf**
3417 Volta Pl., NW
Washington, DC 20007
Sara Conlon, Ph. D., Director

Ali, Muhammad
P.O. Box 76972
Los Angeles, CA 90076
*Retired world heavyweight
champion boxer*

Allam, Mark Whittier
3451 Walnut St.
Philadelphia, PA 19174
*Veterinarian; former university
administrator*

Allegheny International
2 Oliver Plaza
Pittsburgh, PA 15222
Robert J. Buckley, Chairman

Allen, Byron
1875 Century Park East, #2200
Los Angeles, CA 90067
Actor

Allen, George
% CBS Sports
51 W. 52d St.
New York, NY 10019
Football coach & commentator

Allen, Karen
Box 668
San Anselmo, CA 94960
Actress

Allen, Marcus
Los Angeles Raiders
332 Center St.
El Segundo, CA 90245
Prof. football player

Allen, Nancy
1888 Century Park East, #1400
Los Angeles, CA 90067
Dancer; actress

Allen, Peter
9665 Wilshire Blvd., #200
Los Angeles, CA 90212
Singer

Allen, Steve
15201 Burbank Blvd.
Van Nuys, CA 91401
Television humorist; songwriter

Allen, Woody
930 Fifth Ave.
New York, NY 10021
Actor; writer; director

Alley, Kirstie
9169 Sunset Blvd.
Los Angeles, CA 90069
Actress

Allison, Robert Arthur
140 Church St.
Hueytown, AL 35020
Prof. stock car driver

Allman, Gregory Lenoir
% Paragon Agency
560 Arlington Pl.
Macon, GA 31208
Musician; composer

The Allstate Group
40 Allstate Plaza
Northbrook, IL 60062
Donald F. Craib, Jr., Chairman of Board

Allured, Donald
221 95th St., N
Birmingham, AL 35206
U.S. expert on handbell ringing

Allyson, June
865 Comstock Ave.
Los Angeles, CA 90024
Actress

Alopecia Areata Foundation
P.O. Box 5027
Mill Valley, CA 94941
Support group for people who have suffered permanent hair loss

Alpert, Herb
% A & M Records
1416 N. La Brea Ave.
Hollywood, CA 90028
Record company executive, musician

Alpo
Allen Products
RD 3
Allentown, PA 18103
Joseph Sestak, President—dog food company

al-Qaddafi, Colonel Muammar
State Offices
Tripoli, Libya
Head of State, Libya—since 1969

Alston, Walter Emmons
Dodger Stadium
1000 Elysian Park Ave.
Los Angeles, CA 90012
Former major league baseball manager, Los Angeles Dodgers

Alternatives to Abortion International
Hillcrest Hotel, Suite 511
231 16th St.
Toledo, OH 43624
Core Maier, Executive Director

Altman, Nancy Addison
Ryan's Hope
433 W. 53d St.
New York, NY 10019
Actress

Altman, Robert B.
1861 S. Bundy Dr.
Los Angeles, CA 90025
Film director; writer; producer

Alzado, Lyle
Los Angeles Raiders
332 Center St.
El Segundo, CA 90245
Prof. football player

Aman, Reinhold
331 S. Greenfield Ave.
Waukesha, WI 53186
Expert on profanity & cursing

Ameche, Don
5555 Melrose Ave.
Los Angeles, CA 90038
Actor

American Anorexia Nervosa Assn.
133 Cedar Ln.
Teaneck, NJ 07666
Estelle Miller, Founder

American Automobile Assn.
8111 Gatehouse Rd.
Falls Church, VA 22042
Mr. J. B. Creal, President

25

American Bar Assn.
1155 E. 60th St.
Chicago, IL 60637
*Thomas H. Gonser, Executive
Director*

American Broadcasting Co.
1330 Avenue of the Americas
New York, NY 10019
Leonard H. Goldenson, Chairman

American Can Co.
American Ln.
Greenwich, CT 00830
W. S. Woodside, Chairman

American Checker Federation
3475 Belmont Ave.
Baton Rouge, LA 70808
W. B. Grandjean, Secretary, editor

American Chiropractic Assn.
1916 Wilson Blvd.
Arlington, VA 22201
*Gerald M. Brassard, Executive
Director*

American Council of the Blind
1211 Connecticut Ave., NW
Suite 506
Washington, DC 20036
*Oral O. Miller, National
Representative*

American Dental Assn.
211 E. Chicago Ave.
Chicago, IL 60611
John M. Coady, Executive Director

American Diabetes Assn.
2 Park Ave.
New York, NY 10016
*Robert S. Bolan, Executive Vice
President*

American Digestive Disease Society
420 Lexington Ave., #1644
New York, NY 10017
*Martin I. Hossner, Executive
Director*

American Express Co.
American Express Plaza
New York, NY 10004
James D. Robinson III, Chairman

American Federation of Labor &
Congress of Industrial Organizations
(AFL-CIO)
815 16th St., NW
Washington, DC 20006
Lane Kirkland, President

American Federation of Teachers
11 Dupont Circle, NW
Washington, DC 20036
Albert Shanker, President

American Foundation of Jewish
Fighters, Camp Inmates and Nazi
Victims (Holocaust)
823 UN Plaza
New York, NY 10017
*Soloman Zinstein, President,
American Jewish fighters*

American Life Lobby (Right to Life)
% America's Family Center
Rte. #6, Box 162-F
Stafford, VA 22554
Judie Brown, President

American Medical Assn.
535 N. Dearborn St.
Chicago, IL 60610
*James H. Sammons, MD, Executive
Vice President*

American Meteorological Society
45 Beacon St.
Boston, MA 02108
*Kenneth C. Spengler, Executive
Director*

American Mosquito Control Assn.
5545 E. Shields Ave.
Fresno, CA 93727
*Thomas D. Mulhern, Executive
Director*

American Motors Corp.
2777 Franklin Rd.
Southfield, MI 48034
W. Paul Tippitt, Jr., Chairman

26

American Safety Razor Co.
Razor Blade Ln.
Verona, VA 24482
John R. Baker, Chairman

American Schizophrenia Assn.
Huxley Institute for Biosocial
Research
219 E. 31st St.
New York, NY 10016
Albracht Heyer, Executive Director

**American Society for Artificial
Internal Organs**
National Office
Box C
Boca Raton, FL 33482
Karen K. Burke, Executive Director

**American Society of Clinical
Hypnosis**
2250 E. Devon Ave., Suite 336
Des Plains, IL 60018
*William F. Hoffman, Jr., Executive
Director*

**American Society for the Prevention
of Cruelty to Animals (ASPCA)**
441 E. 92d St.
New York, NY 10028
*Dr. John F. Kullberg, Executive
Director*

American Stock Exchange
86 Trinity Pl.
New York, NY 10006
Arthur Levitt, Jr., Chairman

American Youth Enterprises
1533 S. Hi Point
Los Angeles, CA 90035
Tony L. Harris, Director

Ames, Charles Oakes
200 Park Ave.
New York, NY 10166
Stockbroker

Ames, Frank Anthony
National Symphony Orchestra
Kennedy Center for the Performing
Arts
Washington, DC 20566
Percussionist

Ames, Louise Bates
310 Prospect St.
New Haven, CT 06511
Child psychologist

Amory, Cleveland
140 W. 57th St.
New York, NY 10019
*Author; critic; animal-protection
activist*

Amos, John
15301 Ventura Blvd., #345
Sherman Oaks, CA 91403
Actor

Amos, Wally (Famous)
7181 W. Sunset Blvd.
Los Angeles, CA 90046
Cookie maker

Amsterdam, Morey
1290 Avenue of the Americas
Suite 264
New York, NY 10019
Actor; writer; producer

**Amyotrophic Lateral Sclerosis
Society of America (Lou Gehrig's
disease)**
4348 Van Nuys Blvd.
Sherman Oaks, CA 91403
Eames Bishop, President

**Anagnostopoulos, Constantine
Efthymios**
University of Chicago
950 E. 59th St.
Chicago, IL 60637
Cardiac surgeon

Andersen, Adel Edward
1616 H St., NW
Washington, DC 20006
*Farm organization executive (Master
National Grange)*

Andersen, Eric
% Vanguard Recording Society Inc.
71 W. 23d St.
New York, NY 10010
Composer; singer

27

Anderson, Bradley Jay
1439 Pebble Beach
Yuma, AZ 85364
Cartoonist

Anderson, Duwayne Marlo
Clemens Hall
SUNY at Buffalo
Buffalo, NY 14260
Polar scientist

Anderson, George Lee ("Sparky")
Detroit Tigers
Tiger Stadium
Detroit, MI 48216
Prof. baseball team manager

Anderson, Commodore Henry H., Jr.
New York Yacht Club
37 W. 44th St.
New York, NY 10036
Yachtsman

Anderson, Ian
% Premier Talent Agency
3 E. 54th St.
New York, NY 10022
Rock musician

Anderson, Jack
1401 16th St., NW
Washington, DC 20036
Columnist

Anderson, John Bayard
College of Law
University of Illinois
Urbana-Champaign
Urbana, IL 61801
Former U.S. Congressman (R), Illinois, 1961–1979; educator

Anderson, Kenny
Cincinnati Bengals
200 Riverfront Stadium
Cincinnati, OH 45202
Prof. football player

Anderson, Loni
8961 Sunset Blvd., Suite B
Los Angeles, CA 90069
Actress

Anderson, Lynn
Permian Records
3122 Sale St.
Dallas, TX 75219
Singer

Anderson, Marian
Marianna Farms
Joe's Hill Rd.
Danbury, CT 06811
Singer

Anderson, Poul William
% Scott Meredith
845 Third Ave.
New York, NY 10022
Science fiction author

Anderson, Raymond Charles
University of California, Irvine
101 City Drive South
Orange, CA 92668
Family physician

Anderson, Robert E.
5150 Rosecrans Ave.
Hawthorne, CA 90250
Toy manufacturing company executive (Mattel, Inc.)

Anderson, Will
P.O. Box 352
Croton Falls, NY 10519
Collector of beer paraphernalia

Andress, Ursula
9000 Sunset Blvd., #1112
Los Angeles, CA 90069
Actress

Andretti, Mario
53 Victory Ln.
Nazareth, PA 18064
Prof. race car driver

Andrew, Prince
Buckingham Palace
London, England
Son of Queen Elizabeth II

Andrews, Bart
Box 727
Hollywood, CA 90028
TV historian

Andrews, Julie
P.O. Box 666
Beverly Hills, CA 90213
Actress

Andrus, Cecil D.
900 Parkhill
Boise, ID 83702
*Former Secretary of the Interior (D),
1977–1981*

Angelou, Maya
% Dave Le Camera
Lordly & Dame Inc.
51 Church St.
Boston, MA 02116
Author

Angley, Rev. Ernest
Grace Cathedral
1055 Canton Rd.
Akron, OH 44312
TV evangelist

Anheuser-Busch Companies, Inc.
One Busch Pl.
St. Louis, MO 63118
August A. Busch III, Chairman

Anka, Paul
Box 100
Carmel, CA 93921
Singer; songwriter

Anne, Princess
Gatcombe Park
Gloucestershire, England
Daughter of Queen Elizabeth II

Ann-Margret
9665 Wilshire Blvd., #200
Beverly Hills, CA 90212
Actress

Ant, Adam
Box 4QT
London, W1A, England
Singer/rock group

Anti-Communist League of America
3100 Park Newport, Suite #101
Newport Beach, CA 92660
*John K. Crippen, Executive
Secretary*

Anton, Susan
15910 Ventura Blvd., #1602
Encino, CA 91436
Actress

Apple Computer, Inc.
20525 Mariani Dr.
Cupertino, CA 95014
Steven P. Jobs, Chairman

Arafat, Yasir
Palais Essaada La Marsa
Tunis, Tunisia
PLO leader

Aragones, Sergio
Mad magazine
485 Madison Ave.
New York, NY 10022
Cartoonist

Arby's Inc.
One Piedmont Center
3565 Piedmont Rd., NE
Atlanta, GA 30305
*J. T. McMahon, Chief Operating
Officer*

Arcaro, Eddie
ABC Sports
1330 Avenue of the Americas
New York, NY 10019
*Former jockey; sports broadcasting
journalist*

Archer, Ann
141 El Camino Dr., #110
Beverly Hills, CA 90212
Actress

Archerd, Army
Variety
1400 N. Cahuenga Ave.
Los Angeles, CA 90028
Entertainment columnist

Archibald, Nate
Boston Celtics
Boston Gardens
North Station
Boston, MA 02114
Prof. basketball player

Arden, Eve
% Glenn Rose
9665 Wilshire Blvd.
Beverly Hills, CA 90210
Actress

Ariyoshi, George R.
State Capitol
Honolulu, HI 96813
Governor of Hawaii, 1974–present

Arkin, Alan Wolf
141 El Camino Dr., #110
Beverly Hills, CA 90212
Actor

Arkoff, Samuel Z.
9200 Sunset Blvd., PH 3
Los Angeles, CA 90069
Motion picture executive; producer

Arledge, Roone
% ABC
1330 Avenue of the Americas
New York, NY 10019
ABC TV executive

Armani, Giorgio
650 Fifth Ave.
New York, NY 10019
Fashion designer

Armstrong, Anne
President's Foreign Intelligence
Advisory Board
Executive Office Bldg.
Washington, DC 20500
Chairperson

Armstrong, Garner Ted
Box 2525
Tyler, TX 75710
Television evangelist

Armstrong, Herbert W.
Worldwide Church of God
300 W. Green St.
Pasadena, CA 91105
Evangelist

Armstrong, Neil
RR #2, General Delivery
Lebanon, OH 45036
*Former astronaut, first man to walk
on the moon*

Arnason, Hjorvardur Harvard
4 E. 89th St.
New York, NY 10028
Art historian

Arnaz, Desi, Sr.
1920 Ocean Front
Del Mar, CA 92014
Actor; singer

Arnaz, Lucie Desiree
% Lucille Ball Productions
P.O. Box 900
Beverly Hills, CA 90213
Actress

Arness, James
Box 10480
Glendale, CA 91209
Actor

Arnod, Danny
% ABC
1438 N. Gower
Hollywood, CA 90028
Writer; director; producer

Arnold, Eddy
Box 97
Brentwood, TN 37027
Actor

Arnold, Gary Howard
1150 15th St., NW
Washington, DC 20005
Film critic

Arnold, Harry Loren, Jr.
Queens Physicians Office Bldg.
1380 Lusitana St., #412
Honolulu, HI 96813
Dermatologist; editor; author

30

Aronson, Howard Isaac
Department of Linguistics
University of Chicago
Chicago, IL 60637
Linguist; educator

Arquette, Rosanna
9255 Sunset Blvd., #910
Los Angeles, CA 90069
Actress

Arthur, Beatrice
151 El Camino
Beverly Hills, CA 90212
Actress

Arum, Robert
450 Park Ave.
New York, NY 10022
Lawyer; sports events promoter

ASH
2013 H St., NW
Washington, DC 20006
*John F. Banzhaf, Executive Director
(Action on Smoking and Health)*

Ashby, Hal
% Directors' Guild of America
7950 Sunset Blvd.
Hollywood, CA 90046
Film director

Ashe, Arthur
U.S. Tennis Assn.
51 E. 42d St.
New York, NY 10017
Former prof. tennis player

Asher, Frederick
1866 Sheridan Rd.
Highland Park, IL 60035
Mail-order company executive

Ashford & Simpson
% G. Sciffer
1155 N. La Cienega Blvd.
Los Angeles, CA 90069
Song team

Ashley, Elizabeth
151 El Camino
Beverly Hills, CA 90212
Actress

Asimov, Isaac
10 W. 66th St., Apt. 33A
New York, NY 10023
Author; biochemist

Asner, Ed
4348 Van Nuys Blvd., Suite 207
Sherman Oaks, CA 91403
*Actor; president of Screen Actors
Guild*

Aspin, Les
House Office Bldg.
Washington, DC 20515
*U.S Congressman (D), Wisconsin,
1971–present*

Assante, Armand
11726 San Vicente Blvd., #300
Los Angeles, CA 90049
Actor

The Associated Press
50 Rockefeller Plaza
New York, NY 10020
Frank Batten, Chairman

**Association of Professional Baseball
Physicians**
606 24th Avenue South
Minneapolis, MN 55454
Dr. Harvey O'Phelan, Chairman

Astaire, Fred
ICM
8899 Beverly Blvd.
Los Angeles, CA 90048
Actor; dancer

Astin, John Allen
Box 385
Beverly Hills, CA 90213
Actor; director; writer

Astin, Patty Duke
1888 Century Park East, #1400
Los Angeles, CA 90067
Actress

Astor, Mary
Motion Picture Country Home
23450 Calabasas Rd.
Woodland Hills, CA 91302
Actress

31

Atari, Inc.
1265 Borregas Ave.
Sunnyvale, CA 94086
Raymond Kassar, Chairman

Athow, Kirk Leland
Department of Plant Pathology
Purdue University
West Lafayette, IN 47907
Plant pathologist

Atkins, Chet
806 17th Avenue South
Nashville, TN 37203
Musician

Atkins, Christopher
8966 Sunset Blvd.
Los Angeles, CA 90069
Actor

Atlantic Richfield Co.
515 S. Flower St.
Los Angeles, CA 90071
Robert O. Anderson, Chairman

Attenborough, Sir Richard (Samuel)
1888 Century Park East, #1400
Los Angeles, CA 90067
Actor; producer; director

Atwater, Dr. Lynn
Department of Sociology
Seton Hall University
South Orange, NJ 07079
Author, The Extramarital
Connection: Sex, Intimacy, and
Identity *(a study of married women
who have affairs)*

AuCoin, Les
House Office Bldg.
Washington, DC 20515
*U.S. Congressman (D), Oregon,
1975–present*

Auer, Peter Louis
220 Devon Rd.
Ithaca, NY 14850
Plasma physicist, educator

Auerbach, Arnold Jacob ("Red")
Boston Celtics
Boston Garden
North Station
Boston, MA 02114
Prof. basketball executive

Austin, Tracy Ann
888 17th St., NW, #1200
Washington, DC 20006
Prof. tennis player

Autry, Orvon Gene
% Golden West Broadcasters
5858 W. Sunset Blvd.
Hollywood, CA 90028
*Singer; actor; radio entertainer;
broadcasting executive*

Avalon, Frankie
Richard O. Linke
4055 Kraft Ave.
Studio City, CA 91604
Singer

Avedon, Richard
407 E. 75th St.
New York, NY 10021
Photographer

Avildsen, John Guilbert
45 E. 89th St.
New York, NY 10028
Film director

Avis, Inc.
1114 Avenue of the Americas
New York, NY 10036
David J. Mahoney, Chairman

Avon Products, Inc.
9 W. 57th St.
New York, NY 10019
David W. Mitchell, Chairman

A & W Beverages, Inc.
1271 Avenue of the Americas
New York, NY 10020
Monroe Lowenkron, President

Axton, Hoyt Wayne
P.O. Box 614
Tahoe City, CA 95730
Singer; composer

32

Aykroyd, Dan
9200 Sunset Blvd , #428
Los Angeles, CA 90069
Actor

Aznavour, Charles
4 Avenue de Lieulee
78 Galluis, France
Singer; actor

B

Babbitt, Bruce Edward
Office of Governor
State Capitol, West Wing
Phoenix, AZ 85007
Governor of Arizona (D),
1978–present

Bacall, Lauren (Betty Joan Perske)
% STE
888 Seventh Ave.
New York, NY 10019
Actress

Bach, Barbara
% Bruce Grakal
1427 Seventh St.
Santa Monica, CA 90401
Actress

Bacharach, Burt
151 El Camino
Beverly Hills, CA 90212
Pianist; composer

Bachrach, Louis Fabian, Jr.
44 Hunt St.
Watertown, MA 02172
Portrait photographer

Bacon, James
Los Angeles Herald Examiner
1111 S. Broadway
Los Angeles, CA 90051
Syndicated entertainment columnist

Bacon, Kevin
7319 Beverly Blvd., #1
Los Angeles, CA 90036
Actor

Badham, John MacDonald
7475 Mulholland Dr.
Los Angeles, CA 90046
Motion picture director

Badran, Mudar
Office of the Prime Minister
Amman, Jordan
Prime Minister, Jordan—since 1980

Baeder, John
P.O. Box 5174
FDR Station
New York, NY 10022
Diner expert

Baer, Max, Jr.
10433 Wilshire Blvd., Suite 104
Los Angeles, CA 90024
Actor; producer; director

Baez, Joan
P.O. Box 1026
Menlo Park, CA 94025
Folk singer

34

Bailey, James
Houston Rockets
The Summit
Houston, TX 77046
Prof. basketball player

Bailey, Pearl
Box L
Lake Havasu City, AZ 86403
Singer

Bain, Barbara
% Bushell
9440 Santa Monica Blvd.
Beverly Hills, CA 90210
Actress

Bain, Conrad Stafford
1901 Avenue of the Stars
Los Angeles, CA 90067
Actor

Baio, Scott
5555 Melrose Ave.
Los Angeles, CA 90038
Actor

Baird, William Britton
40 Fifth Ave.
New York, NY 10011
Puppeteer

Baker, Bubba
Detroit Lions
1200 Featherstone Rd.
Box 4200
Pontiac, MI 48057
Prof. football player

Baker, Carol
ICM
8899 Beverly Blvd.
Los Angeles, CA 90048
Actress

Baker, Dusty
Los Angeles Dodgers
Dodger Stadium
1000 Elysian Park Ave.
Los Angeles, CA 90012
Prof. baseball player

Baker, Howard H., Jr.
Senate Office Bldg.
Washington, DC 20510
*U.S. Senator (R), Tennessee,
1966–present*

Baker, James Anderson
The White House
1600 Pennsylvania Ave., NW
Washington, DC 20500
*White House chief of staff, Reagan
Administration, 1981–present*

Baker, Joe Don
23339 Hatteras St.
Woodland Hills, CA 91364
Actor

Baker Street Irregulars
(Sherlock Holmes)
33 Riverside Dr.
New York, NY 10023
Julian Wolff, Commissionaire

Bakke, Allan
Mayo Clinic
200 First St., SW
Rochester, MN 55901
*Bakke decision—Supreme Court
decision against using racial quotas
for school admittance*

Bakshi, Ralph
7950 Sunset Blvd.
Los Angeles, CA 90046
Motion picture producer; director

Bald-Headed Men of America
40006 Arendell St.
Morehead City, NC 28557
Bald-headed John Capps, Founder

Baldridge, Malcolm
Department of Commerce
14th St. & Constitution Ave., NW
Washington, DC 20230
Secretary

Baldwin, James
% Edward Acton Inc.
17 Grove St.
New York, NY 10014
Writer

Ball, Lucille
P.O. Box 900
Beverly Hills, CA 90213
Actress; comedienne

Ballard, Greg
Washington Bullets
1 Harry S. Truman Dr.
Landover, MD 20786
Prof. basketball player

Ballard, Kaye
448 W. 44th St.
New York, NY 10036
Actress

Bally Manufacturing Corp.
2640 W. Belmont Ave.
Chicago, IL 60618
Robert E. Mullane, Chairman

Balsam, Martin Henry
141 El Camino Dr., #110
Beverly Hills, CA 90212
Actor

Bancroft, Anne
P.O. Box 900
Beverly Hills, CA 90213
Actress

Bancroft, John Basil
Dean's Office of Natural Science
Centre
University of Western Ontario
London, ON N6A 5B7
Ontario, Canada
Virologist

Bani Sadr, Abolhassan
16 Avenue Pont Royal
94230 Cachan
France
*Former President of Iran,
1977–1978*

Bankamerica Corp.
555 California St.
San Francisco, CA 94104
Leland S. Prussia, Chairman

Banks, Ernest (Ernie)
P.O. Box 10613
Chicago, IL 60610
*Baseball executive (Chicago Cubs);
former baseball player*

Banner, Bob
Pacific Design Center
8687 Melrose Ave., Suite M-20
Los Angeles, CA 90069
Television producer; director

Barbeau, Adrienne
P.O. Box 1334
North Hollywood, CA 91604
Actress

Barber, George
25 Juniper Ln.
Riverside, CT 06878
Big bands expert

Barbera, Joseph
Hanna-Barbera Productions
3400 W. Cahuenga Blvd.
Hollywood, CA 90068
*Motion picture & TV producer;
cartoonist*

Barbour, John
% Press Department, NBC
30 Rockefeller Plaza
New York, NY 10020
Comedian; writer

Bardot, Brigitte
La Madrique
St. Tropez, France
Actress

Barkin, Ellen
222 N. Canon Dr., #204
Beverly Hills, CA 90212
Actress

Barnard, Dr. Christiaan
The University of Cape Town
Medical School Observatory
Cape Town, 7925, South Africa
*Surgeon, performed world's first
heart-transplant operation*

36

Barnes, Clive Alexander
New York Post
210 South St.
New York, NY 10002
Drama & dance critic

Barnes, George Elton
Wayne Hummer & Co.
175 W. Jackson Blvd.
Chicago, IL 60603
Stockbroker

Barr, Doug
151 El Camino
Beverly Hills, CA 90212
Actor

Barr, Richard David
226 W. 47th St.
New York, NY 10036
Theater producer

Barrett, Rona
P.O. Box 1410
Beverly Hills, CA 90213
Columnist

Barrie, Barbara Ann
151 El Camino
Beverly Hills, CA 90212
Actress

Barrie, George
Fabergé Inc.
1343 Avenue of the Americas
New York, NY 10019
Cosmetics company executive

Barris, Chuck
Chuck Barris Productions
6430 Sunset Blvd.
Hollywood, CA 90028
TV producer

Barrow, Bernard Elliott
Theatre Department
Brooklyn College
Brooklyn, NY 11210
Actor; educator

Barrows, Marjorie
1615 Hinman Ave.
Evanston, IL 60201
Author

Barry, Gene
%0 S. Oppenheim Appel Dixon &
Co.
One Century Plaza
Los Angeles, CA 90067
Actor

Barry, Jack
Barry & Enright Productions Inc.
1888 Century Park East
Los Angeles, CA 90067
TV host; producer

Barry, Marion Shepilov, Jr.
Office of the Mayor
District Bldg.
14th & E Sts.
Washington, DC 20004
*Mayor of Washington (D),
1979–present*

Barrymore, Drew
8350 Santa Monica Blvd., #206
Los Angeles, CA 90069
Actress

Barrymore, John Blyth
8370 Wilshire Blvd.
Los Angeles, CA 90211
*Actor; half brother of Drew
Barrymore, grandson of John
Barrymore*

Barsolana, Frank
3 E. 54th St.
New York, NY 10022
Rock talent agent

Bartkowski, Steve
Atlanta Falcons
Suwanee Rd.
Suwanee, GA 30174
Prof. football player

Bartlett, Hal
9200 Sunset Blvd., Suite 908
Los Angeles, CA 90069
Motion picture producer & director

Barton-Jay, David
175 5th Ave., #3156
New York, NY 10010
Author, The Enema as an Erotic
Art

37

Barty, Billy John
10954 Moorpark St.
North Hollywood, CA 91602
Entertainer

Baryshnikov, Mikhail
American Ballet Theater
890 Broadway
New York, NY 10003
Ballet dancer; ballet director

Basehart, Richard
9255 Sunset Blvd., #1105
Beverly Hills, CA 90069
Actor

Basie, Count (William)
% Willard Alexander Inc.
660 Madison Ave.
New York, NY 10021
Composer; band leader

Baskin-Robbins
3600 N. River Rd.
Franklin Park, IL 60131
*Howard M. Dean, Jr., Chief
Operating Officer*

Bass, Louis Nelson
National Seed Storage Laboratory
Colorado State University
Fort Collins, CO 80523
*Government official; agronomist;
plant physiologist*

Bassey, Shirley
Sergio Novak
Villa Capricorn
55 Via Campone
6816 Bissone, Switzerland
Singer

Basu, Asit Prakas
Department of Statistics
University of Missouri
Columbia, MO 65201
Statistician

Basustow, Stephen
1649 11th St.
Santa Monica, CA 90404
Movie producer & distributor

Bates, Alan (Arthur)
% Michael Linnit
Chatto & Linnit Ltd.
Globe Theatre
Shaftesbury Ave.
London, W 1, England
Actor

Bates, Charles Carpenter
P.O. Box 191
Green Valley, AZ 85614
Oceanographer

Battelle, Kenneth Everette
Kenneth Salon
19 E. 54th St.
New York, NY 10022
Hairdresser

Baur, Captain Hans
Neuwiddersberg 38
8036 Herrsching/Ammersee
Federal Republic of Germany
Hitler's personal pilot

Bausch & Lomb
One Lincoln First Sq.
Rochester, NY 14604
Daniel E. Gill, President

Baxandall, Lee
Naturist Society
P.O. Box 132
Oshkosh, WI 54909
*Founder; expert on nude beaches
and clothes, optional life-styles*

Baxter, Anne
9255 Sunset Blvd., #910
Los Angeles, CA 90069
Actress

Baxter-Birney, Meredith
9255 Sunset Blvd., Suite #1105
Los Angeles, CA 90069
Actress

Bay, Howard
159 W. 53d St.
New York, NY 10019
Stage and film designer

Baylor, Donald Edward
California Angels
Anaheim Stadium
2000 State College Blvd.
Anaheim, CA 92806
Prof. baseball player

Beale, Betty (Mrs. George K. Graeber)
2926 Garfield St., NW
Washington, DC 20008
Columnist

Beals, Jennifer
132 S. Rodeo Dr., Suite 110
Beverly Hills, CA 90212
Actress

Beame, Abraham David
Advisory Committee for
Intergovernmental Relations
1111 20th St., NW
Washington, DC 20575
Former Mayor of New York City (D), 1973–1977

Bean, Alan L.
11711 Memorial Dr., Unit 267
Houston, TX 77024
Retired astronaut

Beaton, Roy Howard
175 Curtner Ave.
San Jose, CA 95125
Nuclear industry executive

Beatty, John Lee
107 W. 86th St.
New York, NY 10024
Scenic designer

Beatty, Warren
J.R.S. Productions
5451 Marathon St.
Hollywood, CA 90038
Actor; director

Beck, Julian
% M. L. Beck
800 West End Ave.
New York, NY 10025
Actor; producer; artist; writer; scenic designer

Beck, Marilyn
P.O. Box 11079
Beverly Hills, CA 90213
The world's most widely syndicated entertainment columnist

Becker, Robert Jerome
229 N. Hammes Ave.
Joliet, IL 60435
Allergist

Beckett, Samuel
% Ed. de Minuit
7 Rue B Palissy
75006 Paris, France
Nobel Prize winner; writer

Bedford, Brian
STE
888 Seventh Ave.
New York, NY 10019
Actor

Beebe, Robert Park
Box 1452
Carmel, CA 93921
Yacht designer

Beene, Geoffrey
550 Seventh Ave.
New York, NY 10018
Fashion designer

Begelman, David
MGM
10202 W. Washington Blvd.
Culver City, CA 90230
Motion picture executive

Beggs, James M.
National Aeronautics and Space
Administration (NASA)
400 Maryland Ave., SW
Washington, DC 20546
Administrator, 1981–present

Behrens, Hildegard
% Columbia Artists Management
165 W. 57th St.
New York, NY 10019
Opera singer

Beinecke, Edwin John
330 Madison Ave.
New York, NY 10017
Trading stamp company executive
(Sperry & Hutchinson)

Belafonte, Harry
Belafonte Enterprises Inc.
157 W. 57th St.
New York, NY 10019
Singer; concert artist; actor

Bel Geddes, Barbara
3970 Overland Ave.
Culver City, CA 90230
Actress

Bell, Buddy
Texas Rangers
Arlington Stadium
P.O. Box 1111
Arlington, TX 76010
Prof. baseball player

Bell, Stephen Scott (Steve)
ABC News
1717 DeSales St., NW
Washington, DC 20036
News correspondent, anchorman

Bell, Terrel H.
Department of Education
400 Maryland Ave., SW
Washington, DC 20202
Secretary

Bellamy, Ralph
116 E. 27th St.
New York, NY 10016
Actor

Bell & Howell Co.
7100 McCormick Rd.
Chicago, IL 60645
Donald N. Frey, Chairman

Beller, Kathleen
9255 Sunset Blvd., #1105
Los Angeles, CA 90069
Actress

Bellson, Louis
Box L
Lake Havasu, AZ 86403
Drummer

Bench, Johnny
Cincinnati Reds
100 Riverfront Stadium
Cincinnati, OH 45202
Former prof. baseball player

Benchley, Peter Bradford
Ashley Famous Agency Inc.
1301 Avenue of the Americas
New York, NY 10019
Author

Benedict, Dirk
1801 Century Park East, Suite 1132
Los Angeles, CA 90067
Actor; singer

Benford, Timothy
1464 Whippoorwill Way
Mountainside, NJ 07092
Expert on World War II

Bengelsdorf, Irving Swen
256 S. Arden Blvd.
Los Angeles, CA 90004
Science writer

Benjamin, Richard
222 N. Canon Dr., #204
Beverly Hills, CA 90212
Actor

Benko, Paul Charles
73 Garrison Ave.
Jersey City, NJ 07306
Chess grand master

Bennett, Harve
% Harve Bennett Productions
Paramount Studios
5451 Marathon St.
Los Angeles, CA 90038
TV & movie producer

Bennett, Lemond
Atlanta Falcons
Suwanee Rd.
Suwanee, GA 30174
Prof. football player

Bennett, Michael
890 Broadway
New York, NY 10003
Producer; director; choreographer;
writer

Bennett, Robert Frederick
5100 W. 95th St.
Prairie Village, KS 66208
Lawyer; former Governor of Kansas
(R), 1975–1979

Bennett, Tony
Agency for Performing Arts
120 W. 57th St.
New York, NY 10019
Entertainer

Benson, George
CBS
51 W. 52d St.
New York, NY 10019
Musician

Benson, Robby
1888 Century Park East, #1400
Los Angeles, CA 90067
Actor

Benton, Barbi
P.O. Box 3999
Pasadena, CA 91103
Actress

Bentsen, Lloyd M., Jr.
Senate Office Bldg.
Washington, DC 20510
U.S. Senator (D), Texas,
1971–present

Beresford, Bruce
151 El Camino
Beverly Hills, CA 90212
Actor

Bergen, Candice
1888 Century Park East, #1400
Los Angeles, CA 90067
Actress

Bergen, Polly
9229 Sunset Blvd., #813
Los Angeles, CA 90069
Business executive; actress

Bergeron, Victor J.
20 Cosmo Pl
San Francisco, CA 94109
Restaurateur, founded Trader Vic
chain

Bergman, Alan
Freedman & Freedman
911 Gateway West
Los Angeles, CA 90067
Lyricist

Bergman, Ingmar
620 36 Faro
Sweden
Film director

Bergman, Jules Verne
7 W. 66th St.
New York, NY 10023
Broadcast journalist

Bergman, Marilyn Keith
Freeman & Freeman
911 Gateway West
Los Angeles, CA 90067
Author; lyricist

Bergman, Martin
641 Lexington Ave.
New York, NY 10022
Film producer

Bergstein, Stanley Francis
333 N. Michigan Ave.
Chicago, IL 60601
Harness racing executive

Berkowitz, David
% Attica State Prison
Attica, NY 14011
Son of Sam, convicted mass
murderer

Berle, Milton
151 El Camino
Beverly Hills, CA 90212
Actor

Berlin, Irving
1290 Avenue of the Americas
New York, NY 10019
Composer

Berlitz Schools of Languages of America, Inc.
Research Park, Bldg. O
1101 State Rd.
Princeton, NJ 08540
Raphael G. Alberola, Chief Operating Officer

Bernardi, Herschel
1800 Avenue of the Stars, #500
Los Angeles, CA 90067
Actor

Bernazard, Tony
Seattle Mariners
419 Second Ave.
Seattle, WA 98104
Prof. baseball player

Bernstein, Jay
1888 Century Park East, #622
Los Angeles, CA 90067
Starmaker, manager

Bernstein, Leonard
205 W. 57th St.
New York, NY 10019
Composer

Bernt, Benno Anthony
Ray-O-Vac
101 E. Washington Ave.
Madison, WI 53703
Battery manufacturing company executive

Berra, Dale
Pittsburgh Pirates
600 Stadium Circle
Pittsburgh, PA 15212
Prof. baseball player

Berra, Lawrence ("Yogi")
Sutherland Rd.
Montclair, NJ 07042
Former prof. baseball player; former baseball coach (New York Mets); baseball coach (New York Yankees)

Berry, Chuck (Charles Edward Anderson Berry)
Bob Astor Management
23 Holly Dr.
La Place, LA 70068
Singer; composer

Berry, Ken
2115 Beverly Dr., #201
Beverly Hills, CA 90212
Actor

Bertinelli, Valerie
P.O. Box 1409
Beverly Hills, CA 90210
Actress

Beruh, Joseph
1650 Broadway
New York, NY 10036
Drama and film producer

Best, James Knowland
1901 Avenue of the Stars, Suite 500
Los Angeles, CA 90067
Actor

Better Education Thru Simplified Spelling, Inc.
2340 E. Hammond Lake Dr.
Bloomfield Hills, MI 48013
Chuck Kleber, President

Betty Crocker
9200 Wayzata Blvd.
Minneapolis, MN 55426
Steven H. Warhover, General Manager

Biaggi, Mario
2428 Rayburn House Office Bldg.
Washington, DC 20515
U.S. Congressman, New York (D), 1969–present

BIC Corp.
Wiley St.
Milford, CT 06460
Robert P. Adler, Chairman

Biden, Joseph R., Jr.
Senate Office Bldg.
Washington, DC 20510
U.S. Senator (D), Delaware, 1972–present

Big Bird
Children's Television Workshop
1 Lincoln Plaza
New York, NY 10023
Sesame Street *character*

Bignone, Major General Reynaldo
Office of the President
Buenos Aires, Argentina
President, Argentina—since 1982

Bikel, Theodore
% William Morris Agency
1350 Avenue of the Americas
New York, NY 10019
Actor, singer

Bilandic, Michael
Bilandic, Meistein, Richman,
Hallslinger and Young
33 N. La Salle St.
Chicago, IL 60602
Lawyer; former Mayor of Chicago
(D), 1977–1979

Bill, Tony
73 Market St.
Venice, CA 90291
Producer; director; actor

Billingsley, Barbara
3330 Barham Blvd., #1
Los Angeles, CA 90069
Actress

Bilson, Bruce
% Downwind Enterprises
4444 Radford Ave.
North Hollywood, CA 91607
Motion picture & television director

Bird, Caroline
60 Gramercy Park North
New York, NY 10010
Author, The Good Years: Life in
the 21st Century

Bird, Larry
Boston Celtics
Boston Garden
North Station
Boston, MA 02114
Prof. basketball player

Bird, Rose Elizabeth
350 McAllister St.
San Francisco, CA 94102
Chief Justice, California Supreme
Court, 1977–present

Birdsong, Otis
New Jersey Nets
185 E. Union Ave.
East Rutherford, NJ 07073
Prof. basketball player

Birmingham, Stephen
% Brandt & Brandt
1501 Broadway
New York, NY 10036
Author

Birnbaum, Robert Jack
86 Trinity Pl.
New York, NY 10006
Stock Exchange executive

Birney, David Edwin
Mab Productions Ltd.
% Zeiderman
10850 Wilshire Blvd.
Los Angeles, CA 90024
Actor

Bisexual Center
P.O. Box 26227
San Francisco, CA 94117
David N. Louren, Ed. D., President

Bisset, Jacqueline
ICM
8899 Beverly Blvd.
Los Angeles, CA 90048
Actress

Bixby, Bill
315 S. Beverly Dr., #211
Los Angeles, CA 90212
Actor

Black, Joe
PGA
100 Avenue of Champions
Palm Beach Gardens, FL 33410
Prof. golfer

Black, Shirley Temple (Mrs. Charles A. Black)
115 Lakeview Dr.
Woodside, CA 94062
Former ambassador; former actress

Black, William
425 Lexington Ave.
New York, NY 10017
Philanthropist; restaurant executive

Blackmun, Harry
U.S. Supreme Court
Washington, DC 20543
Supreme Court Justice, 1970–present

Blackwell, Lloyd Phalti
1212 Dubach St.
Ruston, LA 71270
Forester; employment consultant

Blackwell, Richard
719 S. Los Angeles St.
Los Angeles, CA 90014
Designer; fashion consultant; lists 10 best- and worst-dressed personalities of the year

Blaine, Vivian
% Becker & London
15 Columbus Circle
New York, NY 10023
Actress

Blair, Linda
1888 Century Park East, #622
Los Angeles, CA 90067
Actress

Blair, William Draper, Jr.
The Nature Conservancy
1800 N. Kent St.
Arlington, VA 22209
Conservationist

Blake, Robert
409 N. Camden Dr., #202
Beverly Hills, CA 90210
Actor

Blake, Stewart Prestley
734 Bliss Rd.
Longmeadow, MA 01106
Retired ice-cream company executive

Blanc, Mel
266 Toyopa Dr.
Pacific Palisades, CA 90272
Voice of Bugs Bunny, Porky Pig, etc.

Bloch, Henry Wollman
4410 Main St.
Kansas City, MO 64111
Tax preparation company executive (H & R Block)

Block, H & R, Inc.
4410 Main St.
Kansas City, MO 64111
Richard A. Bloch, Chairman

Block, Herbert Lawrence (Herblock)
Washington Post
Washington, DC 20005
Editorial cartoonist

Block, John Russling
U.S. Department of Agriculture
Office of the Secretary
14th St. & Independence Ave., SW
Washington, DC 20250
Secretary

Bloom, Claire
% Michael Linnit
Chatto & Linnit Ltd.
Globe Theatre
Shaftesbury Ave.
London, WI, England
Actress

Bloomingdale's
1000 Third Ave.
New York, NY 10022
Marvin S. Traub, Chairman

Blount, Lisa
7473 Mulholland Dr.
Los Angeles, CA 90046
Actress

Blount, Melvin Cornell (Mel)
Pittsburgh Steelers
Three Rivers Stadium
Pittsburgh, PA 15212
Prof. football player

44

Blue, Vida Rochelle
San Francisco Giants
Candlestick Park
San Francisco, CA 94124
Prof. baseball player

Blue Cross Assn.
676 St. Clair
Chicago, IL 60611
Bernard R. Tresnowski, President

Blue Shield Assn.
676 St. Clair
Chicago, IL 60611
Walter J. McNerney, President

BMW of North America
Campus 3
Montvale, NJ 07645
Fred Peterson, Manager

The Boeing Company
7755 E. Marginal Way South
Seattle, WA 98124
T. A. Wilson, Chairman

Boethea, Elvin
Houston Oilers
P.O. Box 1516
Houston, TX 77001
Prof. football player

Bogarde, Dirk
06 Chateauneuf De Grasse
France
Actor

Bogdanovich, Peter
ICM
8899 Beverly Blvd.
Los Angeles, CA 90048
Movie producer; director

Bohlin, John David
Code SC-7 NASA Headquarters
Washington, DC 22546
Space scientist

Bolger, Ray
618 N. Beverly Dr.
Beverly Hills, CA 90210
Actor

Bolger, William F.
U.S. Postal Service
475 L'Enfant Plaza, SW
Washington, DC 20260
Postmaster General, 1978–present

Bombeck, Erma
Field Newspaper Syndicate
1703 Kaiser Ave.
Irvine, CA 92714
Author; columnist

Bondurant, Bob
Highways 37 & 121
Sonoma, CA 95476
Runs school of high-performance driving

Bonerz, Peter
10201 W. Pico Blvd.
Los Angeles, CA 90035
Actor; director

Bono, Sonny (Salvatore)
Bono's Restaurant
8478 Melrose Ave.
Los Angeles, CA 90069
Singer; composer; restaurateur

Bonsall, Joseph Sloan, Jr.
% Jim Halsey Co. Inc.
5800 E. Skelly Dr.
Tulsa, OK 74135
Singer; member vocal group

Boone, Debby
9255 Sunset Blvd., #519
Los Angeles, CA 90069
Singer

Boone, Pat (Charles Eugene Boone)
ICM
8899 Beverly Blvd.
Los Angeles, CA 90048
Singer; actor

Borden, Inc.
277 Park Ave.
New York, NY 10017
E. J. Sullivan, Chairman

Borg, Bjorn
U.S. Tennis Assn.
51 E. 42d St.
New York, NY 10017
Prof. tennis player

Borge, Victor
ICM
40 W. 57th St.
New York, NY 10019
Comedian; pianist

Boschwitz, Rudy
Senate Office Bldg.
Washington, DC 20510
U.S. Senator (R), Minnesota,
1979–present

Bosley, Tom
ABC Press Relations
1330 Avenue of the Americas
New York, NY 10019
Actor

Bossy, Michael
New York Islanders
Nassau Coliseum
Uniondale, NY 11553
Prof. hockey player

Bothmer, Bernard V.
Brooklyn Museum
Brooklyn, NY 11238
Egyptologist; museum curator

Bottoms, Timothy
% Robert Raison Assocs.
9575 Lime Orchard Rd.
Beverly Hills, CA 90210
Actor

Bourgue, Pierre
4101 E. Sherbrooke St.
Montreal, PQ H1X 2B2
Canada
Nurseryman

Bouton, Jim
121 Cedar Ln.
Teaneck, NJ 07666
Owner big-league cards;
manufactures personalized baseball
cards; former baseball player

Bowen, Otis Ray
Department of Family Medicine
Long Hospital
1100 W. Michigan St.
Indianapolis, IN 46223
Former Governor of Indiana (R),
1973–1981; physician

Bowie, David
9665 Wilshire Blvd., #200
Beverly Hills, CA 90212
Musician; actor

Bowman, William Scott
Buffalo Sabres
Memorial Auditorium
Buffalo, NY 14202
Prof. hockey coach

Bowyer, (Charles) Stuart
Department of Astronomy
University of California, Berkeley
Berkeley, CA 94720
Astronomer; educator

Boy, John Buckner
U.S. Sugar Corp.
Clewiston, FL 33440
Sugar company executive

Boyce, Marian
RD 2
Watkins Glen, NY 14891
Salt & pepper shaker collector

Boyle, Barbara Dorman
11600 San Vicente Blvd.
Los Angeles, CA 90049
Film company executive (New
World Pictures)

Boyle, Peter
1888 Century Park East, #1400
Los Angeles, CA 90067
Actor

Bradbury, Ray Douglas
% Alfred A. Knopf Inc.
201 E. 50th St.
New York, NY 10022
Author of science fiction

Bradley, Bill
Senate Office Bldg.
Washington, DC 20510
U.S. Senator (D), New Jersey,
1979–present

Bradley, Ed
CBS News
524 W. 57th St.
New York, NY 10019
News correspondent

Bradley, Patricia Ellen
PGA
100 Avenue of Champions
Palm Beach Gardens, FL 33410
Prof. golfer

Bradley, Thomas (Tom)
Office of Mayor
City Hall
Los Angeles, CA 90012
Mayor (N-P), 1973–present

Bradshaw, Terry
Pittsburgh Steelers
Three Rivers Stadium
Pittsburgh, PA 15212
Prof. football player

Brady, James S.
The White House Office
1600 Pennsylvania Ave.
and Executive Office Bldg.
Washington, DC 20500
*Press secretary, 1981–present,
wounded in attempted presidential
assassination*

Bragg, Darrell Brent
2357 Main Mall UBC
Vancouver, BC V6T 2AZ
Canada
Nutritionist

Branch, Clifford (Cliff)
Los Angeles Raiders
332 Center St.
El Segundo, CA 90245
Prof. football player

Brand, Robert
505 West End Ave.
New York, NY 10024
Theatrical lighting designer

Brand, Vance DeVoe
Code CB, Lyndon B. Johnson
Space Center
Houston, TX 77058
Astronaut

Brando, Marlon
Tetiaroa Island
Tahiti
Actor

Branigan, Laura
Grand Trine Management
128 N. La Peer Dr.
Los Angeles, CA 90048
Singer

Braun, Edward Joseph
4904 N.W. 33d
Oklahoma City, OK 73122
Private investor

Bream, Julian
% Basil Douglas Ltd.
8 St. George's Terr.
London, NW1 8XJ, England
Classical guitarist

Breck
Shulton, Inc.
One Cyanamid Plaza
Wayne, NJ 07470
P. C. Baker, President

Breed, Allen Forbes
320 First St., NW
Washington, DC 20534
Correctional administrator

Brennan, Eileen Regina
1888 Century Park East, #1400
Los Angeles, CA 90067
Actress

Brennan, William, Jr.
U.S. Supreme Court
Washington, DC 20543
Supreme Court Justice, 1956–present

Brenner, David
William Morris Agency
1350 Avenue of the Americas
New York, NY 10019
Comedian

Brett, George Howard
Kansas City Royals
Harry S. Truman Sports Complex
P.O. Box 1969
Kansas City, MO 64141
Prof. baseball player

Bridges, Beau (Lloyd Vernet, III)
1888 Century Park East, #1400
Los Angeles, CA 90067
Actor

Bridges, Lloyd
1888 Century Park East, #1400
Los Angeles, CA 90067
Actor

Bridges, Todd
933 N. La Brea Ave.
Los Angeles, CA 90038
Actor

Brink, Linda H.
Harvard Medical School
25 Shattuck St.
Boston, MA 02115
Immunoparasitologist

Brinkley, Christie
151 El Camino
Beverly Hills, CA 90212
Model; actress

Brinkley, David
ABC News
1330 Avenue of the Americas
New York, NY 10019
News commentator

Brioni, Marquis Savini Glaetano
79 Via Barberini
Rome, Italy 00186
High-fashion design executive

Brisson, Fredrick
Brisson Productions Inc.
745 Fifth Ave.
New York, NY 10022
Theatrical producer

Bristol Myers Co.
345 Park Ave.
New York, NY 10022
*Richard L. Gelb, Chairman—
makers of Excedrin, Ban*

Britt, Mai
Box 525
Zephr Cove, NV 89448
Actress

Broccoli, Albert Romolo
G. S. Davis
1801 Century Park East, #1850
Los Angeles, CA 90067
Motion picture producer

Brock, Alice May
443 Commercial St.
Provincetown, MA 02657
*Restaurateur; author; former owner
of Alice's Restaurant*

Brock, Lou
13468 Forest Lake Dr.
St. Louis, MO 63141
Former baseball player

Brock, William E., III
Office of the Special Representative
for Trade Negotiations
1800 G St., NW
Washington, DC 20506
*Special representative for trade
negotiations*

Broderick, Matthew
151 El Camino
Beverly Hills, CA 90212
Actor

Brodie, John Riley
% NBC Sports Press Department
30 Rockefeller Plaza
New York, NY 10020
*TV sportscaster; former prof.
football player*

Brody, Clark Louis
1621 Colfax St.
Evanston, IL 60201
Clarinetist

Brody, Stuart Steven
389 Fifth Ave.
New York, NY 10016
Jewelry designer & manufacturer

Brokaw, Tom
NBC
30 Rockefeller Plaza
New York, NY 10020
Newscaster

Brolin, James
ICM
8899 Beverly Blvd.
Los Angeles, CA 90048
Actor

Bronson, Charles (Charles Buchinsky)
9169 Sunset Blvd.
Los Angeles, CA 90069
Actor

Brooke, Edward William
% O'Connor & Hannan
1919 Pennsylvania Ave., NW
Washington, DC 20006
Lawyer; former Senator (R), Massachusetts, 1967–1979

Brooke, Sorrell
4000 Warner Blvd.
Burbank, CA 91505
Actor

Brooks, Albert
% Gelfand and Macnow
1888 Century Park East
Los Angeles, CA 90067
Actor; writer; director

Brooks, Donald Marc
158 E. 70th St.
New York, NY 10021
Designer

Brooks, Herbert Paul
N.Y. Rangers
Madison Square Garden
4 Pennsylvania Plaza
New York, NY 10001
Hockey coach

Brooks, Mel
P.O. Box 900
Beverly Hills, CA 90213
Director; writer; actor

Brothers, Joyce Diane (Mrs. Milton Brothers)
151 El Camino
Beverly Hills, CA 90212
Psychologist

Brotman, Pierce
4024 Radford Ave.
Studio City, CA 91604
Actor

Brown, Helen Gurley
% Cosmopolitan
224 W. 57th St.
New York, NY 10019
Author; editor

Brown, J. Carter
Commission of Fine Arts
708 Jackson Pl., NW
Washington, DC 20006
Chairman

Brown, James
% Joyce Agency
435 E. 79th St.
New York, NY 10021
Singer; broadcasting executive

Brown, Jerry
450 N. Roxbury Dr.
Beverly Hills, CA 90210
Former Governor of California, 1974–1982

Brown, Jim
Columbia Pictures
Columbia Plaza
Burbank, CA 91505
Former football player; actor

Brown, John Y.
State Capitol
Frankfort, KY 40601
Governor of Kentucky, 1980–present

Brown, Louise
Oldham, England
First test-tube baby

Brown, Phyllis George
Cave Hill Ln.
Lexington, KY 40511
Former Miss America; sports commentator

Brown, Robert K.
Survive magazine
5735 Arapahoe Ave.
Boulder, CO 80303
*Publisher, Survive, magazine
devoted to surviving a nuclear
holocaust*

Browne, Dik
% King Features
235 E. 45th St.
New York, NY 10017
Cartoonist

Browne, Jackson
% Peter Golden & Assocs.
1952 Cross Roads of the World
Hollywood, CA 90028
Singer; songwriter

Brunner, Scott
New York Giants
Giants Stadium
East Rutherford, NJ 07073
Prof. football player

Bryan, Leslie Aulls
34 Fields
East Champaign, IL 61820
Transportation economist

Bryan, Richard
Office of Governor
Capitol Bldg.
Carson City, NV 89710
*Governor of Nevada (D),
1983–present*

Bryant, Anita Jane
% Protect America's Children
300 Broad St.
Selma, AL 36701
*Entertainer; antihomosexual
crusader*

Bryant, Bobby Lee
Minnesota Vikings
9520 Viking Dr.
Eden Prairie, MN 55344
Prof. football player

Brynner, Yul
% Mitch Leigh Co.
1414 Avenue of the Americas
New York, NY 10079
Actor

Brzezinski, Zbigniew
% School of Government
Columbia University
New York, NY 10027
*Former Assistant to the President for
National Security affairs,
1977–1981; author*

Buchwald, Art
1750 Pennsylvania Ave., NW
Washington, DC 20006
Columnist

Buckingham, Lindsey
Penguin Promotions
1420 N. Beachwood Dr.
Los Angeles, CA 90028
Rock Musician

Buckley, Betty
7319 Beverly Blvd., #1
Los Angeles, CA 90036
Actress

Buckley, William F.
150 E. 35th St.
New York, NY 10016
*Writer; author; publisher; TV
commentator; leading conservative
voice*

Buckner, Bill
Chicago Cubs
Wrigley Field
Chicago, IL 60613
Prof. baseball player

Budget Rent-A-Car
200 N. Michigan Ave.
Chicago, IL 60601
Morris Beizberg, President

Buffaloe, Bob
3965 Pikes Peak Ave.
Memphis, TN 38108
Coca-Cola memorabilia collector

Buffkins, Archie Lee
Executive Suite
Kennedy Center
Washington, DC 20566
Performing arts administrator

Bufman, Zev
311 W. 43d St., #900
New York, NY 10036
Producer; theater chain executive

Bugliosi, Vincent T.
9171 Wilshire Blvd., #424
Beverly Hills, CA 90210
Lawyer who prosecuted Charles Manson

Bumpers, Dale
Senate Office Bldg.
Washington, DC 20510
U.S. Senator (D), Arkansas, 1975–present

Burdick, Quentin Northrop
451 Russell Senate Office Bldg.
Washington, DC 20510
U.S. Senator (D), North Dakota, 1960–present

Burger, Warren
U.S. Supreme Court
Washington, DC 20543
Chief Justice, Supreme Court, 1969–present

Burger King Corp.
P.O. Box 520783
Miami, FL 33152
Norman E. Brinker, Chief Executive Officer

Burghoff, Gary
% Robert Crystal
146 S. Spalding Dr.
Beverly Hills, CA 90212
Actor

Burleson, Paul R.
California Angels
Anaheim Stadium
2000 State College Blvd.
Anaheim, CA 92803
Prof. baseball player

Burnett, Carol
141 El Camino Dr., #110
Beverly Hills, CA 90212
Actress; comedienne; singer

Burnett, James Eugene, Jr.
National Transportation Safety Board
800 Independence Ave., SW
Washington, DC 20594
Chairman

Burns, George
1040 N. Las Palmas
Hollywood, CA 90038
Comedian

Burr, Raymond
Box 678
Geyserville, CA 95441
Actor

Burrows, Stephen Gerald
10 W. 57th St.
New York, NY 10019
Clothing designer

Burstyn, Ellen
Ferry House, Box 217
Washington Spring Rd.
Snedens Landing
Palisades, NY 10964
Actress

Burton, Phillip L.
House Office Bldg.
Washington, DC 20515
U.S. Congressman (D), California, 1963–present

Burton, Richard (Richard Jenkins)
9004 Ashcroft Ave.
Los Angeles, CA 90048
Actor

Busey, Gary
1888 Century Park East, #1400
Los Angeles, CA 90067
Actor

Bush, Barbara Pierce
The White House
1600 Pennsylvania Ave.
Washington, DC 20501
Wife of U.S. Vice President

Bush, George
The White House
1600 Pennsylvania Ave.
Washington, DC 20501
Vice President of the United States

Buss, Jerry Hatten
Los Angeles Lakers
The Forum
3900 W. Manchester Blvd.
　　or
P.O. Box 10
Inglewood, CA 90306
Real-estate company executive;
basketball team owner

Butkus, Dick
Hel-Nik Farms
Route 5, Box 204
Deland, FL 32720
Former prof. football player

Butler, Jerry
Buffalo Bills
1 Bills Dr.
Orchard Park, NY 14127
Prof. football player

Buxom Belles International
27856 Palomino Dr.
Warren, MI 48093
Joan Kiauka, President

Buzzi, Ruth
141 El Camino Dr., #205
Beverly Hills, CA 90212
Comedienne

Byrd, Robert C.
Senate Office Bldg.
Washington, DC 20510
U.S. Senator (D), West Virginia,
1959–present

C

Caan, James
1888 Century Park East, #1400
Los Angeles, CA 90067
Actor; director

Caesar, Sid
132 Lasky Dr.
Beverly Hills, CA 90212
Actor; comedian

Cage, Nicolas
1901 Avenue of the Stars, #840
Los Angeles, CA 90067
Actor

Cagney, James
P.O. Box 287
Stanfordville, NY 12581
Actor

Cahn, Sammy
2049 Century Park East
Los Angeles, CA 90067
Songwriter

Caldwell, Sarah
% Boston Opera Co.
539 Washington St.
Boston, MA 02111
Opera producer; conductor; stage director & administrator

Caldwell, Taylor (Janet)
(Mrs. William Robert Prestie)
Ivanhoe Ln.
Greenwich, CT 06830
Author

Califano, Joseph
Califano, Ross & Heineman
1775 Pennsylvania Ave., NW
Washington, DC 20006
Former Secretary, Health, Education and Welfare (D), 1977–1979

Caliguiri, Richard S.
Office of Mayor
City Hall
414 Grant St.
Pittsburgh, PA 15219
Mayor of Pittsburgh (D), 1977–1981

Callas, Charlie
1290 Avenue of the Americas, #264
New York, NY 10019
Comedian; actor

Callaway, Ely Reeves, Jr.
32720 Rancho California Rd.
Temecula, CA 92390
Vintner

53

Callaway, Paul Smith
Washington Cathedral
Mount St. Alban
Washington, DC 20016
Organist

Calrissian, Lando
Lucasfilm
P.O. Box 8669
Universal City, CA 91608
Star Wars *character*

Calvin Klein Jeans
1400 Broadway
New York, NY 10018
Carl Rosen, Chairman

Cameron, Colin Campbell
Paia, HI 96779
*Pineapple company and land
development executive*

Campanella, Joseph Mario
% TAT Communications
1901 Avenue of the Stars
Los Angeles, CA 90067
Actor

Campbell, Earl Christian
Houston Oilers
P.O. Box 1516
Houston, TX 77001
Prof. football player

Campbell, Glen
9200 Sunset Blvd., #823
Los Angeles, CA 90069
Entertainer

Campbell, James Arthur
Detroit Tigers
Tiger Stadium
Detroit, MI 48216
Prof. baseball executive

Campbell, William Richard
Boston Red Sox
24 Yawkey Way
Boston, MA 02215
Prof. baseball pitcher

Campbell Soup Company
Campbell Place
Camden, NJ 08101
*John T. Dorrance, Jr., Chairman &
Director*

Cannon, Dyan
1888 Century Park East, #1400
Los Angeles, CA 90067
Actress

Canova, Diana
7319 Beverly Blvd., #1
Los Angeles, CA 90036
Actress

Cap'n Crunch
Quaker Oats Co.
Merchandise Mart Plaza
Chicago, IL 60654
Spokescaptain

Caponi, Donna
PGA
100 Avenue of Champions
Palm Beach Gardens, FL 33410
Prof. golfer

Capote, Truman
870 UN Plaza, #22G
New York, NY 10017
Writer

Cappelletti, John Raymond
San Diego Chargers
P.O. Box 20666
San Diego, CA 92120
Prof. football player

Capra, Frank
P.O. Box 98
La Quinta, CA 92253
Motion picture producer & director

Caprano, Albert
550 Seventh Ave.
New York, NY 10018
Fashion designer

Cardin, Pierre
59 Rue du Faubourg
Saint-Honore
Paris, 8e France
Fashion designer

54

CARE
600 First Ave.
New York, NY 10016
*Philip Johnston, Ph.D., Executive
Director*

Carew, Rod
California Angels
Anaheim Stadium
2000 State College Blvd.
Anaheim, CA 92803
Prof. baseball player

Carlin, George
Warner Bros.
75 Rockefeller Plaza
New York, NY 10019
Comedian

Carlton, Steven Norman
Philadelphia Phillies
P.O. Box 7575
Philadelphia, PA 19101
Prof. baseball player

Carmen, Gerald P.
General Services Administration
18th and F Sts., NW
Washington, DC 20405
Administrator, 1981–present

Carmichael, Harold
Philadelphia Eagles
Veterans Stadium
Philadelphia, PA 19148
Prof. football player

Carnation Co.
5045 Wilshire Blvd.
Los Angeles, CA 90036
H. E. Olson, Chairman

Carne, Judy
Carne Lodge
Chapel Brampton
Northamptonshire
England
Actress

Carner, Jo Anne
PGA
100 Avenue of Champions
Palm Beach Gardens, FL 33410
Prof. golfer

Carnes, Kim
1112 N. Sherbourne Dr.
Los Angeles, CA 90069
Rock singer; songwriter

Carney, Art
ICM
8899 Beverly Blvd.
Los Angeles, CA 90048
Actor

Caroline, Princess
Grimaldi Palace
Monte Carlo, Monaco
or
80 Avenue Foch
Paris, France
Princess of Monaco

Carpenter, John Howard
9454 Wilshire Blvd.
Beverly Hills, CA 90212
Film writer; director

Carr, Allan
1220 Benedict Canyon Dr.
Beverly Hills, CA 90210
*Film producer; celebrity
representative*

Carradine, David
2444 Wilshire Blvd.
Santa Monica, CA 90403
Actor

Carradine, Keith Ian
ICM
8899 Beverly Blvd.
Los Angeles, CA 90048
Actor

Carrol, Joe Barry
Golden State Warriors
Oakland Coliseum
Oakland, CA 94621
Prof. basketball player

Carroll, Diahann
151 El Camino
Beverly Hills, CA 90212
Actress; singer

Carroll, Pat
% L. B. Sanders
1900 Avenue of the Stars, #510
Los Angeles, CA 90067
Actress

Carson, Johnny
3000 W. Alameda
Burbank, CA 91523
Talk show host

Carter, Billy
Tidwell Industries
Haleyville, AL 35565
*Brother of former President Jimmy
Carter*

Carter, Gary
Montreal Expos
P.O. Box 500
Station M
Montreal, PQ H1V 3P2
Canada
Prof. baseball player

Carter, Jimmy (James Earl, Jr.)
75 Spring St.
Atlanta, GA 30303
*Former President of United States,
1976–1981*

Carter, Lynda
151 El Camino
Beverly Hills, CA 90212
Actress; singer

Carter, Nell
% Richard Astor
119 W. 57th St.
New York, NY 10019
Actress; singer

Carter, Rosalynn Smith
75 Spring St.
Atlanta, GA 30303
*Wife of former President of United
States, Jimmy Carter*

Cartland, Barbara
Camfield Pl., Hatfield
Hertfordshire, England
Author

Cartwright, Angela
Rubber Boots Store
10143 Riverside Dr.
Toluca Lake, CA 91602
Actress

Cartwright, Bill
New York Knicks
Madison Square Garden Center
4 Pennsylvania Plaza
New York, NY 10001
Prof. basketball player

Casals, Rosemary
Women in Sports Inc.
9945 Young Dr.
Beverly Hills, CA 90212
Prof. tennis player

Casey, Howard Wayne
7764 N.W. 71st St.
Miami, FL 33166
*Performer; songwriter; record
producer*

Casey, William J.
Central Intelligence Agency
Washington, DC 20505
Director, 1981–present

Cash, Johnny
711 Summerfield Dr.
Hendersonville, TN 37075
Singer; actor

Cash, June Carter
P.O. Box 508
Hendersonville, TN 37075
Singer

Casper, David John
Oakland Raiders
7850 Edgewater Dr.
Oakland, CA 94621
Prof. football player

Casper, William Earl, Jr.
PGA
100 Avenue of Champions
Palm Beach Gardens, FL 33410
Prof. golfer

Cassavetes, John
9056 Santa Monica Blvd., #201
Los Angeles, CA 90069
Actor; director

Cassidy, David Bruce
William Morris Agency
1350 Avenue of the Americas
New York, NY 10019
Actor; singer

Cassidy, Paul James
18070 Rancho St.
Encino, CA 91316
Radio industry executive (Storer Broadcasting)

Cassidy, Shaun
151 El Camino
Beverly Hills, CA 90212
Actor; singer

Cassini, Oleg Lolewski
257 Park Avenue South
New York, NY 10010
Designer; manufacturer

Castaneda, Carlos
% University of California Press
2223 Fulton St.
Berkeley, CA 94720
Anthropologist; author

Castellino, Francis Joseph
College of Science
University of Notre Dame
South Bend, IN 46556
University dean

Castro, Fidel
Palacio del Gobierno
Havana, Cuba
President of Cuba—since 1959

Cates, Gilbert
9200 Sunset Blvd.
Los Angeles, CA 90069
Director; producer

Cauthen, Steve
% Barry Hills
Lambourne, England
Jockey

Cavanaugh, James Henry
The White House
1600 Pennsylvania Ave.
Washington, DC 20500
Consultant to President Ronald Reagan, 1981–present

Cavett, Dick
WNET
Channel 13
356 W. 58th St.
New York, NY 10019
Entertainer

CBS Inc.
51 W. 52d St.
New York, NY 10019
Thomas Wyman, Chairman

Cey, Ron
Chicago Cubs
Wrigley Field
Chicago, IL 60613
Prof. baseball player

Chacko, George Kuttickal
University of Southern California
Office
5510 Columbia Pike
Arlington, VA 22204
Consultant; educator

Chagall, David
P.O. Box 85
Agoura, CA 91301
Author; marketing research consultant

Chagall, Marc
Villa la Colline
Quartier les Gardettes
16570 St. Paul, France
Artist

Chamberlain, Richard
1888 Century Park East, #1400
Los Angeles, CA 90067
Actor

Chamberlain, Wilt
16633 Ventura Blvd.
Encino, CA 91436
Former prof. basketball player

Chamber of Commerce of the United States
1615 H St., NW
Washington, DC 20062
Richard L. Lesner, President

57

Chambers, Marilyn
4528 W. Charleston Blvd.
Las Vegas, NV 89102
Pornography film star

Chambliss, Chris
Atlanta Braves
P.O. Box 4064
Atlanta, GA 30302
Prof. baseball player

Champion, Marge
(Marjorie Celeste Belcher)
10889 Wilshire Blvd., #1160
Los Angeles, CA 90024
Actress; dancer

Champlin, Charles Davenport
Los Angeles Times
Times-Mirror Sq.
Los Angeles, CA 90053
Writer; critic

Chancellor, John Wm.
% NBC
30 Rockefeller Plaza
New York, NY 10020
News correspondent

Chandler, Otis
Los Angeles Times
Times-Mirror Sq.
Los Angeles, CA 90053
Publisher

Chandler, Robert
CBS News
524 W. 57th St.
New York, NY 10019
TV news executive

Channa, Muhammad Alam
Sewhan, Pakistan
World's tallest man, 8 feet 3 inches

Channing, Carol
151 El Camino
Beverly Hills, CA 90212
Actress

Channing, Stockard
151 El Camino
Beverly Hills, CA 90212
Actress

Chaplenko, George
73 Alexander St.
Edison, NJ 08817
Expert on telescope building

Chaplenko, Tanya
73 Alexander St.
Edison, NJ 08817
Egg decorating expert

Chaplin, Geraldine
William Morris Agency
1350 Avenue of the Americas
New York, NY 10019
Actress

Chapman, Bruce K.
Bureau of the Census
Department of Commerce
14th St. & Constitution Ave.
Washington, DC 20230
Director, 1981–present

Chapman, Graham
2 Park Square West
London, NWI, England
Performer; writer

Charisse, Cyd (Tula Ellice Finklea)
132 Lasky Dr.
Beverly Hills, CA 90212
Actress; dancer

Charles, Prince
Kensington Palace
London, W8, England
Prince of Wales

Charles, Ray (Ray Charles Robinson)
% NTI
P.O. Box 82
98 Cuttermill Rd., #343
Great Neck, NY 11021
Musician; singer; composer

Charlie the Tuna
Star-Kist Foods Inc.
582 Tuna St.
Terminal Island, CA 90731
Mascot for Star-Kist Foods

Chartoff, Robert Irwin
% Press Relations, United Artists
729 Seventh Ave.
New York, NY 10019
Film producer

Chase, Chevy
8966 Sunset Blvd.
Los Angeles, CA 90069
Actor

Chavez, Cesar
La Paz
Keene, CA 93531
Union official

Cheech & Chong
32020 Pacific Coast Hwy.
Malibu, CA 90265
Comedians

Chef Boy-ar-dee
American Home Foods
685 Third Ave.
New York, NY 10017
Spokeschef

Cher
% Press Office Ltd.
555 Madison Ave.
New York, NY 10022
Singer

Chesebrough-Pond's Inc.
33 Benedict Pl.
Greenwich, CT 06830
Ralph E. Ward, Chairman

Cheshire, Maxine
(Mrs. Herbert W. Cheshire)
Los Angeles Times
Times-Mirror Sq.
Los Angeles, CA 90053
Columnist

Chicago Tribune
435 N. Michigan Ave.
Chicago, IL 60611
James Squires, Editor

Child, Julia
125 Western Ave.
Boston, MA 02134
Chef; TV show host

Childhood Sensuality Circle
P.O. Box 5164
San Diego, CA 92105
*Vavila Davila, Editor—Total
children's liberation*

Children of Gay Parents
8306 Wilshire Blvd., #222
Beverly Hills, CA 90211
Lona Lloyd, President

Children of the Night
1800 N. Highland Avenue, #128
Hollywood, CA 90028
*Lois Lee, Executive Director—help
organization for runaways &
prostitutes*

Ching-kuo, Chiang
18 Chang An East Rd.
First Section
Taiwan, Republic of China
President, 1978–present

Chiquita Branch, Inc.
1271 Avenue of the Americas
New York, NY 10020
*Michael J. Lakis, Chief Operating
Officer*

Chisholm, Shirley
85 Livingston St.
Brooklyn, NY 11201
*Former Congresswoman (D),
1969–1983; teacher*

Chong, Thomas
% Monterey Peninsula Artists
P.O. Box 7308
Carmel, CA 93921
Comedian; writer; director; musician

Christie, Julie
ICM
40 W. 57th St.
New York, NY 10019
Actress

Christopher, Warren
1800 M St., NW
Washington, DC 20036
*Helped negotiate Iran hostage
release*

Christopher, William
20th Century-Fox
10211 Pico Blvd.
Los Angeles, CA 90064
Actor

Chrysler Corp.
12000 Lynn Townsend Dr.
Highland Park, MI 48203
L. A. Iacocca, Chairman

Chung, Connie
NBC
30 Rockefeller Plaza
New York, NY 10020
TV anchorwoman

Cimino, Michael
151 El Camino
Beverly Hills, CA 90212
Film director; writer

Citicorp
399 Park Ave.
New York, NY 10043
Walter B. Wriston, Chairman

**Citizens Committee for the Right to
Keep and Bear Arms**
1601 114th St., SE, #151
Bellevue, WA 98004
Alan M. Gottlieb, Chairman

Claiborne, Craig
Doubleday & Co.
245 Park Ave.
New York, NY 10017
Chef; author

Claiborne, Liz (Elisabeth)
1441 Broadway
New York, NY 10018
Women's clothing designer

Clairol, Inc.
345 Park Ave.
New York, NY 10022
Bruce S. Gelb, President

Clapton, Eric
% Robert Stigwood Organization
1775 Broadway
New York, NY 10019
Rock musician

Clark, Candy
% Pat McQueeney
146 N. Almont Dr., #8
Los Angeles, CA 90048
Actress

Clark, Dick
% Dick Clark Productions
3003 W. Olive Ave.
Burbank, CA 91505
Performer; producer

Clark, Fred
Orlando Helicopter Airways
P.O. Box 2802
Orlando, FL 32802
*Manufactures a camper that sleeps
six with shower, air conditioning,
color TV, etc.*

Clark, Jack
San Francisco Giants
Candlestick Park
San Francisco, CA 94124
Prof. baseball player

Clark, Mary Higgins
200 Central Park South
New York, NY 10019
Author

Clark, Petula
P.O. Box 498
Quakertown, PA 18951
Singer

Clark, Ramsey
Clark, Wulf & Levine
113 University Pl.
New York, NY 10003
Lawyer; former Attorney General

Clark, Roy
% Jim Halsey Co. Inc.
5800 E. Skelly Dr.
Tulsa, OK 74135
Singer; musician; business executive

60

Clark, William P.
Department of State
2201 C St., NW
Washington, DC 20520
*Assistant to the President for
National Security Affairs,
1981–present*

Clarke, Arthur C.
Leslies House
25 Barnes Pl.
Colombo, 7, Sri Lanka
Author, 2001

Clarke, Mae
Motion Picture Country Home
23450 Calabasas Rd.
Woodland Hills, CA 91302
Actress

Clarke, Stanley Marvin
8817 Rangely Ave.
Los Angeles, CA 90048
Musician; composer

Clavell, James
Dell Publishing Co. Inc.
1 Dag Hammerskjold Plaza
New York, NY 10017
Author

Clayburgh, Jill
William Morris Agency
1350 Avenue of the Americas
New York, NY 10019
Actress

Cleary, Beverly Atlee
% William Morrow
105 Madison Ave.
New York, NY 10016
Author

Cliburn, Van
% Shaw Concerts Inc.
1995 Broadway
New York, NY 10023
Concert pianist

The Clorox Co.
1221 Broadway
Oakland, CA 94612
C. S. Hatch, Chairman

Clower, Jerry
Box 12514
Nashville, TN 37212
Comedian; author

Coalition for Better Television
P.O. Box 1398
Tupelo, MS 38801
Rev. Donald E. Wildmon, Founder

Coburn, James
409 N. Camden Dr., #105
Beverly Hills, CA 90210
Actor

Coca, Imogene
% Actors Equity Assn.
1500 Broadway
New York, NY 10036
Actress; comedienne

The Coca-Cola Co.
310 North Ave., NW
Atlanta, GA 30313
Roberto C. Goizueta, Chairman

Cocaine Hot Line
Fair Oaks Hospital
19 Prospect St.
Summit, NJ 07901
Dr. Mark S. Gold, Coordinator

Coco, James
% Paul H. Wolfowitz
59 E. 54th St.
New York, NY 10022
Actor

Cody, Iron Eyes
9172 Sunset Blvd., #2
Los Angeles, CA 90069
Actor; environmentalist

Coffey, Linda
415 11th Ave., SE
Minneapolis, MN 55414
*Haute Canine, baker of gourmet
snacks for dogs*

Cohen, Marshall Harris
Astronomy Department
California Institute of Technology
Pasadena, CA 91125
Radio astronomer; educator

Cohen, Sam
4640 Admiralty Way
Marina Del Rey, CA 90291
Inventor of the neutron bomb

Cohn, Roy Marcus
39 E. 68th St.
New York, NY 10021
Lawyer

Colbert, Claudette
Dellerive Wt. Peter
Barbados, West Indies
Actress

Cole, Natalie
Capitol Records
1750 Vine St.
Hollywood, CA 90028
Singer

Cole, Mrs. Nat King
South House
Tyringham, MA 01264
Widow of Nat Cole; singer

Coleman, Cy
161 W. 54th St.
New York, NY 10023
Pianist; composer

Coleman, Dabney
1888 Century Park East, #1400
Los Angeles, CA 90067
Actor

Coleman, Gary
261 S. Robertson Blvd.
Beverly Hills, CA 90211
Actor

Coles, Robert
75 Mount Auburn St.
Cambridge, MA 02138
Child psychiatrist; educator; author

Coley, John Ford
% Twin Trumpets Productions
10100 Santa Monica Blvd., #1095
Los Angeles, CA 90067
Musician; composer

Colgate-Palmolive Co.
300 Park Ave.
New York, NY 10022
*Keith Crane, Chairman—makers of
Fab, Baggies*

Collins, Jackie
Simon & Schuster
1230 Avenue of the Americas
New York, NY 10020
Author

Collins, Joan
151 El Camino
Beverly Hills, CA 90212
Actress

Collins, Judy
P.O. Box 1296
Cathedral Station
New York, NY 10025
Singer

Collins, Marva
Westside Preparatory School
4146 West Chicago Ave.
Chicago, IL 60651
*Schoolteacher, excels in the
educating of hard-to-teach
youngsters*

Collinsworth, Chris
Cincinnati Bengals
200 Riverfront Stadium
Cincinnati, OH 45202
Prof. football player

**Colter, Jessi (Mirriam Joan Johnson
Jennings)**
% Neil Reshen
54 Main St.
Danbury, CT 06810
Singer

Comaneci, Nadia
Gheorgie Cheorghin DEJ
Romania
Gymnast

Comden, Betty
% The Dramatists Guild
234 W. 44th St.
New York, NY 10036
Writer; dramatist; lyricist; performer

Comfort, Alex
Simon & Schuster
1230 Avenue of the Americas
New York, NY 10020
Author, The Joy of Sex

Commodore International Ltd.
950 Rittenhouse Rd.
Norristown, PA 19403
Irving Gould, Chairman

Communist Party of the United States of America
235 W. 23d St., 7th Fl.
New York, NY 10011
Gus Hall, General Secretary

Como, Perry
305 Northern Blvd., 3A
Great Neck, NY 11021
Singer

Compton, Ann Woodruff
ABC News
1717 De Sales St., NW
Washington, DC 20036
News correspondent

Comstock, Bruce
Cameron Balloons U.S.
3600 Elizabeth Rd.
Ann Arbor, MI 48103
Hot air balloon collector

Conboy, John Joseph
7800 Beverly Blvd.
Los Angeles, CA 90036
Television producer

Concepcion, Dave
Cincinnati Reds
100 Riverfront Stadium
Cincinnati, OH 45202
Prof. baseball player

Concern for Dying
250 W. 57th St.
New York, NY 10107
Mrs. Henry W. Levinson, Executive Director—euthanasia

Conkling, John A.
Washington College
Washington Ave.
Chestertown, MD 21620
Fireworks expert

Connally, John
First City National Bank Bldg.
Houston, TX 77002
Former Governor, Texas, 1963–1969; former Secretary of Treasury, 1971–1972; wounded in assassination of President John F. Kennedy

Conners, Bernard F.
9110 Sunset Blvd., #240
Los Angeles, CA 90069
Author; ex-FBI agent

Connery, Sean
1888 Century Park East, #1400
Los Angeles, CA 90067
Actor

Conniff, Ray
P.O. Box 36
Encino, CA 91316
Conductor; composer; arranger

Connors, Chuck
Star Route, Box 725-73
Tehachapi, CA 93561
Actor

Connors, James Scott (Jimmy)
Gerald Ln.
Belleville, IL 60507
Prof. tennis player

Connors, Mike
4348 Van Nuys Blvd.
Sherman Oaks, CA 91403
Actor

Conrad, Robert
15301 Ventura Blvd., #345
Sherman Oaks, CA 91403
Actor

Conrad, William
1888 Century Park East, #1400
Los Angeles, CA 90067
Actor; producer; director

Consagra, Sophie Chandler
American Academy in Rome
Via Masina 5
Rome, Italy
Director

Convy, Bert
151 El Camino
Beverly Hills, CA 90212
Actor

Conway, Tim
Phil Weltman
425 S. Beverly Dr.
Beverly Hills, CA 90212
Comedian

Cooke, Alistair
Nassau Point
Cutchogue, NY 11935
Author

Cooley, Dr. Denton
3014 Del Monte Dr.
Houston, TX 77019
Heart surgeon

Coolidge, Rita
811 16th Avenue South
Nashville, TN 37203
Singer; musician

Cooney, Gerry
1511 K St., NW, #843
Washington, DC 20005
Boxer

Coors Co., Adolph
Golden, CO 80401
William K. Coors, Chairman

Copland, Aaron
% Boosey & Hawkes Inc.
24 W. 57th St.
New York, NY 10019
Composer

Coppola, Carmine
Coppola Co.
916 Kearny St.
San Francisco, CA 94133
Composer; conductor

Coppola, Francis Ford
Coppola Co.
915 Kearny St.
San Francisco, CA 94133
Film writer; producer; director

Corby, Ellen
Motion Picture Country Home
23450 Calabasas Rd.
Woodland Hills, CA 91302
Actress

Corman, Roger
7950 Sunset Blvd.
Los Angeles, CA 90046
Director; producer

Corona, Juan
Vacaville State Prison
Vacaville, CA 95688
Convicted mass murderer of migrant workers

Corrick, Ann Marjorie
113 Felix St., #6
Santa Cruz, CA 95060
Journalist

Cort, Bud
9255 W. Sunset Blvd., #1105
Hollywood, CA 90069
Actor

Corwin, Norman
1840 Fairburn Ave.
Los Angeles, CA 90025
Writer; director; producer

Cosby, Bill
1900 Avenue of the Stars, #1900
Century City, CA 90067
Actor; entertainer

Cosell, Howard (Howard William Cohen)
ABC-TV
1330 Avenue of the Americas
New York, NY 10019
Sportscaster

Cosmic Cat
901 Pope Ave.
Hagerstown, MD 21221
Leon Seidman, co-owner—world's largest producer of catnip

Cosmopolitan
224 W. 57th St.
New York, NY 10019
Helen Gurley Brown, Editor

Costello, Elvis
% Columbia Records
51 W. 52d St.
New York, NY 10019
Musician; songwriter

Cotten, Joseph
6363 Wilshire Blvd.
Los Angeles, CA 90048
Actor

Couch Potatoes
Robert Armstrong
Pittschool Rd.
Dixon, CA 95620
Robert Armstrong, Head Spud—society of television watchers

Count Dracula Society
334 W. 54th St.
Los Angeles, CA 90037
Donald A. Reed, President

Courtney, Jacqueline Dianna
Press Relations
ABC Entertainment
1330 Avenue of the Americas
New York, NY 10019
Actress

Cousteau, Jacques
Musée Oceanografique
Saint Martin, Monaco
Marine biologist

Cowers, Al
Seattle Mariners
419 Second Ave.
Seattle, WA 98104
Prof. baseball player

Cox, Archibald
Glesen Ln.
Wayland, MA 01778
Lawyer; director, Watergate prosecution

Craig, Jim
36 N. Main St.
North Easton, MA 02356
Prof. hockey player

Crane, Daniel B.
Longworth House Office Bldg.
Washington, DC 20515
Congressman (R) Illinois, 1979–present, reprimanded for having sexual relations with a congressional page

Crane, Irving Donald
270 Yarmouth Rd.
Rochester, NY 14610
Pocket billiards player

Cranston, Alan
229 Russell Office Bldg.
Washington, DC 20510
U.S. Senator (D), California, 1969–present; 1984 presidential candidate

Crenshaw, Ben
PGA
100 Avenue of Champions
Palm Beach Gardens, FL 33410
Prof. golfer

Cribbs, Joe
Buffalo Bills
1 Bills Dr.
Orchard Park, NY 14127
Prof. football player

Crist, Judith
180 Riverside Dr.
New York, NY 10024
Film & drama critic

Crofts, Dash
% Day 5 Productions
216 Chatsworth Dr.
San Fernando, CA 91340
Singer; songwriter

Cromwell, Nolan
Los Angeles Rams
2327 W. Lincoln Ave.
Anaheim, CA 92801
Prof. football player

Cronkite, Walter
CBS News
51 W. 52d St.
New York, NY 10019
Radio-TV news correspondent

Crosby, Kathryn
400 S. Burnside Ave., #12H
Los Angeles, CA 90036
Actress; author; widow of Bing

Crosby, Mary
% Jules Sharr Enterprises
9145 Sunset Blvd.
Los Angeles, CA 90069
Actress

Crosby, Norm
P.O. Box 48559
Los Angeles, CA 90048
Comedian

Cross, Christopher
Warner Bros.
3300 Warner Blvd.
Burbank, CA 91505
Singer

Crothers, Joel
222 E. 44th St.
New York, NY 10017
Actor

Crowley, Neal
P.O. Box 784
Pacific Palisades, CA 90272
Toy soldier collector

Crown, David Allan
3103 Jessie Ct.
Fairfax, VA 22030
Criminologist

Crystal, Billy
151 El Camino
Beverly Hills, CA 90212
Actor

C3PO
P.O. Box 2009
San Rafael, CA 94912
Robot, Star Wars

Cullum, John
ICM
8899 Beverly Blvd.
Los Angeles, CA 90048
Actor; singer

Cummings, Constance
68 Old Church St.
London, SW3, England
Actress

Cunningham, Billy
Philadelphia 76ers
Veterans Stadium
P.O. Box 25040
Philadelphia, PA 19147
Prof. basketball coach

Cunningham, Sam
New England Patriots
Schaefer Stadium
Foxboro, MA 02035
Prof. football player

Cunningham, Sean S.
7950 Sunset Blvd.
Los Angeles, CA 90046
Film director; producer

Cuomo, Mario M.
State Capitol
Albany, NY 12248
*Governor of New York (D),
1983–present*

Curtin, Jane
1888 Century Park East, #1400
Los Angeles, CA 90067
Actress

Curtis, Jamie Lee
8642 Melrose Ave., #200
Los Angeles, CA 90069
Actress

Curtis, Tony
P.O. Box 540
Beverly Hills, CA 90213
Actor

D

Daily Racing Form, Inc.
1701 S. Bimini Pl.
Los Angeles, CA 90004
Michael P. Sandler, Publisher

Dali, Salvador
Port Lligat
Cadeques, Spain
Artist

Daltrey, Roger
MCA
70 Universal City Plaza
Universal City, CA 91510
Rock singer, The Who

D'Amato, Alfonse M.
Senate Office Bldg.
Washington, DC 20510
*U.S. Senator (R), New York,
1981–present*

Damon, Cathryn
151 El Camino
Beverly Hills, CA 90212
Actress

Danforth, John C.
Senate Office Bldg.
Washington, DC 20510
*U.S. Senator (R), Missouri,
1977–present*

Dangerfield, Rodney
1118 First Ave.
New York, NY 10010
Comedian; actor

Daniel, Margaret Truman
830 Park Ave.
New York, NY 10028
*Daughter of late President Harry S.
Truman*

Daniels, Charlie
210 25th Avenue North, #500
Nashville, TN 37203
Country rock band

Dannay, Frederick
29 Byron Ln.
Larchmont, NY 10538
Writer

Danner, Blythe
9000 Sunset Blvd., #315
Los Angeles, CA 90069
Actress

Danner, William D.
Trak, Inc.
187 Neck Rd.
Ward Hill, MA 01830
*Invented the waxless cross-country
ski*

68

Dannon Co.
2211 38th Ave.
Long Island City, NY 11101
Jay Johnson, President

Danson, Ted
9220 Sunset Blvd., #202
Los Angeles, CA 90069
Actor

Darren, James
P.O. Box 1088
Beverly Hills, CA 90213
Actor

D'Aubuisson, Roberto
Office of the President
San Salvador, El Salvador
*President of Constituent Assembly,
El Salvador—since 1982*

David, Hal
Elm Dr.
East Hills, NY 11576
Lyricist

Davidson, John Arthur
New York Rangers
Madison Square Garden
4 Pennsylvania Plaza
New York, NY 10001
Prof. hockey player

Davis, Ann B.
1365 Holmby Dr.
Los Angeles, CA 90024
Actress

Davis, Bette (Ruth Elizabeth)
% Gottlieb, Schiff, Ticktin,
Sternklar and Singer
555 Fifth Ave.
New York, NY 10017
Actress

Davis, David H.
% Distasio
710 Shore Rd.
Spring Lake Heights, NJ 07762
Prof. bowler

Davis, Lynn
% Don Purcell
300 W. 55th St.
New York, NY 10019
Author of Guide to the Personal
Ads, *book on how to advertise for
the perfect mate*

Davis, Mac
9255 Sunset Blvd., #1115
Los Angeles, CA 90069
Singer; songwriter

Davis, Ossie
10000 Santa Monica Blvd., #305
Los Angeles, CA 90067
Actor; author

Davis, Patti
1888 Century Park East, Suite 1616
Los Angeles, CA 90067
*Actress; daughter of President
Ronald Reagan*

Davis, Ron
Minnesota Twins
Hubert H. Humphrey Metrodome
501 Chicago Avenue South
Minneapolis, MN 44415
Prof. baseball player

Davis, Sammy, Jr.
151 El Camino
Beverly Hills, CA 90212
Entertainer

Davis, Walter
Phoenix Suns
Funk's Greyhound Bldg.
2910 N. Central
Phoenix, AZ 85012
Prof. basketball player

Dawkins, Darryl
New Jersey Nets
185 E. Union Ave.
East Rutherford, NJ 07073
Prof. basketball player

Dawson, Richard
% ABC Press Relations
1330 Avenue of the Americas
New York, NY 10019
Game show host; actor

69

Day, Doris
Box 223163
Carmel, CA 93922
Actress

Dean, Charles H., Jr.
Tennessee Valley Authority
Woodward Bldg.
15th and H Sts., NW
Washington, DC 20444
or
New Sprankle Bldg.
Knoxville, TN 37902
Chairman

Dean, Dizzy
Wiggins, MS 39577
Former prof. baseball player

Dean, Jimmy
1341 W. Mockingbird Ln.,
Suite 1100 E
Dallas, TX 75247
Meat processing company executive;
entertainer

DeBakey, Dr. Michael
Baylor College of Medicine
1200 Moursund Ave.
Houston, TX 77030
Heart specialist

Debbie Dox Foundation for Severe
Facial Deformities
P.O. Box 11082
Chattanooga, TN 37401
Dr. Thelma S. Elliot, President

DeCarlo, Yvonne
721 N. La Brea Ave., #201
Los Angeles, CA 90038
Actress

DeConcini, Dennis
Senate Office Bldg.
Washington, DC 20510
U.S. Senator (D), Arizona,
1977–present

De Cordova, Frederick Timmins
3000 W. Alameda
Burbank, CA 91523
TV producer-director

Dee, Ruby
10000 Santa Monica Blvd., #305
Los Angeles, CA 90067
Actress

De Fuccio, Jerry
Mad
485 Madison Ave.
New York, NY 10022
Comic book collector

De Givenchy, Hubert
Givenchy
3 Avenue George V
75008 Paris, France
Fashion designer

De Guire, Frank C.
Pabst Brewing Co.
917 Juneau Ave.
P.O. Box 642
Milwaukee, WI 53201
Brewing company executive

de Havilland, Olivia Mary
BP 156 75764
Paris, Cedex 16 France
Actress

Delahanty, Tom
4314 Briggs Chaney Rd.
Bettsville, MD 20705
Policeman who, in saving President
Reagan, got shot

de la Madrid Hurtado, Miguel
Office of the President
Mexico City, Mexico
President, Mexico—since 1982

Delaney, Kim
All My Children
101 W. 67th St.
New York, NY 10023
Actress

De La Renta, Oscar
550 Seventh Ave.
New York, NY 10018
or
Brook Hill Farm
Skiff Mountain Rd.
Kent, CT 06757
Fashion designer

70

De Laurentiis, Dino
Hamersley Hill
Pawling, NY 12564
Film director

Del Monte Corp.
One Market Plaza
San Francisco, CA 94105
*Richard H. Ward, Chairman of
Board*

De Lorean, John
% James Srodes
Editorial Department
Putnam Publishing
200 Madison Ave.
New York, NY 10016
Former auto manufacturer

Del Rio, Dolores
Salvador Novo 127
Mexico City, D.F., Mexico
Actress

Delta Air Lines
Hartsfield Atlanta International
Airport
Atlanta, GA 30320
W. T. Beebe, Chairman

DeLuise, Dom
% EBM
132 S. Rodeo Dr.
Beverly Hills, CA 90212
Actor

Deneuve, Catherine
10 Avenue George V
75008 Paris, France
Actress

DeNiro, Robert
9 E. 41st St., #1000
New York, NY 10017
Actor

Dennis, Sandy
Blake-Glenn Agency
409 N. Camden Dr.
Beverly Hills, CA 90210
Actress

Dent, Bucky
Texas Rangers
Arlington Stadium
P.O. Box 1111
Arlington, TX 76010
Prof. baseball player

Denver, John
9744 Wilshire Blvd., #400
Los Angeles, CA 90212
Singer; songwriter

**de Oliveira Figueiredo, General
Joao Baptista**
Office of the President
Brasilia, Brazil
President, Brazil—since 1979

DePalma, Brian
Fetch Productions
1600 Broadway
New York, NY 10019
Film director & writer

Derek, Bo
1888 Century Park East, #1400
Los Angeles, CA 90067
Actress

Dern, Bruce Macleish
1888 Century Park East, #1400
Los Angeles, CA 90067
Actor

De Sade, Dr.
Fetish Times
B & D Co.
P.O. Box 7109
Van Nuys, CA 91409
Executive editor

Deukmejian, George
State Capitol
Sacramento, CA 95814
*Governor of California,
1983–present*

Devane, William
ICM
8899 Beverly Blvd.
Los Angeles, CA 90069
Actor

Devine, Vaughan P.
St. Louis Cardinals
200 Stadium Plaza
St. Louis, MO 63102
Prof. football team executive

DeVito, Danny
9229 Sunset Blvd., #422
Los Angeles, CA 90069
Actor

Devo
P.O. Box 6868
Burbank, CA 91510
Rock group

DeWein, Sibyl
1696 Valley Rd.
Clarksville, TN 37040
Barbie Doll collector

Dewey, A. J.
Miami Dolphins
3550 Biscayne Blvd.
Miami, FL 33137
Prof. football player

Dewhurst, Colleen
Flood Farm
Boutonville Rd.
South Salem, NY 10590
Actress

DeWitt, Joyce
William Morris Agency
1350 Avenue of the Americas
New York, NY 10019
Actress

Diamond, Neil
9744 Wilshire Blvd., #507
Beverly Hills, CA 90212
Singer; composer

Diana, Princess
Kensington Palace
London, W8, England
Princess of Wales; Prince Charles's wife

Dibbs, Edward George
% U.S. Tennis Assn.
51 E. 42d St.
New York, NY 10017
Prof. tennis player

Dickinson, Angie
409 N. Camden Dr., #202
Beverly Hills, CA 90210
Actress

Dietrich, Marlene
9200 Sunset Blvd., #823
Los Angeles, CA 90069
Actress

Di Giovanni, Mario
15400 Albright St.
Pacific Palisades, CA 90272
Christopher Columbus expert

Dignity After Death
668 Monroe Ave.
Rochester, NY 14607
Laura Lyn Senft, Founder— organization protesting commercialization of John Lennon after his death

Diller, Barry
5451 Marathon St.
Los Angeles, CA 90038
Motion picture company executive (Paramount Pictures)

Diller, Phyllis
% Phil Dil Productions Ltd.
One Dag Hammarskjold Plaza
New York, NY 10017
Comedienne; author

Dillon, Matt
P.O. Box 800
Old Chelsea Station
New York, NY 10011
Actor

DiMaggio, Joe
2150 Beach St.
San Francisco, CA 94123
Former prof. baseball player

Dire Straits
5 Kendal Pl,
London, W1, England
Rock group

Dirt Band, The
Box 1915
Aspen, CO 81611
Rock group

Dixon, Donna
151 El Camino
Beverly Hills, CA 90212
Actress

DOC
127 Chase Rd.
Manhasset, NY 11030
*Dr. Alan Blum, Founder (Doctors
Ought to Care)*

Dockstader, Frederick T.
165 W. 66th St.
New York, NY 10023
*Museum director of Indian arts
(Museum of the American Indian,
New York)*

Dole, Elizabeth Hanford
Department of Transportation
400 Seventh St., SW
Washington, DC 20590
Secretary, 1983–present

Dole, Robert
Senate Office Bldg.
Washington, DC 20510
*U.S. Senator (R), Kansas,
1960–present*

Dolenz, Mickey
115 University Ave.
Los Gatos, CA 95030
*Musician; former member of The
Monkees*

Dolly Madison
P.O. Box 1627
Kansas City, MO 64141
*Bertram J. Cohn, Chairman—ice-
cream company*

Domenici, Pete V.
Dirksen Senate Office Bldg
Suite 4239
Washington, DC 20510
*U.S. Senator (R), New Mexico,
1972–present*

Donahue, Elinor
9200 Sunset Blvd., #909
Los Angeles, CA 90212
Actress

Donahue, Phil
WGN-TV
2501 Bradley Pl.
Chicago, IL 60618
Talk show host

Donovan, Raymond J.
Department of Labor
200 Constitution Ave., NW
Washington, DC 20210
Secretary, 1981–present

Doobie Bros.
13251 Ventura Blvd.
Studio City, CA 91604
Rock group

Doolittle, James H.
P.O. Box 6087
Carmel, CA 93921
General

Dorsett, Tony Drew
Dallas Cowboys
6116 N. Central Expwy.
Dallas, TX 75206
Prof. football player

dos Santos, Jose Eduardo
Office of President
Luanda, Angola
President, Angola—since 1979

Doubleday & Co.
245 Park Ave.
New York, NY 10017
John Sargent, Chairman

Doughboy
Pillsbury Center
Minneapolis, MN 55402
Pillsbury mascot

Douglas, Cathleen Curran Hefferan
815 Connecticut Ave., NW
Washington, DC 20006
Widow of Supreme Court Justice;
lawyer; conservationist

Douglas, Kirk
Bryna Co.
141 El Camino Dr.
Beverly Hills, CA 90212
Actor; motion picture producer

Douglas, Michael Kirk
4000 Warner Blvd.
Burbank, CA 91505
Actor; film producer

Douglas, Mike
151 El Camino
Beverly Hills, CA 90212
TV personality

Douglas, Suzanne
Intro magazine
P.O. Box Intro
Studio City, CA 91604
Publisher, specializing in personal
ads for singles

Dow, Tony
TK Tal
119 San Vicente Blvd.
Los Angeles, CA 90211
Wally on Leave It to Beaver

Dow Chemical Co.
The Dow Center
Midland, MI 48640
Robert W. Lundeen, Chairman

Dow Jones & Co.
22 Cortlandt St.
New York, NY 10007
Warren H. Phillips, Chairman

Down, Lesley-Anne
147-149 Wardour St.
London, V1V 3TB, England
Actress

Drea
8231 De Longpre Ave., #1
West Hollywood, CA 90046
Porno writer & director

Drew, John
Atlanta Hawks
100 Techwood Dr., NW
Atlanta, GA 30303
Prof. basketball player

Drexler, Paul
Art Dreco Institute
323 Noe St.
San Francisco, CA 94114
Expert on art dreco (art so ugly, it's
beautiful)

Dreyfuss, Richard Stephan
8966 Sunset Blvd.
Los Angeles, CA 90069
Actor

Dr. Hook
Box 121017
Nashville, TN 37212
Rock group

Driesson, Dan
Cincinnati Reds
100 Riverfront Stadium
Cincinnati, OH 45202
Prof. baseball player

Dr Pepper Co.
5523 E. Mockingbird Ln.
Dallas, TX 75206
W. W. Clements, Chairman

Duan, Le
Office of the Secretary-General
Hanoi, Vietnam
Secretary-General, Vietnam—since
1960

Duffy, Patrick
11726 San Vicente Blvd., #300
Los Angeles, CA 90049
Actor

Dukakis, Michael S.
State Capitol
Boston, MA 02201
Governor of Massachusetts (D),
1983–present

74

Dukes, David
ICM
8899 Beverly Blvd.
Los Angeles, CA 90048
Actor

Dun & Bradstreet Corp.
299 Park Ave.
New York, NY 10017
Harrington Drake, Chairman

Dunaway, Faye
151 El Camino
Beverly Hills, CA 90212
Actress

Duncan, Sandy
151 El Camino
Beverly Hills, CA 90212
Actress

Dunkin' Donuts Inc.
P.O. Box 317
Randolph, MA 02368
William Rosenberg, Chairman

Du Pont, Pierre S., IV
State Capitol
Dover, DE 19901
*Governor of Delaware (R),
1977–present*

**Du Pont de Nemours & Co., Inc.,
E. I.**
1007 Market St.
Wilmington, DE 19898
Edward G. Jefferson, Chairman

Dupree, Billy Joe
Dallas Cowboys
6116 N. Central Expwy.
Dallas, TX 75206
Prof. football player

Duran Duran
Capitol Records
1750 Vine St.
Hollywood, CA 90028
Rock group

Duran, Roberto
Box 157
Arena Colon
Panama City, Panama
Boxer

Durocher, Leo (Leon Ernst)
Simon & Schuster
1230 Avenue of the Americas
New York, NY 10020
Former prof. baseball club manager

Dussault, Nancy Elizabeth
222 N. Canon Dr., #204
Beverly Hills, CA 90210
Actress; singer

Duvall, Robert
% John H. Duvall of Old Towne
Ltd.
P.O. Box 784
Alexandria, VA 22313
Actor

Duvall, Shelley
4151 Prospect Ave.
Los Angeles, CA 90028
Actress; producer

Dylan, Bob
Box 264
Cooper Station, NY 10003
Singer; songwriter

Dymally, Mervyn M.
House Office Bldg.
Washington, DC 20515
*U.S. Congressman (D), California,
1981–present*

E

E. A., Mrs.
Box 2666
Van Nuys, CA 91401
Seller of child pornography

Eagleton, Thomas Francis
1209 Dirksen Senate Office Bldg.
Washington, DC 20510
U.S. Senator (D), Missouri,
1968–present

Eakin, Thomas Capper
2729 Shelley Rd.
Shaker Heights, OH 44122
Sports promotion executive

Earle, Sylvia Alice
California Academy of Sciences
Golden Gate Park
San Francisco, CA 94118
Oceanographer

Earley, James
6509 Hillmont Dr.
Oakland, CA 94605
Expert on medieval warfare

Eastern Airlines, Inc.
Miami International Airport
Miami, FL 33148
Frank Borman, Chairman

Eastman, Daniel
8033 Sunset Blvd., #1040
Los Angeles, CA 90046
Makeup artist to stars

Eastman Kodak Co.
343 State St.
Rochester, NY 14608
Walter A. Fallon, Chairman

Eastwood, Clint
Box 125
Pebble Beach, CA 93953
Actor; director

Eastwood, Warwick
3565 New Haven Rd.
Pasadena, CA 91107
Expert on horseless carriages

Ebsen, Buddy
8150 Beverly Blvd., #206
Los Angeles, CA 90048
Actor; dancer

Eden, Barbara Jean
% Plant-Cohen Co.
9777 Wilshire Blvd.
Beverly Hills, CA 90212
Actress

Eder, Shirley
16500 N. Park Dr.
Southfield, MI 48075
Syndicated entertainment columnist

Edwards, John
Associated Piano Craftsmen, Inc.
19 Emerson Plaza
Emerson, NJ 07630
Player piano expert

Edwards, Ralph
1717 N. Highland Ave.
Hollywood, CA 90028
Former host, This Is Your Life

Edwards, Vince
P.O. Box 642
Malibu, CA 90265
Actor

Ehrlichman, John Daniel
P.O. Box 5559
Santa Fe, NM 87502
Author; radio & TV commentator

Eichorn, Lisa
1888 Century Park East, #1400
Los Angeles, CA 90067
Actress

Eikerenkoetter, Frederick Joseph, II
910 Commonwealth Ave.
Boston, MA 02215
Evangelist; educator; lecturer

Eisenberg, Kenneth Sawyer
1000 Connecticut Ave., NW
Washington, DC 20036
Restoration expert

Eisenstaedt, Alfred
Time Inc.
Rockefeller Center
New York, NY 10020
Photojournalist

Elaine Powers Figure Salons
105 W. Michigan Ave.
Milwaukee, WI 53203
Andrew C. Lien, President

Elam, Jack
Box 5718
Santa Barbara, CA 93108
Actor

Elder, Robert Lee
% Lee Elder Enterprises
1725 K St., NW, #1202
Washington, DC 20006
Prof. golfer

Elias, Taslim O.
United Nations
1 UN Plaza
New York, NY 10017
*President, International Court of
Justice (World Court)*

Elizabeth, Queen
Clarence House
London, SW1, England
Queen Mother

Elizabeth Arden, Inc.
Park Avenue Plaza
55 E. 52d St.
New York, NY 10022
J. F. Ronchetti, President

Elizabeth II, Queen
Buckingham Palace
London, SW1, England
Ruler of England

El Korimiy, Ibrahim
Ein Ghessin, Egypt
Oldest living man (born 1823)

Elliman, Yvonne
% Alive Enterprises Inc.
8600 Melrose Ave.
Los Angeles, CA 90069
Singer

Elliot, Robert B.
% Random House Inc.
201 E. 50th St.
New York, NY 10022
Comedian

Ellis, Perry Edwin
575 Seventh Ave.
New York, NY 10018
Fashion designer

77

Ellsberg, Daniel
90 Norwood Ave.
Kensington, CA 94707
*Writer; lecturer; former government
official; political activist*

Encyclopædia Britannica, Inc.
425 N. Michigan Ave.
Chicago, IL 60611
Robert P. Gwinn, Chairman

Engel, Georgia Bright
850 Seventh Ave., #1201
New York, NY 10019
Actress

English, Alex
Denver Nuggets
McNichols Sports Arena
1635 Clay St.
Denver CO 80204
Prof. basketball player

English Leather, Inc.
Union Street Extension
Northvale, NJ 07647
Stephen H. Mayer, Chairman

Enough Is Enough Club
Box 925
Hurst, TX 76053
*C. F. Sullivan, Founder—fans of
Monday night football who believe
program would be better without
Howard Cosell and other
distractions*

Enstar
5051 Westheimer, #2200
Houston, TX 77056
O. Charles Honig, Chairman

Environmental Action
1346 Connecticut Ave., NW, #731
Washington, DC 20036
Elizabeth Davenport, Coordinator

Ephron, Nora
ICM
40 W. 57th St.
New York, NY 10019
Author

Epilepsy Foundation of America
4351 Garden City Dr.
Landover, MD 20781
William McLin, Executive Director

Ershad, Lieutenant General H. M.
Dacca, Bangladesh
*Head of government, Bangladesh—
since 1982*

Ervin, Sam J., Jr.
P.O. Box 69
Morganton, NC 28655
Headed Senate Watergate hearings

Erving, Julius
Philadelphia 76ers
Veterans Stadium
P.O. Box 25040
Philadelphia, PA 19147
Prof. basketball player

Eskimo Pie Corp.
530 E. Main St.
Richmond, VA 23219
F. N. Hord, Chief Operating Officer

Esposito, Philip Anthony
Phil Esposito Management Corp.
200 McGrath Hwy.
Somerville, MA 02143
*Former prof. ice hockey player;
announcer & scout (New York
Rangers)*

E.T.
4000 Warner Blvd.
Burbank, CA 91505
Extraterrestrial

Evans, Daryl
San Francisco Giants
Candlestick Park
San Francisco, CA 94124
Prof. baseball player

Evans, Dwight
Boston Red Sox
24 Yawkey Way
Boston, MA 02215
Prof. baseball player

Evans, Heloise
% King Features Syndicate
235 E. 45th St.
New York, NY 10017
Columnist

Evans, Linda
9000 Sunset Blvd., #1112
Los Angeles, CA 90069
Actress

Evans, Robert
Paramount Pictures Corp.
202 N. Canon Dr.
Beverly Hills, CA 90210
Motion picture producer

Everett, Chad
ICM
8899 Beverly Blvd.
Los Angeles, CA 90069
Actor

Everly Brothers
Don: 2510 Franklin Rd.
Nashville, TN 37204

Phil: 1940 E. 18th Ave.
Denver, CO 80206
Music group

Evert Lloyd, Christine Marie
U.S. Tennis Assn.
51 E. 42d St.
New York, NY 10017
Prof. tennis player

Evren, Kenan
Office of the President
Ankara, Turkey
President, Turkey—since 1980

EWOKS
Lucasfilm
P.O. Box 8669
Universal City, CA 91608
Brown furry characters from Return
of the Jedi

Ex-Moon
P.O. Box 62
Brookline, MA 02146
*Steven Hassan, President—former
Moonies*

Exxon Corp.
1251 Avenue of the Americas
New York, NY 10020
C. C. Garvin, Jr., Chairman

F

Fahd, King
Royal Palace
Riyadh, Saudi Arabia
Ruler of Saudi Arabia

Fairchild, Morgan
P.O. Box 8170
Universal City, CA 91608
Actress

Fairy Investigation Society
1 Lakelands Close
Stillorgan, Blackrock
Dublin, Ireland
Mr. Leslie Sheppard, President

Falk, Peter
1888 Century Park East, #1400
Los Angeles, CA 90067
Actor

Falwell, Rev. Jerry
Moral Majority Inc.
P.O. Box 190
Forest, VA 24551
*TV evangelist; head of Moral
Majority*

Family Circle magazine
488 Madison Ave.
New York, NY 10022
Arthur Hettich, Editor

Fanfani, Amintore
Office of the Prime Minister
Rome, Italy
Prime Minister, Italy—since 1982

Farberware
1500 Bassett Ave.
Bronx, NY 10461
Al S. Rummelsburg, Chairman

Fargo, Donna
P.O. Box 15743
Nashville, TN 37215
Singer

Farr, Jamie
ICM
8899 Beverly Blvd.
Los Angeles, CA 90048
Actor

Farrell, Mike
9220 Sunset Blvd., #202
Los Angeles, CA 90069
Actor

Farrow, Mia
135 Central Park West
New York, NY 10023
or
RFD
Vineyard Haven, MA 02568
Actress

Father's Day Council
47 W. 34th St.
New York, NY 10001
*Theodore M. Kaufman, Executive
Director*

Fauci, Dr. Anthony
National Institute of Allergy and
Infectious Diseases
Bethesda, MD 20014
AIDS expert

Fawcett, Farrah
ICM
8899 Beverly Blvd.
Los Angeles, CA 90048
Actress

Feiffer, Jules
325 West End Ave.
New York, NY 10023
Cartoonist

Feinstein, Dianne
Office of the Mayor
City Hall
San Francisco, CA 94102
Mayor (D), 1978–present

Feld, Irving
3201 New Mexico Ave., NW
Washington, DC 20016
Circus producer

Feldon, Barbara
1888 Century Park East, #1400
Los Angeles, CA 90067
Actress

Feldstein, Martin S.
Council of Economic Advisers
(CEA)
Executive Office Building
Washington, DC 20506
Chairman, 1977–present

Feliciano, Jose
8425 W. Third St., #207
Los Angeles, CA 90048
Singer

Fell, Norman
151 El Camino
Beverly Hills, CA 90212
Actor

Fellini, Federico
141A Via Margutta 110
Rome, Italy
Director

Females for Felons
51 E. 42d St., #517
New York, NY 10017
*Ralph Sturges, Coordinator—
supplies volunteer female sexual
partners to men in prison*

Ferguson, Joe
Buffalo Bills
1 Bills Drive
Orchard Park, NY 14127
Prof. football player

Ferragamo, Vincent
Los Angeles Rams
2327 W. Lincoln Ave.
Anaheim, CA 92801
Prof. football player

Ferrare, Christine
% James Srodes
Editorial Department
Putnam Publishing
200 Madison Ave.
New York, NY 10016
Model; wife of John De Lorean

Ferrer, Jose Vicente
2 Pennsylvania Plaza
New York, NY 10001
Producer; director; actor

Ferry, Robert Dean
Washington Bullets
1 Harry S. Truman Dr.
Landover, MD 20786
Prof. basketball team executive

Fetchit, Stepin
Motion Picture Home
23388 Mulholland Dr.
Woodland Hills, CA 91364
Actor

Fiedler, Bobbi
House Office Bldg.
Washington, DC 20515
U.S. Congresswoman (R),
California, 1981–present

Field, Sally
1888 Century Park East, #1400
Los Angeles, CA 90067
Actress

Fields, Debbie
P.O. Box 680370
Park City, UT 84060
Owner of Mrs. Fields Cookies

Fields, Kim
P.O. Box 5973-322
Sherman Oaks, CA 91413
Actress

Fingers, Roland Glen (Rollie)
Milwaukee Brewers
Milwaukee County Stadium
Milwaukee, WI 53214
Prof. baseball player

Fink, Robert L.
205 Ralston
Converse, TX 78109
Founder, National Fink Week

Finney, Albert
25 Dover St.
London, W1, England
Actor

Firestone Tire & Rubber Co., The
1200 Firestone Pkwy.
Akron, OH 44317
John J. Nevin, President

Fisher, Carrie
10350 Santa Monica Blvd., #210
Los Angeles, CA 90025
Actress

Fisher, Eddie
% Gene Williams Entertainments
306 Church St.
Horseshoe Bend, AR 72512
Singer

Fisher Toys
606 Girard
East Aurora, NY 14052
Franklyn S. Barry, Chief Operating
Officer

Fisk, Carlton
Chicago White Sox
Comiskey Park
324 W. 35th St.
Chicago, IL 60616
Prof. baseball player

Fitzgerald, Ella
% Norman Granz
451 N. Canon Dr.
Beverly Hills, CA 90210
Singer

FitzGerald, Garret
Office of the Prime Minister
Dublin, Ireland
Prime Minister, Ireland—since 1982

Flanagan, Michael Kendall
Baltimore Orioles
Memorial Stadium
Baltimore, MD 21218
Prof. baseball player

Fleetwood, Mick
% Penguin Promotions
1420 N. Beachwood Dr.
Los Angeles, CA 90028
Musician

Fleming, John Vincent
Department of English
Princeton University
Princeton, NJ 08540
Educator

Flesher, Fran
17809 Glenhelen Rd.
Devore, CA
Owner/operator of Tree House Fun
Ranch, largest nudist colony in
Southern California

Fletcher, Cliff
Calgary Flames
P.O. Box 1540
Station M
Calgary, AB T2P 3B9
Canada
Prof. hockey executive

Fletcher, Louise
% International Creative
Management
8899 Beverly Blvd.
Los Angeles, CA 90048
Actress

Floating Hospital
275 Madison Ave.
New York, NY 10016
*Jeffers, Susan, Ph.D., Executive
Director*

Flynt, Larry Claxton
2029 Century Park East, #3800
Los Angeles, CA 90067
Publisher, Hustler *magazine;
wounded in assassination attempt*

Foch, Nina
P.O. Box 1884
Beverly Hills, CA 90213
Actress; teacher

Fogelberg, Daniel Grayling
% Front Line Management
8280 Melrose Ave.
Los Angeles, CA 90069
Composer

Fonda, Jane
8642 Melrose Ave., #200
Los Angeles, CA 90069
Actress

Fonda, Peter
% International Creative
Management
8899 Beverly Blvd.
Los Angeles, CA 90048
Actor

Fontaine, Joan
9229 Sunset Blvd., #306
Los Angeles, CA 90069
Actress

Fonteyne De Arias, Dame Margot
% Royal Opera House
Covent Garden
London, WC2, England
Ballerina

Foray, June
22745 Erwin St.
Woodland Hills, CA 91364
Voice of Rocky and Natasha on
Bullwinkle *cartoons*

Forbes, Malcolm Stevenson
60 Fifth Ave.
New York, NY 10011
Publisher, Forbes *magazine*

Ford, Mrs. Betty
P.O Box 927
Rancho Mirage, CA 92270
Former First Lady

Ford, Eileen Otte
344 E. 59th St.
New York, NY 10022
Modeling agency executive

Ford, Gerald Rudolph, Jr.
P.O. Box 927
Rancho Mirage, CA 92270
Former President, 1974–1976

Ford, Glenn
9255 Sunset Blvd., #910
Los Angeles, CA 90069
Actor

Ford, Harrison
222 N. Canon Dr., #204
Beverly Hills, CA 90210
Actor

Ford, Henry, II
The American Rd.
Dearborn, MI 48126
*Automobile manufacturing company
executive*

Ford, Steven
CBS-TV
7800 Beverly Blvd.
Los Angeles, CA 90036
*Actor; son of former President
Gerald Ford*

83

Ford, Tennessee Ernie
P.O. Box 31–552
San Francisco, CA 94131
Entertainer

Ford Motor Co.
The American Rd.
Dearborn, MI 48126
Philip Caldwell, Chairman

Foreigner
1790 Broadway, PH
New York, NY 10019
Rock group

Foreman, Walter Eugene
New England Patriots
Schaefer Stadium
Foxboro, MA 02035
Prof. football player

Forman, Milos
% Robert Lantz
114 E. 55th St.
New York, NY 10022
Film director

Forsythe, John
Box 60257
Terminal Annex Station
Los Angeles, CA 90060
Actor

Fosse, Bob
ICM
40 W. 57th St.
New York, NY 10019
Director

Foster, George
New York Mets
William A. Shea Stadium
Roosevelt Ave. & 126th St.
Flushing, NY 11368
Prof. baseball player

Foster, Jodie
ICM
40 W. 57th St.
New York, NY 10019
Actress

Four Guys
P.O. Box 2138
Nashville, TN 37214
Singing group

4-H Program
Extension Service
Department of Agriculture
Washington, DC 20250
*Dr. Eugene Williams, National
Director*

Fouts, Daniel Francis
San Diego Chargers
P.O. Box 20666
San Diego, CA 92120
Prof. football player

Fowler, Ann R.
22612 Foothill Blvd., #210
Hayward, CA 94541
*Trichodemolist—permanently
removes hair*

Fowler, Mark
Federal Communications
Commission
1919 M St., NW
Washington, DC 20554
Chairman

Fox, Jim
10176 Page Dr.
Mentor-on-the-Lake, OH 44060
Expert on license plates

Fox, Michael J.
% Lax Management
9105 Carmelita Ave., #1
Beverly Hills, CA 90210
Actor

Foxworth, Robert
3970 Overland Ave.
Culver City, CA 90230
Actor

Foxx, Redd
933 N. La Brea Ave.
Los Angeles, CA 90038
Actor; comedian

Foyt, A.J.
6415 Toledo
Houston, TX 77008
Prof. race car driver

Fragrance Foundation
116 E. 19th St.
New York, NY 10003
Annette Green, Executive Director

Frampton, Peter
Box 8
Croton-on-Hudson, NY 10520
Rock musician

Franciosa, Anthony
151 El Camino
Beverly Hills, CA 90212
Actor

Francis, Anne
P.O. Box 5417
Santa Barbara, CA 93108
Actress

Francis, Dick Stanley
% Penny Chase Blewbury
Oxfordshire, England
Author

Francis, Genie
120 El Camino Dr., #104
Beverly Hills, CA 90212
Actress

Franklin, Aretha
% Rev. Cecil Franklin
16919 Stansbury
Detroit, MI 48235
Singer

Franklin, Bonnie
1888 Century Park East, #1400
Los Angeles, CA 90067
Actress

Frazier, Joe
2917 N. Broad St.
Philadelphia, PA 19132
*Former heavyweight champion
boxer*

Free, World B.
Golden State Warriors
Oakland Coliseum
Oakland, CA 94621
Prof. basketball player

Freebies magazine
P.O. Box 20283
Santa Barbara, CA 93101
Lynn Carlisle, Managing Editor

Fregosi, Jim
California Angels
Anaheim Stadium
2000 State College Blvd.
Anaheim, CA 92803
Prof. baseball player

French, Victor
1888 Century Park East, #1400
Los Angeles, CA 90067
Actor; director; teacher

Friars Club
57 E. 55th St.
New York, NY 10022
*Walter C. Goldstein, Executive
Director*

Friday, Nancy
Simon & Schuster
1230 Avenue of the Americas
New York, NY 10020
Author

Friedan, Betty
1 Lincoln Plaza
New York, NY 10023
Feminist

Friedkin, William
124 Udine Way
Los Angeles, CA 90024
Author

Friedman, Milton
Hoover Institution
Stanford University
Stanford, CA 94305
Nobel Prize winner

Frigidaire Co.
WC Box 4900
3555 S. Kettering Blvd.
Dayton, OH 45449
Richard F. Zoellner, President

Frito-Lay, Inc.
Frito-Lay Tower
Exchange Park
Dallas, TX 75235
D. Wayne Calloway, President

Fromme, Lynette ("Squeaky")
Federal Reformatory for Women
Alderson, WV 24910
Would-be assassin of Gerald Ford

Frost, David
46 Egerton Crescent
London, SW3, England
Author; producer; columnist

Fuller Brush Co.
2800 Rock Creek Pkwy., #400
North Kansas City, KS 64116
Leonard D. Dunlap, President

Furness, Betty
% NBC News
30 Rockefeller Plaza
New York, NY 10020
*Broadcast journalist; consumer
adviser; actress*

Furstenberg, Egon Edvard von
50 W. 57th St., #501
New York, NY 10019
Fashion designer

G

Gabet, Sharon
222 E. 44th St.
New York, NY 10017
Actress

Gable, John
Theodore Roosevelt Assn.
P.O. Box 720
Oyster Bay, NY 11771
Theodore Roosevelt expert

Gabor, Eva
9255 Sunset Blvd., #1115
Los Angeles, CA 90069
Actress

Gabor, Zsa Zsa
721 N. La Brea Ave., #201
Los Angeles, CA 90038
Actress

Gabriel, John
433 W. 53d St.
New York, NY 10019
Actor

Gacy, John W.
Lock Box 711
Menard, IL 62259
Murderer, death row

Gainey, Robert Michael
Montreal Canadiens
2313 W. St. Catherine St.
Montreal, PQ H3H 1N2
Canada
Prof. hockey player

Galbraith, John Kenneth
30 Francis Ave.
Cambridge, MA 02138
Economist

Gallo
Gallo Vineyards
P.O. Box 1130
Modesto, CA 95353
Julio Gallo, President

Gallup, Dr. George, II
The Great Rd.
Princeton, NJ 08540
Pollster

Gandhi, Indira
1 Safdarjung Rd.
New Delhi 110011
India
*Premier of India 1966–1977,
1980–present*

Gap Stores, Inc., The
P.O. Box 60
San Bruno, CA 94066
*Donald Fisher, Chairman—clothing
stores*

Garagiola, Joe
% FSM Inc.
One Rockefeller Plaza
New York, NY 10020
Radio-TV personality

Garbo, Greta
450 E. 52d St.
New York, NY 10022
Actress

Garcia, David
Cleveland Indians
Cleveland Stadium
Cleveland, OH 44114
Prof. baseball team executive

Garcia, Jerome John
Grateful Dead
P.O. Box 1065
San Rafael, CA 94902
Guitarist; composer

Gardner, Ava
34 Ennismore Gardens
London, SW7, England
Actress

Garfunkel, Art
CBS
51 W. 52d St.
New York, NY 10019
Musician

Garner, James
141 El Camino Dr., #110
Beverly Hills, CA 90212
Actor

Garner, Phil
Houston Astros
Astrodome
P.O. Box 288
Houston, TX 77001
Prof. baseball player

Garnier, Peggy
639 S. Irena St.
Redondo Beach, CA 90277
*Founder and musical director of
Happy Time Pipers National Chorus
of the National Council of Senior
Citizens*

Garr, Teri
1888 Century Park East, #1400
Los Angeles, CA 90067
Actress

Garriott, Owen K.
Johnson Space Center
Houston, TX 77058
Astronaut

Garvey, Steve
San Diego Padres
P.O. Box 2000
San Diego, CA 92120
Prof. baseball player

Gastineau, Mark
New York Jets
598 Madison Ave.
New York, NY 10022
Prof. football player

Gavin, John
Box 961
Beverly Hills, CA 90213
or
Paseo de la Reforma
305 Mexico City 5, D.C.
Mexico
*Actor; business executive;
ambassador*

Gaye, Marvin
Motown Records
6255 Sunset Blvd.
Los Angeles, CA 90028
Singer; songwriter

Gayle, Crystal
800 S. Robertson, #5
Los Angeles, CA 90048
Singer

Gaynor, Janet
P.O. Box 38
Palm Springs, CA 92262
Actress

Geary, Tony
% Jim Warren
4732 Radford Ave.
North Hollywood, CA 91607
Actor

Geisel, Theodore S. (Dr. Seuss)
7301 Encellia Dr.
La Jolla, CA 92037
*Author of Dr. Seuss children's
books*

Gelbart, Larry
9255 Sunset Blvd., #609
Los Angeles, CA 90069
TV producer

Gemayel, Amin
Office of the President
Beirut, Lebanon
President, Lebanon—since 1982

General Electric Co.
3135 Easton Turnpike
Fairfield, CT 06431
John F. Welsh, Jr., Chairman

General Foods
250 North St.
White Plains, NY 10625
*James L. Ferguson, Chairman—
makers of Oscar Mayer, Jell-O,
Tang, Kool-Aid, Birds Eye, etc.*

General Lee
4000 Warner Blvd.
Burbank, CA 91505
"Dukes" car in The Dukes of
Hazzard

General Mills, Inc.
9200 Wayzata Blvd.
Minneapolis, MN 55440
*H. Brewster Atwater, Jr.,
Chairman—makers of Yoplait,
Gorton Fish, Saluto Foods*

General Motors Corp.
General Motors B109
Detroit, MI 48202
Roger B. Smith, Chairman

George, Wally
P.O. Box 787
Hollywood, CA 90028
Conservative TV broadcaster

Georgia-Pacific Corp.
133 Peachtree St., NE
Atlanta, GA 30303
Robert E. Floweree, Chairman

Gerber Products Co.
445 State St.
Fremont, MI 49412
Aahor J. Frehs, Chairman

Gere, Richard
545 Madison Ave., #800
New York, NY 10022
Actor

Gerhard, Maestro
5 Embarcadero Center
San Francisco, CA
Body hair stylist

Gerulaitis, Vitas Kevin
% U.S. Tennis Assn.
51 E. 42d St.
New York, NY 10017
Prof. tennis player

Gervin, George
San Antonio Spurs
HemisFair Arena
P.O. Box 530
San Antonio, TX 78292
Prof. basketball player

Getty Oil Co.
3810 Wilshire Blvd.
Los Angeles, CA 90010
Sidney R. Peterson, Chairman

Gettys, Loyd Bryant
P.O. Box 378
David City, NE 68632
Numismatist

Getz, Stan
Jack Whittemore
80 Park Ave.
New York, NY 10016
Saxophonist

Gibb, Andy
% Martin Hewlett
8335 Sunset Blvd.
Los Angeles, CA 90069
Singer

Gibb, Barry
% Robert Stigwood Organization
1775 Broadway
New York, NY 10019
Vocalist; songwriter

Gibb, Maurice
% Robert Stigwood Organization
1775 Broadway
New York, NY 10019
Vocalist; songwriter

Gibb, Robin
% Robert Stigwood Organization
1775 Broadway
New York, NY 10019
Vocalist; songwriter

Gibbs, Joe Jackson
Washington Redskins
P.O. Box 17247
Dulles International Airport
Washington, DC 20041
Prof. football coach

Gibbs, Marla
8461 S. Vermont Ave.
Los Angeles, CA 90044
Actress

Gibson, Henry
151 El Camino
Beverly Hills, CA 90212
Comedian

Gibson, Kirk
Detroit Tigers
Tiger Stadium
Detroit, MI 48216
Prof. baseball player

Gibson, Mel
151 El Camino
Beverly Hills, CA 90212
Actor

Gibson, Robert
New York Mets
William A. Shea Stadium
Roosevelt Ave. & 126th St.
Flushing, NY 11368
Baseball coach; former prof.
baseball player

Gielgud, Sir John
South Pavillion
Wotten Underwood
Aylesbury, Buckinghamshire
England
Actor

Gilbert, Rod Gabriel
New York Rangers
Madison Square Garden
4 Pennsylvania Plaza
New York, NY 10001
Prof. hockey player

Gilboa, Netta
2520 N. Lincoln Ave., #120
Chicago, IL 60614
Expert on child pornography

Gilford, Jack
ICM
40 W. 57th St.
New York, NY 10019
Actor; comedian

Gillan, Kevin W.
#11448-086
P.O. Box 1000
Milan, MI 48160
Prisoner; former head of world's
largest LSD manufacturing and
distribution operation

Gillette Co., The
Prudential Tower Bldg.
Boston, MA 02199
Colman M. Mocklei, Jr., Chairman

Gillies, Clark
New York Islanders
Nassau Coliseum
Uniondale, NY 11553
Prof. hockey player

Ginsberg, Allen
261 Columbus Ave.
San Francisco, CA 94133
Poet

Gish, Lillian
430 E. 57th St.
New York, NY 10022
Actress

Glaser, Paul Michael
% Leiderman/Oberman Inc.
10850 Wilshire Blvd.
Los Angeles, CA 90024
Actor

Glass, Ron
Harriet R. Modler
3359 Wade St.
Los Angeles, CA 90066
Actor

Gleason, Jackie
Inverrary
Lauderhill, FL 33319
Actor; comedian

Glenn, John H.
Senate Office Bldg.
Washington, DC 20510
*U.S. Senator (D), Ohio,
1974–present; 1984 presidential
candidate*

Godiva Chocolatier, Inc.
E. Neversink Rd.
Reading, PA 19606
John Moon, Vice President

Godunov, Alexander Boris
% Loree Rodkin Management
2729 Ellison Dr.
Beverly Hills, CA 90210
Ballet dancer

Goldberg, Leonard
Twentieth Century-Fox
P.O. Box 900
Beverly Hills, CA 90213
Television & movie producer

Goldwater, Barry Morris
337 Russell Bldg.
Washington, DC 20510
*U.S. Senator (R), Arizona,
1953–1965, 1969–present*

Goldwyn, Samuel John, Jr.
1041 N. Formosa Ave.
Los Angeles, CA 90046
Motion picture producer

Gonzales, Richard A.
Caesars Palace
Tennis Shop
3570 Las Vegas Blvd.
Las Vegas, NV 89109
Prof. tennis player

Gonzalez Marquez, Felipe
Office of the Prime Minister
Madrid, Spain
Prime Minister, Spain—since 1982

Good Housekeeping **magazine**
959 Eighth Ave.
New York, NY 10019
Wade Nichols, Editor

Good Humor Corp.
40 New Dutch Ln.
Fairfield, NJ 07006
H. M. Tibbetts, President

Goodman, Benny
200 E. 66th St.
New York, NY 10021
Orchestra conductor; clarinetist

Goodman, Dody
721 N. La Brea Ave., #201
Los Angeles, CA 90038
Actress; comedienne

Goodman, Linda
% Press Relations
Manny Unltd.
137 Hayden St.
Cripple Creek, CO 80813
Author

Goodman, Dr. William, & James Price
P.O. Box 1314
Lynchburg, VA 24505
Author, Life with Falwell and Falwell, *an unauthorized biography*

Goodrich Co., B. F.
500 S. Main
Akron, OH 44318
John Dong, Chairman

Goodson, Mark
375 Park Ave.
New York, NY 10022
TV producer

Goodstein, David B.
6400 Canoga Ave., #311
Woodland Hills, CA 91367
Owner, publisher of the Advocate, *world's largest newsmagazine for gay men & women*

Goodyear Tire and Rubber Co.
1144 E. Market
Akron, OH 44316
Charles J. Pilliod, Jr., Chairman

Goolagong Cawley, Evonne
80 Duntroon Ave.
Roseville, New South Wales, Australia
Prof. tennis player

Goralnick, Murray
The Beverly Hills Computer Store
2080 Century Park East
Los Angeles, CA 90067
President

Gordon, Cyrus Herzi
637 East Bldg.
New York University
Washington Sq.
New York, NY 10003
Orientalist; educator

Gordon, Ellen
7401 S. Cicero Ave.
Chicago, IL 60629
Candy company executive

Gordon, Gale
Tub Canyon Farm
P.O. Box 126
Borrego Springs, CA 92004
Actor

Gordon, Ruth
200 W. 57th St., #1203
New York, NY 10019
Actress

Gordy, Berry
6255 Sunset Blvd., #1800
Los Angeles, CA 90028
Founder of Motown Records

Goring, Robert Thomas
New York Islanders
Nassau Coliseum
Uniondale, NY 11553
Prof. hockey player

Gorman, James
245 W. 104th St.
New York, NY 10025
Author, First Aid for Hypochondriacs

Gorme, Eydie
P.O. Box 5140
Beverly Hills, CA 90210
Singer

Gorshin, Frank
P.O. Box 48559
Los Angeles, CA 90048
Impressionist; singer; comedian; actor

Gossert, Harold & Eunice
6597 Flabtown Rd.
Waynesboro, PA 17268
World's heaviest couple (782 lb.)

Gossett, Louis, Jr.
151 El Camino
Beverly Hills, CA 90212
Actor

Gould, Elliott
9000 Sunset Blvd., #315
Los Angeles, CA 90069
Actor

Gould, Susan
P.O. Box 35372
Detroit, MI 48235
Owns and operates Susan's Pets, an erotic-gift mail-order business

Goulder, Joseph
1300 Lamar
Houston, TX 77010
Author, Alligators in Our Sewers, and Other American Credos

Goulet, Robert Gerard
ICM
40 W. 57th St.
New York, NY 10019
Singer; actor

Gowdy, Curtis
Curt Gowdy Broadcasting Inc.
33 Franklin St.
Lawrence, MA 01840
Sportscaster

Grade, Lew
ITC Entertainment Ltd.
17 Great Cumberland Pl.
London, W1H 1AG, England
Entertainment corporation executive

Gradishar, Randy
Denver Broncos
5700 Logan Street
Denver, CO 80216
Prof. football player

Graham, D. Robert
Office of Governor
The Capitol
Tallahassee, FL 32301
Governor of Florida (D), 1979–present

Graham, Virginia
Prentice-Hall
Route 9-W
Englewood Cliffs, NJ 07632
Radio, TV & theatrical performer; lecturer

Graham, William Franklin (Billy)
1300 Harmon Pl.
Minneapolis, MN 55403
Evangelist

Gramm, Phil
House Office Bldg.
Washington, DC 20515
U.S. Congressman (R), Texas, 1979–present

Grandy, Fred
151 El Camino
Beverly Hills, CA 90212
Actor

Grant, Cary
% Fabergé
1345 Avenue of the Americas
New York, NY 10019
Actor

Grant, Hank
Hollywood Reporter
6715 Sunset Blvd.
Los Angeles, CA 90028
Entertainment columnist

Grant, Lee
151 El Camino
Beverly Hills, CA 90212
Actress

Grant, Dr. Toni
3321 S. La Cienega Blvd.
Los Angeles, CA 90016
Radio psychologist

Gray, Erin
9100 Wilshire Blvd., #460
Beverly Hills, CA 90212
Actress

Gray, Hanna Holborn
University of Chicago
5855 University Ave.
Chicago, IL 60637
President

Gray, Linda
3970 Overland Ave.
Culver City, CA 90230
Actress

Gray, Melvin Dean
St. Louis Cardinals
200 Stadium Plaza
St. Louis, MO 63102
Prof. football player

Gray, Paul Edward
111 Memorial Drive
Cambridge, MA 02142
University president (Massachusetts Institute of Technology)

Gray Panthers
3635 Chestnut St.
Philadelphia, PA 19104
Margaret Kuhn, National Convenor

Green, Adolph
211 Central Park West
New York, NY 10024
Playwright, lyricist

Green, George Dallas
Chicago Cubs
Wrigley Field
Clark & Addison Sts.
Chicago, IL 60613
Manager, prof. baseball team

Green, Gordon
1200 Main Tower Bldg.
Dallas, TX 75202
Expert on TV & films of the 1940s & 1950s

Greene, Lorne
Box 1653
Burbank, CA 91507
Actor

Greene, Mean Joe
Pittsburgh Steelers
Three Rivers Stadium
Pittsburgh, PA 15212
Prof. football player

Greene, Shecky
1245 Rancho Dr.
Las Vegas, NV 89106
Entertainer

Greenwood, David
Chicago Bulls
333 N. Michigan Ave.
Chicago, IL 60601
Prof. basketball player

Greyhound Corp., The
Greyhound Tower
Phoenix, AZ 85077
Gerald H. Trautman, Chairman

Grich, Robert Anthony
California Angels
Anaheim Stadium
2000 State College Blvd.
Anaheim, CA 98203
Prof. baseball player

Griese, Robert Allen
106 Washington Rd.
West Point, NY 10996
Prof. football player

Griffin, Alfredo
Toronto Blue Jays
Box 7777
Adelaide St. P.O.
Toronto, ON M5C 2K7
Canada
Prof. baseball player

Griffin, Merv Edward
1541 N. Vine St.
Hollywood, CA 90028
Entertainer; TV producer

Griffith, Andy
Richard O. Linke
4055 Kraft Ave.
Studio City, CA 91604
Actor

Griffith Laboratories
12200 S. Central Ave.
Alsip, IL 60658
Carroll L. Griffith, Chairman—meat additives

Grodin, Charles
ICM
40 W. 57th St.
New York, NY 10019
Actor

94

Groebli, Werner Fritz
% U S Figure Skating Assn.
20 First St.
Colorado Springs, CO 80906
Prof. ice skater

Grogan, Steve
New England Patriots
Schaefer Stadium
Foxboro, MA 02035
Prof. football player

Groh, David
120 El Camino Dr., #206
Beverly Hills, CA 90212
Actor

Grossinger, Paul
Grossinger Hotel
Grossinger, NY 12734
Hotel executive

Grossman, Dr. Richard
4910 Van Nuys Blvd., #306
Sherman Oaks, CA 91403
Plastic surgeon; burn specialist

Ground Zero (Nuclear)
806 15th St., NW, #421
Washington, DC 20036
*Dr. Roger Molander, Executive
Director*

Guardian Angels
982 E. 89th St.
Brooklyn, NY 11236
Curtis Sliwa, Founder

Guidry, Ron
New York Yankees
Yankee Stadium
Bronx, NY 10451
Prof. baseball player

Guillaume, Robert
1438 N. Gower, #567
Los Angeles, CA 90028
Actor; singer

Guinness, Sir Alec
Kettle Brook Meadows
Petersfield, Hampshire
England
Actor

Guinness Book of World Records
Sterling Bros.
419 Park Avenue South
New York, NY 10016
*Norris McWhirter, Editor and
Compiler*

Gulf Oil Corp.
439 Seventh Ave.
Pittsburgh, PA 15219
James E. Lee, Chairman

Gumbel, Bryant
NBC
30 Rockefeller Plaza
New York, NY 10020
Host, Today *show*

Guthrie, Arlo
250 W. 57th St., #1304
New York, NY 10019
Folk singer; composer

Guttenberg, Steve
9255 Sunset Blvd., #1115
Los Angeles, CA 90069
Actor

Gwynne, Fred
Hook Rd.
Bedford Village, NY 10506
Actor

H

Haagen-Dazs
1 Amboy Ave.
Woodbridge, NJ 07075
Kevin Hurley, President

Hackett, Buddy
151 El Camino
Beverly Hills, CA 90212
Actor, comedian

Hackman, Gene
9100 Wilshire Blvd., #517
Beverly Hills, CA 90212
Actor

Hackner, Tobias
525 N. Laurel Ave.
Los Angeles, CA 90048
Runs club for people with a lingerie fetish

Haddad, Jill
P.O. Box 3584
Bakersfield, CA 93385
Expert in pedophilia, child exploitation & molestation

Haden, Patrick Capper
Los Angeles Rams
2327 W. Lincoln Ave.
Anaheim, CA 92801
Prof. football player

Haggard, Merle Ronald
6988 Ramblin Ln.
P.O. Box 500
Bella Vista, CA 96008
Songwriter; recording artist

Hagman, Larry
3970 Overland Ave.
Culver City, CA 90230
Actor

Haig, Alexander
1155 15th St., NW, #800
Washington, DC 20005
Former Secretary of State, 1980–1982

Hailey, Arthur
Seaway Authors Ltd.
1 Pl. Ville Marie, #1609
Montreal, PQ H3B 2B6
Canada
Author

Haley, Alex
P O Box 3338
Beverly Hills, CA 90212
Author

Hall (Daryl) & Oates (John)
Champion Enterprises
130 W. 57th St.
New York, NY 10019
Rock musicians

Hall, Deidre
Days of Our Lives
3000 W. Alameda
Burbank, CA 91523
Actress

Hall, Dino
Cleveland Browns
Municipal Stadium
Cleveland, OH 44114
Prof. football player

Hall, Joseph
Qtrs. 25 Al
Lee Ave.
Fort Meyers, VA 22211
Freed American hostage from Iran

Hall, Monty
7833 Sunset Blvd.
Los Angeles, CA 90046
Television producer; actor

Hall, Tom T.
Hallnote Music
P.O. Box 40209
Nashville, TN 37204
Songwriter; performer

Halston (Roy Halston Frowick)
645 Fifth Ave.
New York, NY 10022
Fashion designer

Hamel, Veronica
9000 Sunset Blvd., #315
Los Angeles, CA 90069
Actress

Hamill, Dorothy Stuart
% Ice Capades, Inc.
6121 Santa Monica Blvd.
Hollywood, CA 90038
Prof. ice skater

Hamill, Mark
Lucasfilm
P.O. Box 8669
Universal City, CA 91608
Actor

Hamilton, Charles
200 W. 57th St.
New York, NY 10019
World's foremost autograph collector & dealer

Hamilton, George
1900 Avenue of the Stars, #1630
Los Angeles, CA 90067
Actor

Hamilton Beach
P.O. Box 1158
Washington, DC 27889
John J. Flaherty, Chief Operating Officer—home appliances

Hamlisch, Marvin
970 Park Ave., #600
New York, NY 10028
Composer

Hammer, Barbara
Goddess Films
P.O. Box 694
Cathedral Station
New York, NY 10025
Feminist filmmaker

Hand-Gun Control
810 18th St., NW, #705
Washington, DC 20006
Nelson T. Shields, Chairman

Hanes Group
P.O. Box 5416
Winston-Salem, NC 27013
Paul Fulton, Jr., President

Hanna, William Denby
3400 W. Cahuenga Blvd.
Hollywood, CA 90068
Animated cartoon producer

Hardy, Mrs. Oliver (Price)
4055 Tujunga Ave.
North Hollywood, CA 91604
Widow of Oliver Hardy

Harlem Globetrotters Inc.
15301 Ventura Blvd., #430
Sherman Oaks, CA
Art Harvey, President

Harley-Davidson
AMF Inc.
777 Westchester Ave.
White Plains, NY 10604
*W. Thomas York, Chairman—
motorcycles*

Harper, Tess
120 El Camino Dr., #104
Beverly Hills, CA 90212
Actress

Harper, Valerie
151 El Camino
Beverly Hills, CA 90212
Actress

Harrah, Toby
Cleveland Indians
Cleveland Stadium
Cleveland, OH 44114
Prof. baseball player

Harris, Emmy Lou
P.O. Box 4471
North Hollywood, CA 91607
Singer

Harris, Franco
Pittsburgh Steelers
Three Rivers Stadium
Pittsburgh, PA 15212
Prof. football player

Harris, Mrs. Jean
Bedford Hills Correctional Facility
Westchester County
Bedford Hills, NY 10507
*Convicted of murdering Dr. Herman
Tarnower, author of* The Complete
Scarsdale Medical Diet

Harris, Joe Frank
Office of Governor
State Capitol
Atlanta, GA 30334
*Governor of Georgia (D),
1983–present*

Harris, Julie
151 El Camino
Beverly Hills, CA 90212
Actress

Harris, Richard
ICM
8899 Beverly Blvd.
Los Angeles, CA 90048
Actor

Harrison, George
Friar Park Rd.
Henley-on-Thames
England
Musician; former Beatle

Harrison, Gregory
P.O. Box 900
Beverly Hills, CA 90213
Actor

Harrison, Rex Cary
La Renadiere Carsinje 1252
Geneva, Switzerland
Actor

Harry, Deborah
1888 Century Park East, #1400
Los Angeles, CA 90067
*Member, Blondie rock group;
actress*

Hart, Gary
Senate Office Bldg.
Washington, DC 20510
*U.S. Senator (D), Colorado,
1975–present; 1984 presidential
candidate*

98

Hart, James Warren (Jim)
St. Louis Cardinals
200 Stadium Plaza
St. Louis, MO 63102
Prof. football player

Hart, John Lewis
% Field Newspaper Syndicate
401 N. Wabash Ave.
Chicago, IL 60611
Cartoonist

Hartley, Mariette
9454 Wilshire Blvd., #M1
Beverly Hills, CA 90212
Actress

Hartman, David
7 W. 66th St.
New York, NY 10023
TV host

Hartman, David Downs
% Trascott Alyson & Craig Inc.
222 Cedar Ln.
Teaneck, NJ 07666
Actor

Hartz Mountain Corp.
700 S. Fourth St.
Harrison, NJ 07029
Leonard N. Stern, Chairman

Harvey, Paul
360 N. Michigan Ave.
Chicago, IL 60601
Radio commentator

Hasen, Irwin Hanan
% Chicago Tribune
NY News Syndicate Inc.
News Building
220 E. 42d St.
New York, NY 10017
Cartoonist

Hasselhoff, David
8380 Waring Ave., #204
Los Angeles, CA 90069
Actor

Hatch, Orrin G.
Senate Office Bldg.
Washington, DC 20510
U.S. Senator (R), Utah,
1977–present

Hatcher, Mickey
Minnesota Twins
Hubert H. Humphrey Metrodome
501 Chicago Avenue South
Minneapolis, MN 44415
Prof. baseball player

Hatfield, Mark
Rm. 463
Senate Office Bldg.
Washington, DC 20510
U.S. Senator (R), Oregon,
1967–present

Hauser, Gayelord
Hauser Editorial Office
P.O. Box 09398
Milwaukee, WI 53209
Author; nutritionist

Hawke, Bob
Office of Prime Minister
Canberra, Australia
Prime Minister, Australia—since
1983

Hawn, Goldie
8642 Melrose Ave.
Los Angeles, CA 90069
Actress; producer

Hayakawa, Samuel Ichiye
6217 Dirksen Senate Office Bldg.
Washington, DC 20510
U.S. Senator (R), California,
1977–present

Hayden, Sterling
% G. P. Putnam
200 Madison Ave.
New York, NY 10016
Actor

Hayden, Tom
409 Santa Monica Blvd., #214
Santa Monica, CA 90401
Political activist; lecturer; writer

Hayes, Bill, & Susan Seaforth
Burbank Studios
Columbia Pictures Television
Burbank, CA 91505
Performers

Hayes, Elvin
Houston Rockets
The Summit
Houston, TX 77046
Prof. basketball player

Hayes, Isaac
1290 Avenue of the Americas, #264
New York, NY 10019
Composer; singer

Hayes, Peter Lind
3538 Pueblo Way
Las Vegas, NV 89109
Actor

Haynes, Michael James
New England Patriots
Schaefer Stadium
Foxboro, MA 02035
Prof. football player

Hays, Robert
10100 Santa Monica Blvd., #310
Los Angeles, CA 90067
Actor

Hayworth, Rita
132 Lasky Dr.
Beverly Hills, CA 90212
Actress

Hearst, Patty
110 Fifth St.
San Francisco, CA 94103
Victim of kidnap

Hearst Corp., The
959 Eighth Ave.
New York, NY 10019
Randolph A. Hearst, Chairman

Heart
6300 S. Center Blvd., #200
Seattle, WA 98188
Rock group

Hebrew-National Kosher Foods Inc.
5880 Maurice Ave.
Maspeth, NY 11378
Isidore Pines, President

Heckler, Margaret M.
Department of Health & Human
Services
200 Independence Ave., SW
Washington, DC 20201
Secretary

Heinz, H. John, III
Senate Office Bldg.
Washington, DC 20510
*U.S. Senator (R), Pennsylvania,
1977–present*

Heinz Co., H. J.
1062 Progress
Pittsburgh, PA 15212
Henry J. Heinz II, Chairman

Helms, Jesse A.
Senate Office Bldg.
Washington, DC 20510
*U.S. Senator (R), North Carolina,
1973–present*

Hemsley, Sherman
100 Universal City Plaza
Universal City, CA 91608
Actor

Henderson, Florence
151 El Camino
Beverly Hills, CA 90212
Singer; actress

Henderson, Ricky
Oakland Athletics
Oakland Coliseum
Oakland, CA 94621
Prof. baseball player

Hendrick, George
St. Louis Cardinals
Busch Memorial Stadium
250 Stadium Plaza
St. Louis, MO 63102
Prof. baseball player

Henson, Jim
P.O. Box 2495
New York, NY 10001
Puppeteer; creator of Muppets

Hepburn, Audrey
Ville Trotschenatz-Leman
Switzerland
Actress

Hepburn, Katharine
201 Bloomfield Ave.
West Hartford, CT 06117
Actress

Herbeck, Kent
Minnesota Twins
Hubert II. Humphrey Metrodome
501 Chicago Avenue South
Minneapolis, MN 55415
Prof. baseball player

Herpes Handbook
Alternative Treatment Programs
P.O. Box 9428
San Rafael, CA 94912
Dr. Tom Klosinsky, Founder

Herpes Resource Center
Box 100
Palo Alto, CA 94302
Carla F. Hines, Program Director

Hershey Foods Corp.
100 Mansion Road East
Hershey, PA 17033
Harold S. Mohler, Chairman

Hertz Corp.
660 Madison Ave.
New York, NY 10021
Frank A. Olson, Chairman

Hessman, Howard
151 El Camino
Beverly Hills, CA 90212
Actor

Heston, Charlton
9255 Sunset Blvd., #910
Los Angeles, CA 90069
Actor

Hewitt, Christopher
10000 Santa Monica Blvd., #205
Los Angeles, CA 90067
Actor

Hill, Albert Alan
Council on Environmental Quality
722 Jackson Pl., NW
Washington, DC 20006
Chairman, 1981–present

Hill, Benny
% Thames Television
1370 Avenue of the Americas
New York, NY 10019
Performer

Hillerman, John
100 Universal City Plaza
Universal City, CA 91608
Actor

Hilton, Barron
Hilton Hotels Corp.
9880 Wilshire Blvd.
Beverly Hills, CA 90210
Chairman of Board, President and Chief Executive Officer

Hinckley, John, Jr.
St. Elizabeths Hospital
2700 Martin Luther King, Jr., Ave., SE
Washington, DC 20032
Attempted assassination of President Ronald Reagan

Hirohito, Emperor
Office of the Emperor
Tokyo, Japan
Emperor of Japan—since 1926

Ho, Don
International Marketplace
2330 Kalakaua Ave.
Honolulu, HI 96814
Singer

Hobson, Nancy
Victims for Victims
1800 S. Robertson
Bldg. 6, Suite 400
Los Angeles, CA 90035
Rape victim; member of board of
directors of Victims for Victims

Hodel, Donald P.
Department of Interior
1000 Independence Ave., SW
Washington, DC 20585
Undersecretary, 1981–present

Hoffman, Dustin
315 E. 65th St.
New York, NY 10021
Actor

Hog Wild
280 Friend
Boston, MA 02114
David Mercer, President—pig
merchandise store

Hohlweg, Prof. Dr. Walter
Prevenhueberweg 25
8047 Graz, Austria
Discovered sex hormones

Holiday Inns Inc.
3742 Lamar Ave.
Memphis, TN 38195
Roy E. Winegardner, Chairman of
Board

Holistic Life Foundation
1627 10th Ave.
San Francisco, CA 94122
William Staniger, President

Hollings, Ernest F.
Senate Office Building
Washington, DC 20510
U.S. Senator (D), South Carolina,
1966–present; 1984 presidential
candidate

Holly, Mrs. Buddy (Diaz)
717 E. Rochelle Blvd.
Irving, TX 75062
Widow of Buddy Holly

Hollywood Reporter
6715 Sunset Blvd.
Hollywood, CA 90028
Tichi Wilkerson Miles, Editor &
Publisher

Home Oriented Maternity
Experience
511 New York Ave.
Takoma Park
Washington, DC 20012
Esther Herman, Executive Secretary

Honda Motor Co.
100 W. Alondra Blvd.
Gardena, CA 90247
Kent Dellinger, Supervisor

Honecker, Erich
Office of the Secretary
East Berlin, East Germany
First Secretary of Communist party,
East Germany—since 1971

Honetschlager, Lorin
129 W. Juniper
Mesa, AZ 85201
Scorpion milker

Honeywell, Inc.
Honeywell Plaza
Minneapolis, MN 55408
E. W. Spencer, Chairman of the
Board

Hooper, Bob Scott
4330 W. Desert Inn Rd., #3
Las Vegas, NV 89102
Playboy photographer

Hope, Bob
10346 Moorpark
North Hollywood, CA 91602
Entertainer

Hopper, Dennis
Box 1889, Los Gallos
Taos, NM 87571
Actor

Horne, Lena
9255 Sunset Blvd., #318
Los Angeles, CA 90069
Singer

Horner, Bob
Atlanta Braves
P.O. Box 4064
Atlanta, GA 30302
Prof. baseball player

Horsley, Lee
7319 Beverly Blvd., #1
Los Angeles, CA 90036
Actor

Hoschek, John
Motor Bus Society
P.O. Box 7058
Trenton, NJ 08628
Bus expert

House, David
Pretty Girl International
13837 Ventura Blvd.
Sherman Oaks, CA 91403
Runs world's largest nude model agency

Hovanec, Helene
5 Sprucc Ln.
Kingston, NJ 08528
Expert on word puzzles

Howard, Ron
5555 Melrose Ave.
Los Angeles, CA 90038
Actor; director

Howard, Trevor
Rowley Green
Arkley, Hertfordshire
England
Actor

Howard Johnson Co.
220 Forbes Rd.
Braintree, MA 02184
G. Michael Hostage, Chairman of Board

Howell, C. Thomas
113 N. Robertson Blvd.
Los Angeles, CA 90048
Actor

Howland, Beth
4000 Warner Blvd.
Burbank, CA 91505
Actress

Hubcap Collectors Club
Box 54
Buckley, MI 49620
Dennis H. Kuhn, President

Hudson, Rock
151 El Camino
Beverly Hills, CA 90212
Actor

Hug Club
P.O. Box 453
Laguna Beach, CA 92652
Ellen Woods, Chairman—motto: There is no warmer gift than a hug

Hughes, Mike
P.O. Box 727
Hollywood, CA 90028
Former cat burglar

Hughes Aircraft Co.
Centinela Ave. & Teale St.
Culver City, CA 90230
A. E. Puckett, Chairman

Humbard, Rev. Rex Emanuel
2690 State Rd.
Cuyahoga Falls, OH 44223
TV evangelist

Humphrey, Muriel
822 Marquette St., #341
Minneapolis, MN 55402
Widow of former Vice President Hubert Humphrey

Hunger Project
2015 Steiner St.
San Francisco, CA 94115
Joan Holmes, Executive Director

Hunter, Jim ("Catfish")
RR #1, Box 945
Hertford, NC 27944
Former prof. baseball pitcher

Hunt-Wesson Foods
1645 W. Valencia Dr.
Fullerton, CA 92634
Frederick B. Rentschler, President

Hurt, John
60 St. James St.
London, SW1, England
Actor

Hurt, William
7319 Beverly Blvd.
Los Angeles, CA 90036
Actor

Hussein, Saddam
Office of the President
Baghdad, Iraq
President, Iraq—since 1979

Hussein I, King
Box 1055
Amman, Jordan
Ruler

Huston, John
Aptdo Postal 273
Libro Puerta Vallarta
Jalisco, 22261 Mexico
Film director; actor

Hutton, Lauren
9665 Wilshire Blvd., #200
Beverly Hills, CA 90212
Actress; model

Hutton, Timothy
ICM
8899 Beverly Blvd.
Los Angeles, CA 90048
Actor

Hyatt Corp.
9700 W. Bryn Mawr Ave.
Rosemont, IL 60018
Jay A. Pritzker, Chairman

Hyde, Henry J.
House Office Bldg.
Washington, DC 20515
*U.S. Congressman (R), Illinois,
1981–present*

I

Ice Capades, Inc.
6121 Santa Monica Blvd.
Hollywood, CA 90038
Richard Palmer, President

Ideal Toys Corp.
184-10 Jamaica Ave.
Hollis, NY 11423
Lionel A. Weintraub, Chairman

Iglesias, Julio
9665 Wilshire Blvd., #200
Beverly Hills, CA 90212
Singer

Inouye, Daniel K.
Senate Office Bldg.
Washington, DC 20510
U.S. Senator (D), Hawaii,
1963–present

International Barbie Doll Collectors
Club
P.O. Box 79
Bronx, NY 10464
Ruth Cronk, President

International Beer Tasting Society
801 Via Lido Soud
Newport Beach, CA 92663
Martin J. Lockney, Director

International Brotherhood of Old
Bastards
2330 S. Brentwood Blvd.
St. Louis, MO 63144
Brother Cozen P. Bantling,
Supreme Arch Bastard

International Chinese Snuff Bottle
Society
2601 N. Charles St.
Baltimore, MD 21218
John G. Ford, Vice President &
Secretary

International Church of Ageless
Wisdom, Inc.
P.O. Box 101
Wyalusing, PA 18853
Roberta S. Herzog, Archbishop

International Correspondence of
Corkscrew Addicts
275 Windsor St.
Hartford, CT 06120
Homer D. Babbidge, Jr., Executive
Officer

International Dairy Queen, Inc.
5701 Green Valley Dr.
Minneapolis, MN 55437
John W. Mooty, Chairman

International Federation of
Bodybuilders
2875 Bates Rd.
Montreal, PQ H3S 1B7
Canada
Ben Weider, President

International Flavors & Fragrances,
Inc.
521 W. 57th St.
New York, NY 10019
Henry G. Walter, Jr., Chairman

International Frisbee Disc Assn.
P.O. Box 970
San Gabriel, CA 91776
*Dr. Daniel M. Roddick, Executive
Director*

International House of Pancakes
6837 Lankershim Blvd.
North Hollywood, CA 91605
Richard K. Herzer, President

International Telephone &
Telegraph
320 Park Ave.
New York, NY 10022
Rand V. Araskog, Chairman

International Twins Assn.
114 N. Lafayette Dr.
Muncie, IN 47303
Judy Stillwagon, Secretary-Treasurer

Irons, Jeremy
The Lantz Office
888 Seventh Ave.
New York, NY 10019
Actor

Irving, Amy
7319 Beverly Blvd., #1
Los Angeles, CA 90036
Actress

Irving, Julius ("Dr. J.")
Philadelphia 76ers
Veterans Stadium
P.O. Box 25040
Philadelphia, PA 19147
Prof. basketball player

Isaac, William M.
Federal Deposit Insurance Corp.
550 17th St., NW
Washington, DC 20429
Chairman

J

Jabbar, Kareem Abdul
10100 Santa Monica Blvd., #1044
Los Angeles, CA 90067
Prof. basketball player, Los Angeles Lakers

Jackson, Anne (Mrs. Eli Wallach)
% Actors Equity Membership
Department
165 W. 46th St.
New York, NY 10036
Actress

Jackson, Chuck
P.O. Box 538
Templeton, CA 93465
Makes ventriloquist dummies

Jackson, Glenda
51 Harvey Rd.
Blackheath
London, SE3, England
Actress

Jackson, Jesse
Operation PUSH
930 E. 50th St.
Chicago, IL 60615
Civil rights leader; 1984 presidential candidate

Jackson, Kate
9665 Wilshire Blvd., #200
Beverly Hills, CA 90212
Actress

Jackson, Michael
4641 Hayvenhurst Ave.
Encino, CA 91436
Singer

Jackson, Reggie
California Angels
P.O. Box 2000
Anaheim, CA 92803
Prof. baseball player

Jagger, Bianca
Cheyne Walk
Chelsea
London, SW3, England
Actress; former wife of Mick Jagger

Jagger, Mick
Rolling Stones Records
1841 Broadway
New York, NY 10023
Rock singer; songwriter

James, John
Box 60257
Terminal Annex
Los Angeles, CA 90060
Actor

Jan & Dean
Jan: 1111 Linda Flora Dr.
Los Angeles, CA. 90049

Dean: 8912 Burton Way
Beverly Hills, CA 90211
Music group

Jarreau, Al
Warner Bros.
3300 Warner Blvd.
Burbank, CA 91505
Singer

Jaruzelski, General Wojciech
Ministers Two Obrony Narodowej
U1.Klonowa 1, 00-909
Warsaw, Poland
Premier of Poland—since 1981

Jaworski, Ron
Philadelphia Eagles
Veterans Stadium
Philadelphia, PA 19148
Prof. football player

Jefferson, Jesse
New Orleans Saints
1500 Poydras St.
New Orleans, LA 70112
Prof. football player

Jefferson Starship
2400 Fulton St.
San Francisco, CA 94118
Music group

Jenkins, Jackie ("Butch")
East Texas Water Systems Co.
Quinlan, TX 75474
Former child star

Jenner, Bruce
% Sports Media Sales
1901 Avenue of the Stars
Los Angeles, CA 90067
Olympic Gold Medal winner;
spokesman

Jennings, Waylon
141 El Camino Dr., #110
Beverly Hills, CA 90212
Singer

Jewish Defense League
76 Madison Ave.
New York, NY 10016
Rabbi Meir Kahane, Executive
Director

J. Geils Band
8 Cadman Plaza West
Brooklyn, NY 11201
Band

Jillian, Ann
P.O. Box 408
San Ramon, CA 94583
Actress

Joel, Billy
CBS Records
51 W. 57th St.
New York, NY 10019
Singer

Johan, Marie
120 El Camino Dr., #104
Beverly Hills, CA 90212
Dancer—did the dancing in the
movie *Flashdance*

John, Elton
9665 Wilshire Blvd., #200
Los Angeles, CA 90212
Singer; songwriter

John Paul II, Pope
Palazzo Apostolico Vatican
Vatican City, Italy
Head of Roman Catholic Church

Johns and Call Girls United Against
Repression
P.O. Box 1011
Brooklyn, NY 11202
Hugh Montgomery, President

Johnson, Betty
NASA
Houston, TX 77058
Spokesperson for potential
astronauts

Johnson, Cliff
Toronto Blue Jays
Box 7777
Adelaide St. P.O.
Toronto, ON M5C 2K7
Canada
Prof. baseball player

Johnson, Mrs. Lady Bird
78671 Stonewall
Austin, TX 78701
*Widow of President Lyndon B.
Johnson*

Johnson, Loudilla, Loretta, Kay
International Fan Club
Organization
P.O. Box 177
Wild Horse, CO 80862
*Founding members, Loretta Lynn &
Country Music fan clubs*

Johnson, Magic
Los Angeles Lakers
The Forum
3900 W. Manchester Blvd.
　　　　or
P.O. Box 10
Inglewood, CA 90306
Prof. basketball player

Johnson, Marques
Milwaukee Bucks
901 N. Fourth St.
Milwaukee, WI 53203
Prof. basketball player

Johnson, Van
151 El Camino
Beverly Hills, CA 90212
Actor

Johnson & Johnson
501 George St.
New Brunswick, NJ 08903
J. E. Burke, Chairman

Johnston, Jay
Chicago Cubs
Wrigley Field
Chicago, IL 60613
Prof. baseball player

Jolly Green Giant
1100 N. Fourth St.
Le Sueur, MN 56058
Vegetable giant

Jones, Bobby
Philadelphia 76ers
Veterans Stadium
P.O. Box 25040
Philadelphia, PA 19147
Prof. basketball player

Jones, Caldwell
Houston Rockets
The Summit
Houston, TX 77046
Prof. basketball player

Jones, Davy
100 Berkley Sq., #6H
Atlantic City, NJ 08401
*Singer; actor; former member of
rock group The Monkees*

Jones, Ed ("Too Tall")
Dallas Cowboys
6116 N. Central Expwy.
Dallas, TX 75206
Prof. football player

Jones, Grace
A.R.C.
75 Rockefeller Plaza
New York, NY 10019
Singer

**Jones, Drs. Howard D. W. &
Georgeanne**
Norfolk General Hospital
Norfolk, VA 23501
Developed first U.S. test-tube baby

Jones, Ricki Lee
3300 Warner Blvd.
Burbank, CA 91505
Singer

Jones, Tom
CBS Records
51 W. 52d St.
New York, NY 10019
Singer

Jong, Erica
New American Library
1633 Broadway
New York, NY 10019
Writer

Jorgenson, Christine
31752 Grand Canyon Dr.
Laguna Niguel, CA 92677
First transsexual

Journey
Box 404
San Francisco, CA 94101
Rock group

J. S. & A.
235 Anthony Trail
Northbrook, IL 60062
Joe Sugarman, Founder—
organization that takes reservations
for space shuttle

Juan Carlos, King
Palaciode la Zarzuela
Madrid, Spain
Ruler of Spain—since 1975

Jurgensen, Sonny
P.O. Box 53
Mount Vernon, VA 22121
Prof. football player

K

Kahane, Rabbi Meir
76 Madison Ave.
New York, NY 10016
Founder, Jewish Defense League

Kahn, Madeline
151 El Camino
Beverly Hills, CA 90212
Actress

Kamuda, Edward
Titanic Historical Society
P.O. Box 53
Indian Orchard, MA 01151
The Titanic *expert*

Kanaly, Steve
8966 Sunset Blvd.
Los Angeles, CA 90069
Actor

Kane, Carol
151 El Camino
Beverly Hills, CA 90212
Actress

Kapral, Charles
Bldg. 28, Apt. 3
Skytop Gardens
Parlin, NJ 08859
Expert on lunar phenomena

Karmal, Babrak
Office of the President
Kabul, Afghanistan
President, Afghanistan—since 1979

Karsh, Yousuf
Box 1931
Prescott Hwy.
Ottawa, ON
Canada
Photographer

Kasem, Casey
C.U.
7461 Beverly Blvd.
Los Angeles, CA 90036
Radio & TV spokesperson

Kassebaum, Nancy L.
Senate Office Bldg.
Washington, DC 20510
U.S. Senator (R), Kansas,
1979–present

Kaufman, Andy
141 El Camino Dr., #205
Los Angeles, CA 90212
Actor

K. C. & The Sunshine Band
495 S.E. 10th Ct.
P.O. Box 1780
Hialeah, FL 33010
Band

Keach, Stacy
1888 Century Park East, #1400
Los Angeles, CA 90067
Actor

Keaton, Diane
145 Central Park West
New York, NY 10023
Actress

Keds Corp., The
Cambridge Center
Cambridge, MA 02142
Arnold Hiatt, Chairman of Board

Keebler Elves
Keebler Co.
One Hollow Tree Ln.
Elmhurst, IL 60126
Spokeselves for Keebler Cookies

Keeler, Ruby
Balboa Bay Club
1221 W. Coast Hwy, #220
Newport Beach, CA 92661
Actress

Keep America Beautiful
99 Park Ave.
New York, NY 10016
Roger W. Powers, President

Keeshan, Bob
555 W. 57th St.
New York, NY 10019
Captain Kangaroo

Keith, David
8642 Melrose Ave., #200
Los Angeles, CA 90069
Actor

Kellogg Co.
235 Porter
Battle Creek, MI 49016
W. E. Lamothe, Chairman

Kelly, Gene
725 N. Rodeo Dr.
Beverly Hills, CA 90210
Actor

Kelly, Mary-Carol
Scott Newman Foundation
Burbank Studios
4000 Warner Blvd.
Burbank, CA 91505
Executive director, antidrug abuse group of which Paul Newman is president

Kelly Girls
Kelly Services, Inc.
999 W. Big Beaver
Troy, MI 48084
W. R. Kelly, Chairman

Kelsey, Linda
1116 S. Alvira St.
Los Angeles, CA 90035
Actress

Kemp, Jack F.
House Office Bldg.
Washington, DC 20515
U.S. Congressman (R), New York, 1970–present

Kennedy, Edward Moore
Senate Office Bldg.
Washington, DC 20510
U.S. Senator (D), Massachusetts, 1962–present

Kennedy, George
9000 Sunset Blvd., #1112
Los Angeles, CA 90069
Actor

Kennedy, Leon Isaac
9000 Sunset Blvd., #1112
Los Angeles, CA 90069
Actor

Kennedy, Rose Fitzgerald
Hyannis Port, MA 02647
Mother of John, Robert, Edward Kennedy

Kennedy, Terry
San Diego Padres
P.O. Box 2000
San Diego, CA 92120
Prof. baseball player

Kent, Raymond Dennis
555 N. 30th St.
Omaha, NE 68131
Phonetician

Kercheval, Ken
% Two Century Plaza, #2060
2049 Century Park East
Los Angeles, CA 90067
Actor

Kercsmar, Grace
639 WMS
Bethlehem, PA 18015
Cosponsor, Old Maids Day, June 4

Kermit the Frog
P.O. Box 2495
New York, NY 10001
Muppet

Kerr, Deborah
Wyhergut
7250 Klosters
Grisons, Switzerland
Actress

Kerr, Walter F.
230 W. 41st St.
New York, NY 10018
Drama critic; author

Kerwin, Lance
Box 237
Lake Elsinore, CA 92326
Actor

Kesey, Ken
85829 Ridgeway Rd.
Pleasant Hill, OR 97401
Author, One Flew Over the
Cuckoo's Nest

Ketcham, Hank
P.O. Box 800
Pebble Beach, CA 93953
Cartoonist, Dennis the Menace

Keyworth, George A., II
Office of Science & Technology
Policy
Executive Office Building
Washington, DC 20503
Director, 1976–present

Khomeini, Ayatollah Ruhollah
State Offices
Teheran, Iran
Religious head, Iran—since 1979

Kibbe, David
Color Me Beautiful
30 Lincoln Plaza
New York, NY 10023
Color consultant

Kidder, Margot
9100 Wilshire Blvd., #852
Los Angeles, CA 90212
Actress

Kiff, Kaleena
6640 Sunset Blvd., #203
Los Angeles, CA 90028
Actress

Kiley, Daniel Urban
Castle Forest
Charlotte, VT 05445
Landscape architect; planner

Killy, Jean-Claude
73 Val-d'Isere
France
Former prof. skier

Kilpatrick, James L.
White Walnut Hill
Woodville, VA 22749
Syndicated columnist

Kimball International
1549 Royal St.
Jasper, IN 47546
Thomas L. Habig, Chairman

King, Alan
151 El Camino
Beverly Hills, CA 90212
Entertainer

King, B. B.
% Sidney A. Seidenberg
1414 Avenue of the Americas
New York, NY 10019
World famous blues star; singer; guitarist

King, Bernard
New York Knicks
Madison Square Garden Center
4 Pennsylvania Plaza
New York, NY 10001
Prof. basketball player

King, Billie Jean
2029 Century Park East, #1200
Los Angeles, CA 90067
Prof. tennis player

King, Carole
Broysky Stewart Group Inc.
1209 Baylor St.
Austin, TX 78703
Composer; singer

King, Coretta Scott
671 Beckwith St., SW
Atlanta, GA 30314
Lecturer; writer; concert singer; widow of Martin Luther King, Jr.

King, Perry
1888 Century Park East, #1400
Los Angeles, CA 90067
Actor

King, Stephen
Viking Press
40 W. 23d St.
New York, NY 10010
Author

Kingman, David Arthur
New York Mets
William A. Shea Stadium
Roosevelt Ave. & 126th St.
Flushing, NY 11368
Prof. baseball player

Kingsley, Ben
ICM
40 W. 57th St.
New York, NY 10019
Actor

Kinski, Nastassia
ICM
8899 Beverly Blvd.
Los Angeles, CA 90048
Actress

Kipnis, Igor
20 Drummer Ln.
RFD 2
West Redding, CT 06896
Harpsichordist

Kirby, Durward
Box 374, Rte. #37
Sherman, CT 06784
Comedian

Kirkland, Gelsey
945 Fifth Ave.
New York, NY 10021
Ballet dancer

Kirkpatrick, Jeane J.
United Nations
1 UN Plaza
New York, NY 10017
Permanent U.S. Representative to United Nations—since 1981

Kirshner, Don
1370 Avenue of the Americas
New York, NY 10019
Entertainer

KISS
P.O. Box 840
Westbury, NY 11590
Rock group

Kissinger, Henry Alfred
1800 K St., NW, #400
Washington, DC 20006
Former Secretary of State, 1973–1977; presidential adviser on Central America

Kitt, Eartha Mae
1290 Avenue of the Americas, #264
New York, NY 10019
Actress; singer

Kittle, Rod
Chicago White Sox
Comiskey Park
324 W. 35th St.
Chicago, IL 60616
Prof. baseball player

Klanwatch (KKK)
1001 S. Hull St.
Montgomery, AL 36101
Randall Williams, Executive Director

Klein, Calvin Richard
205 W. 39th St.
New York, NY 10018
Designer

Klein, Robert
% Rollins & Joffe Inc.
130 W. 57th St.
New York, NY 10019
Comedian; actor

Kleiner, Dick
P.O. Box 25025
Los Angeles, CA 90025
Syndicated entertainment columnist; author

Kline, Kevin
1888 Century Park East, #1400
Los Angeles, CA 90067
Actor

Kloss, John Anthony
10 W. 66th St.
New York, NY 10023
Fashion designer

Klugman, Jack
9200 Sunset Blvd., #909
Los Angeles, CA 90069
Actor

K-Mart Corp.
3100 W. Big Beaver Rd.
Troy, MI 48084
Bernard M. Fauber, Chairman

Knapp, Edward A.
National Science Foundation (NSF)
1800 G St., NW
Washington, DC 20550
Director

Knievel, Robert Craig
(Evel Knievel)
Box 7777
Butte, MT 59701
Stunt motorcyclist

Knight, Gladys
1414 Avenue of the Americas
New York, NY 10019
Singer

Knight, Ted
P.O. Box 642
Pacific Palisades, CA 90272
Actor

Knotts, Don
9454 Wilshire Blvd., #309
Beverly Hills, CA 90212
Actor

Knox, Charles Robert
Buffalo Bills
1 Bills Dr.
Orchard Park, NY 14127
Prof. football coach

Knox, Chuck
Seattle Seahawks
5305 Lake Washington Blvd.
Kirkland, WA 98033
Prof. football coach

Koch, Edward I.
Office of the Mayor
City Hall
New York, NY 10007
Mayor of New York City (D), 1978–present

Koch, Howard Winchel
5451 Marathon St.
Hollywood, CA 90038
Film and TV producer, Academy Awards telecasts

Kohl, Chancellor Helmut
Bundeskanzuramt
Adenauerallee, 139-141
53 Bonn 1, West Germany
Prime Minister, 1982–present

Kollek, Teddy
22 Jaffa Rd.
Jerusalem, Israel
Mayor of Jerusalem, 1978–present

Kolodin, Irving
Saturday Review magazine
150 E. 58th St.
New York, NY 10022
Music critic

Kong, Queen
P.O. Box 504
Harbor City, CA 90710
Erotic lady wrestler

Koosman, Jerry Martin
RR 2
Box 67E
Chaska, MN 55318
Prof. baseball player

Kopell, Bernard Morton
10201 Pico Blvd.
Los Angeles, CA 90046
Actor; writer

Koppel, Ted
ABC-TV
7 W. 66th St.
New York, NY 10023
TV journalist

Korman, Harvey Herschel
% Singer and Lewak
10960 Wilshire Blvd.
Los Angeles, CA 90024
Actor

Kornmuller, Hellmuth
Lake Superior State College
Sault Ste. Marie, MI 49783
*Expert on sauntering—leisurely,
essentially purposeless walking*

Kosinski, Jerzy Nikodem
60 W. 57th St.
New York, NY 10019
Author

Kraft Foods
Kraft Ct.
Glenview, IL 60023
A. W. Woelfle, President

Kramer, Tommy
Minnesota Vikings
9520 Viking Dr.
Eden Prairie, MN 55344
Prof. football player

Krantz, Judith
Crown Publishers
1 Park Ave.
New York, NY 10016
Author

Kraus, Hans Peter
16 E. 46th St.
New York, NY 10017
Rare book dealer; publisher

Krause, Bernard Leo
680 Beach St., #414
San Francisco, CA 94109
*Sonic artist; composer; audio
electronics firm executive*

Kresge, Stanley Sebastian
2401 W. Big Beaver Rd.
Troy, MI 48084
*Founder, executive (S.S. Kresge
Co.)*

Kreskin
3 Oates Terr.
West Caldwell, NJ 07006
Mentalist

Kristofferson, Kris
Monument Entertainment
Corporation of America
21 Music Square East
Nashville, TN 37203
Actor; singer

Kruh, Louis
17 Alfred Road West
Merrick, NY 11566
Expert on cryptology—science of
deciphering codes

Kubek, Anthony Christopher
NBC-TV
30 Rockefeller Plaza
New York, NY 10020
Sports announcer; former prof.
baseball player

Kubrick, Stanley
Borehamwood
England
Film director

Kuhn, Bowie
15 W. 51st St.
New York, NY 10019
Commissioner of baseball

Ku Klux Klan, Invisible Empire,
Knights of the Imperial Wizard
P.O. Box 700
Denham Springs, LA 70726
Bill Wilkinson, Grand Wizard

Kunkin, Arthur
4521 Wallace Ln.
Salt Lake City, UT 84117
Founder of Los Angeles Free Press

Kunstler, William Moses
Center for Constitutional Rights
853 Broadway
New York, NY 10003
Lawyer; author

Kupcinet, Irv
Chicago Sun-Times
401 Wabash Ave.
Chicago, IL 60611
Syndicated entertainment columnist

Kupke, Frederic Lee
Rte. #2, Box 40
Francesville, IN 47946
Freed American hostage from Iran

Kuralt, Charles Bishop
CBS News
524 W. 57th St.
New York, NY 10019
TV news correspondent

Ky, General Nguyen Cao
15701 Sunburst Circle
Huntington Beach, CA 92649
Former President of Vietnam

Kyser, Kay
504 E. Franklin St.
Chapel Hill, NC 27514
Band leader

L

Lacayo, Carmela Gloria
1730 W. Olympic Blvd., #401
Los Angeles, CA 90015
*Corporate executive, political party
official (D)*

Lachman, Morton
4115 B Warner Blvd.
Burbank, CA 91505
Writer; director; producer

Lack, Fredell
4202 S. MacGregor Way
Houston, TX 77021
Concert violinist

Ladd, Alan Walbridge, Jr.
Ladd Co.
Burbank, CA 91501
Motion picture executive

Ladd, Cheryl
151 El Camino
Beverly Hills, CA 90212
Actress

Laffer, Arthur
608 Silver Spur Rd., #229
Rolling Hills Estates, CA 90274
*Supply side economist; inventor of
the Laffer Curve*

LaFleur, Guy
Montreal Canadiens
2313 W. St. Catherine St.
Montreal, PQ H3H 1N2
Canada
Prof. hockey player

Lahti, Christine
7319 Beverly Blvd., #1
Los Angeles, CA 90036
Actress

Laingen, Lowell Bruce
Department of State
Washington, DC 20520
Diplomat

Laird, Campbell
Department of Metallurgy &
Materials Science
University of Pennsylvania
Philadelphia, PA 19104
Metallurgist

Laird, Jack
Universal Studios
Universal City, CA 91608
*Film & TV producer; writer;
director*

118

Laird, Melvin R.
1730 Rhode Island Ave., NW
Washington, DC 20036
*Former Secretary of Defense
1969–1972*

Lake, Arthur
Thunderbird Country Club
Palm Desert, CA 92260
Dagwood on radio & film in
Blondie *series*

Lakein, Alan
2918 Webster St.
San Francisco, CA 94123
*Instructor for a more purposeful way
of life*

Lamarr, Hedy
% Paul J. Sherman
410 Park Ave.
New York, NY 10022
Motion picture actress

Lamas, Lorenzo
3970 Overland Ave.
Los Angeles, CA 90230
Actor

La Master, Frank
San Francisco Giants
Candlestick Park
San Francisco, CA 94124
Prof. baseball player

**Lamberg-Karlovsky, Clifford
Charles**
Peabody Museum
Harvard University
Cambridge, MA 02138
Anthropologist; archaeologist

Lambert, John Harold (Jack)
Pittsburgh Steelers
Three Rivers Stadium
Pittsburgh, PA 15212
Prof. football player

Lamm, Richard D.
State Capitol
Denver, CO 80203
*Governor of Colorado (D),
1975–present*

LaMotta, Vicki
520 East Dr.
North Miami, FL 33162
52-year-old Playmate *centerfold;
wife of former fighter Jake LaMotta*

Lamparski, Richard
3289 Carse Dr.
Los Angeles, CA 90068
*Author, Whatever Became of . . .
series*

Lancaster, Burt
8966 Sunset Blvd.
Los Angeles, CA 90069
Actor

Lanchester, Elsa
% Harold R. Williams
9405 Brighton Way
Beverly Hills, CA 90210
Actress

Land, Bill & Dorothy
Cozy Kitchen Cafe
725 Royal Heights Rd.
Belleville, IL 62223
*Run restaurant for poor people &
don't charge for food*

Land, Edwin Herbert
730 Main St.
Cambridge, MA 02139
Physicist; inventor

Landau, Jacob
Pratt Institute
Brooklyn, NY 11205
Artist

Landau, Martin
9440 Santa Monica Blvd., #400
Beverly Hills, CA 90210
Actor

Lander, David L.
% ABC Public Relations
1330 Avenue of the Americas
New York, NY 10019
Actor

119

Landers, Ann (Mrs. Esther P. Lederer)
Chicago Sun-Times
401 N. Wabash Ave.
Chicago, IL 60611
Columnist

Landesberg, Steve
151 El Camino
Beverly Hills, CA 90212
Actor

Landesman, Ruth
3081 Plaza Blanca
Santa Fe, NM 87501
Houseboat buff

Landis, John
7950 Sunset Blvd.
Los Angeles, CA 90046
Director

Land O' Lakes, Inc.
P.O. Box 116
Minneapolis, MN 55440
Claire Sandness, Chairman

Landon, Alfred M.
Box 1280
Topeka, KS 66601
Former presidential candidate

Landon, Michael (Eugene Maurice Orowitz)
1990 Century Park East, #401
Los Angeles, CA 90067
Actor; writer

Landry, Tom
Dallas Cowboys
6116 N. Central Expwy.
Dallas, TX 75206
Prof. football coach

Lane, Cleo, & John Dankworth
The Old Rectory
Wavendon
Milton Keynes MK 17 8LT
England
Singers/entertainers

Langdon, Sue Ane
7060 Hollywood Blvd., #610
Los Angeles, CA 90028
Actress

Lange, Hope
9200 Sunset Blvd., #1009
Los Angeles, CA 90069
Actress

Lange, Jessica
ICM
8899 Beverly Blvd.
Los Angeles, CA 90048
Actress

Lange, Ted
9021 Melrose Ave., #308
Los Angeles, CA 90069
Actor; director

Langella, Frank
ICM
8899 Beverly Blvd.
Los Angeles, CA 90048
Actor

Lanier, Bob
Milwaukee Bucks
901 N. Fourth St.
Milwaukee, WI 53203
Prof. basketball player

Lansbury, Angela
1650 Broadway
New York, NY 10019
Actress

Lansbury, Edgar George
1650 Broadway
New York, NY 10019
Producer

Lansford, Carney
Oakland Athletics
Oakland Coliseum
Oakland, CA 94621
Prof. baseball player

Lansing, Sherry
Jaffe/Lansing Productions
5555 Melrose Ave.
Los Angeles, CA 90038
Producer

Lanyon, Ellen
(Mrs. Roland Ginzel)
412 Clark St.
Chicago, IL 60610
Artist

Lanyon, Wesley Edwin
American Museum of Natural
History
New York, NY 10024
Ornithologist

Lapalombara, Joseph
8 Reservoir St.
New Haven, CT 06511
Educator (Yale University)

LaPointe, Guy Gerard
Montreal Canadiens
2313 W. St. Catherine St.
Montreal, PQ H3H 1N2
Canada
Prof. hockey player

Larson, Glen
P.O Box 900
Beverly Hills, CA 90213
TV producer; writer

Larson, Jack
449 Skyeway Rd.
Los Angeles, CA 90049
Jimmy Olsen in Superman *TV series*

LaRue (Adrian) Jan (Pieters)
Department of Music
268 Waverly Bldg.
New York University
New York, NY 10003
Musicologist, educator

LaRue, Lash
3639 Walnut Ave.
Long Beach, CA 90807
King of the Bullwhip screen idol

Lasorda, Tom Charles
Dodger Stadium
1000 Elysian Park Ave.
Los Angeles, CA 90012
Prof. baseball team manager

Lasson, Kenneth
3808 Menlo Dr.
Baltimore, MD 21215
Author, Representing Yourself:
What You Can Do Without a
Lawyer

Lau, Laurence
All My Children
101 W. 67th St.
New York, NY 10023
Actor

Lauder, Estée
767 Fifth Ave.
New York, NY 10022
Cosmetics company executive

Laurents, Arthur
Quogue, NY 11959
Playwright

Laurie, Piper (Rosetta Jacobs)
9869 Santa Monica Blvd., #207
Beverly Hills, CA 90212
Actress

Lavin, Linda
4000 Warner Blvd.
Burbank, CA 91505
Actress

Lavine, John
400 S. Beverly Dr., #214
Los Angeles, CA 90212
*Founder of Wonderful World of
Fantasy Productions, firm
specializing in making fantasies
come true*

Lawford, Peter
1880 Century Park East, #819
Los Angeles, CA 90067
Actor

Lawrence, Carol
9220 Sunset Blvd., #306
Los Angeles, CA 90069
Entertainer

Lawrence, Steve
9255 Sunset Blvd., #318
Los Angeles, CA 90069
Entertainer

Laxalt, Paul
Senate Office Bldg.
Washington, DC 20510
*U.S. Senator (R), Nevada,
1974–present*

Lazar, Irving Paul
211 S. Beverly Dr.
Beverly Hills, CA 90212
Artist's representative; lawyer

La-Z Boy Chair Co.
1284 N. Telegraph Rd.
Monroe, MI 48161
Edward M. Knabusch, Chairman

Leach, Reginald Joseph (Reggie)
Philadelphia Flyers
The Spectrum
Pattison Pl.
Philadelphia, PA 19148
Prof. hockey player

Leach, Robin
One Gulf & Western Plaza, 3d Fl.
New York, NY 10023
Syndicated entertainment columnist

Leachman, Cloris
9000 Sunset Blvd., #315
Los Angeles, CA 90069
Actress

Leakey, Richard Erskine
National Museums of Kenya
P.O. Box 40658
Nairobi, Kenya
*Paleoanthropologist; museum
director*

Lear, Norman Milton
1901 Avenue of the Stars
Los Angeles, CA 90067
*Writer, producer, director, TV &
films*

Learned, Michael
255 Albert St.
Ottawa, ON K1P 5V8
Canada
Actress

Leary, Timothy
% Peace Press Inc.
3828 Willat Ave.
Culver City, CA 90230
Psychologist; author

Led Zeppelin
484 Kings Rd.
London SW10 OLF
England
Rock group

Lee, Brenda
Box 24727
Nashville, TN 37202
Singer

Lee, Christopher
9000 Sunset Blvd., #315
Beverly Hills, CA 90210
Actor; author

Lefrak, Samuel J.
97-77 Queens Blvd.
Forest Hills, NY 11374
*Real estate-developer; business
executive*

Lefthanders International
3601 S.W. 29th St., #201
Topeka, KS 66614
*Dean R. Campbell, Chairman,
President*

LeGallienne, Eva
Hillside Rd.
Weston, CT 06883
Actress

Lehman, Deborah
Love Letters Anonymous
P.O. Box 694
New York, NY 10028
*Writer of love letters for tongue-tied
lovers*

Leia, Princess
Lucasfilm
P.O. Box 8669
Universal City, CA 91608
Star Wars character

Leibman, Ron
9000 Sunset Blvd., #315
Los Angeles, CA 90069
Actor

Leigh, Janet
132 Lasky Dr.
Beverly Hills, CA 90212
Actress

Lejins, Peter Pierre
7114 Everfield Dr.
College Heights Estates, MD 20782
Criminologist; sociologist; educator

LeMay, Curtis
1046 Pescadar Dr.
Newport Beach, CA 92660
*Former general; former vice
presidential running mate to George
Wallace*

Lemmon, Jack
Jalem Productions
141 El Camino Dr., #201
Beverly Hills, CA 90212
Actor

Lemon, Chet
Detroit Tigers
Tiger Stadium
Detroit, MI 48216
Prof. baseball player

Lemon, Meadowlark
Bucketeers
30 Rockefeller Plaza
New York, NY 10020
*Former Harlem Globetrotter;
entertainer*

Leonard, Gloria
801 Second Ave.
New York, NY 10017
Publisher High Society; *founder of
Aural Sex Hotline*

Leonard, Sheldon
Sheldon Leonard Productions
315 S. Beverly Dr.
Beverly Hills, CA 90212
TV producer-director

Leopold, Irving Henry
Department of Ophthalmology
California College of Medicine
University of California, Irvine
Irvine, CA 92717
Physician; medical educator

Lerner, Alan Jay
420 Madison Ave.
New York, NY 10017
Playwright; lyricist

LeRoy, Mervyn
9200 Sunset Blvd.
Los Angeles, CA 90069
Motion picture producer

Letterman, David
30 Rockefeller Plaza
New York, NY 10020
Comedian; talk show host; writer

Lever Brothers Co.
390 Park Ave.
New York, NY 10022
Michael R. Angus, Chairman

Levin, Ira
% Harold Ober Assocs.
40 E. 49th St.
New York, NY 10017
Author; playwright

Levine, Joseph Edward
277 Park Ave.
New York, NY 10017
Motion picture producer

Levine, Michael
967 N. La Cienega Blvd.
Los Angeles, CA 90069
Author, The Address Book

Levi Strauss & Co.
Levi's Plaza
1155 Battery St.
San Francisco, CA 94111
Peter E. Haas, Chairman

Lewis, Gary
14068 Lorain, #204
Cleveland, OH 44111
Singer

Lewis, Geoffrey
151 El Camino
Beverly Hills, CA 90212
Actor

Lewis, Jerry
3305 W. Spring Mountain Rd., #1
Las Vegas, NV 89102
Comedian; filmmaker

Lewis, Jerry Lee
Talenthouse Inc.
1719 West End Ave.
Nashville, TN 37203
Country-rock singer; musician

Lewis, M. K., & Rosemary Ruiz
P.O. Box 49031
Los Angeles, CA 90049
Authors, Your Film Acting Career

Lewis, Shari
% J. P. Tarcher
9110 Sunset Blvd.
Los Angeles, CA 90069
Ventriloquist; puppeteer

Liberace (Wlad Ziu Valentino
Liberace)
4993 Wilbur St.
Las Vegas, NV 89119
Pianist; concert artist; composer

Lichtenstein, Roy
P.O. Box 1369
Southampton, NY 11968
Artist

Life magazine
Time & Life Bldg.
Rockefeller Center
New York, NY 10020
*Ralph P. Davidson, Chairman of
Board*

Life Savers, Inc.
40 W. 57th St.
New York, NY 10019
Peter N. Rogers, President

Lightfoot, Gordon Meredith
ICM
40 W. 57th St.
New York, NY 10019
Singer; songwriter

Limbert, John William, Jr.
5310 Moorland Ln.
Bethesda, MD 20014
Freed American hostage from Iran

Lindbergh, Anne Morrow
Scotts Cove
Darien, CT 06820
*Author, widow of Charles
Lindbergh*

Linden, Hal
151 El Camino
Beverly Hills, CA 90212
Actor

Lindfors, Viveca
% Bret Adams Ltd.
36 E. 61st St.
New York, NY 10021
Actress

Lindley, Audra
409 N. Camden Dr., Suite #202
Beverly Hills, CA 90210
Actress

Lindsay, John V.
1 Rockefeller Plaza
New York, NY 10020
*Former Mayor of New York,
1965–1973*

Liney, John Joseph, Jr.
% King Features Syndicate
235 E. 45th St.
New York, NY 10017
Cartoonist

Linkletter, Arthur Gordon
8530 Wilshire Blvd.
Beverly Hills, CA 90211
Radio & TV broadcaster

Lionel Corp.
9 W. 57th St.
New York, NY 10019
Leonard Wasserman, President—
trains

Lipton, Thomas J., Inc.
800 Sylvan Ave.
Englewood Cliffs, NJ 07632
H. M. Tibbetts, President

Lisk, Richie
Seattle Mariners
419 Second Ave.
Seattle, WA 98104
Prof. baseball player

List, Roland
Department of Physics
University of Toronto
Toronto, ON M5S 1A7
Canada
Meteorologist

Lithgow, John
8642 Melrose Ave., #200
Los Angeles, CA 90069
Actor

Little, Cleavon Jake
9255 Sunset Blvd., #1105
Los Angeles, CA 90069
Actor

Little, Elbert Luther, Jr.
Department of Botany
Smithsonian Institution
Washington, DC 20560
Dendrologist; botanist

Little, Richard
P.O. Box 262
Carteret, NJ 07008
Minister; singer

Little, Sally
PGA
100 Avenue of Champions
Palm Beach Gardens, FL 33410
Prof. golfer

Little People of America
Box 126
Owatonna, MN 55060
Charles Bedow, Executive Officer

Little River Band
88 Richardson St.
Albert Park
Melbourne 3206, Australia
Rock group

Littler, Gene Alec
P.O. Box 1949
Rancho Santa Fe, CA 92067
Prof. golfer

Liu, Kuo-Sung
Chinese U Shatin
NT Hong Kong
Artist

Living Bank (Donor)
P.O. Box 6725
Houston, TX 77005
Mrs. Glen W. Karsten, President

Livingood, Clarence S.
Henry Ford Hospital
Detroit, MI 48202
Dermatologist

Lloyd, Christopher
222 N. Canon Dr.
Beverly Hills, CA 90210
Actor

LoBianco, Tony
7319 Beverly Blvd., #1
Los Angeles, CA 90036
Actor

Locke, Sondra
151 El Camino
Beverly Hills, CA 90212
Actress

Lockhart, June
132 Lasky Dr.
Beverly Hills, CA 90212
Actress

Locklear, Heather
9200 Sunset Blvd., #931
Los Angeles, CA 90069
Actress

Lodge, Henry Cabot
275 Hale St.
Beverly, MA 09115
*Former government official; author;
lecturer*

Loews Corp.
666 Fifth Ave.
New York, NY 10103
Laurence A. Tisch, Chairman

Lofton, James
Green Bay Packers
1265 Lombardi Ave.
Green Bay, WI 54303
Prof. football player

Logan, Joshua
435 E. 52d St.
New York, NY 10022
Playwright; director; producer

Loggins, Kenny
Columbia Records
51 W. 52d St.
New York, NY 10019
Rock singer; songwriter

Lollobrigida, Gina
Via Appino Antica 223
Rome, Italy
Actress

Long, Russell B.
Senate Office Bldg.
Washington, DC 20510
*U.S. Senator (D), Louisiana,
1951–present*

Long, Shelley
8966 Sunset Blvd.
Los Angeles, CA 90069
Actress

Lopes, Davey
Oakland Athletics
Oakland Coliseum
Oakland, CA 94621
Prof. baseball player

Lopez, Nancy
1 Erieview Plaza
Cleveland, OH 44114
Prof. golfer

Lopez, Priscilla
William Morris Agency
1330 Avenue of the Americas
New York, NY 10019
Actress

Lopez, Trini
% Don Sterling
260 S. Beverly Dr.
Beverly Hills, CA 90212
Singer

Lopez Portillo, Jose
Palacio Nacional Mexico
DF Mexico
*Former President of Mexico,
1976–1982*

Lord, Jack
% J. W. Hayes
132 S. Rodeo Dr.
Beverly Hills, CA 90212
Actor; director; artist; producer

Loren, Sophia
Chalet Daniel Burgenstock
Lucerne, Switzerland
Actress

Loring, Gloria Jean
% The Light Agency
113 N. Robertson Blvd.
Los Angeles, CA 90048
Singer; actress

Loring, Lisa
357 W. 55th St., #1-K
New York, NY 10019
Actress, played Wednesday on The
Addams Family

Los Angeles Times
Times-Mirror Co.
Times-Mirror Sq.
Los Angeles, CA 90053
W. Thomas Johnson, Publisher

Losers Anonymous
P O Box 152
Miami Springs, FL 33266
Al Stubvlefield, President

Lott, Ronnie
San Francisco 49ers
1255 Post St.
San Francisco, CA 94109
Prof. football player

Love Canal Home Owners Assn.
P.O. Box 7097
Arlington, VA 22207
Lois Marie Gibbs, President

Lovell, James A., Jr.
Centel Bus Systems Inc.
5725 E. River Rd.
Chicago, IL 60631
Former astronaut, aboard Apollo 8, first journey to the moon

Lowe, Rob
11726 San Vicente Blvd., #300
Los Angeles, CA 90049
Actor

Loy, Myrna
9255 Sunset Blvd., #505
Los Angeles, CA 90069
Actress

Lucas, George
P.O. Box 2009
San Rafael, CA 94912
Film director; screenwriter

Lucas, Maurice
Phoenix Suns
Funk's Greyhound Bldg.
2910 N. Central
Phoenix, AZ 85012
Prof. basketball player

Lucci, Susan
% Rogers and Cowan
122 E. 42d St.
New York, NY 10168
Actress

Luce, Clare Boothe
4 Sutton Pl.
New York, NY 10023
Playwright; former Congresswoman; former ambassador

Luckinbill, Laurence George
% Lucille Ball Productions
P.O. Box 900
Beverly Hills, CA 90213
Actor

Ludlum, Robert
% Henry Morrison
58 W. 10th St.
New York, NY 10011
Author

Luening, Otto
460 Riverside Dr.
New York, NY 10027
Composer; conductor; flutist

Lugar, Richard G.
Senate Office Bldg.
Washington, DC 20510
U.S. Senator (R), Indiana, 1977–present

LuLu
12 Richmond Bldgs.
Dean St.
London, W1, England
Singer

Lumet, Sidney
% LAH Film Corp.
156 W. 56th St., 2d Fl.
New York, NY 10019
Director

Luo, Jay
Boise State University
Boise, ID 83725
Youngest college graduate (12 years old), plans graduate school at Stanford

Luzinski, Greg
Chicago White Sox
Comiskey Park
324 W. 35th St.
Chicago, IL 60616
Prof. baseball player

Lyman, Dorothy
% Jacksina & Freedman
1501 Broadway
New York, NY 10036
Actress

Lynley, Carol Ann
15301 Ventura Blvd., #345
Sherman Oaks, CA 91403
Actress

Lynn, Fred
California Angels
Anaheim Stadium
2000 State College Blvd.
Anaheim, CA 92803
Prof. baseball player

Lynn, Janet
4215 Marsh Ave.
Rockford, IL 61111
Prof. figure skater

Lynn, Loretta Webb
(Mrs. Oliver Lynn, Jr.)
P.O. Box 23470
Nashville, TN 37202
Singer

Lynn, Dame Vera
4 Sandhurst Ave.
Bispham, Blackpool
Lancashire FY2 9AV
England
Singer

M

McAdoo, Bob
Los Angeles Lakers
The Forum
3900 W. Manchester Blvd.
or
P.O. Box 10
Inglewood, CA 90306
Prof. basketball player

McAlpine, Trevor
Warner Beach, South Africa
Kills sharks with bare hands

MacArthur, James
132 Lasky Dr.
Beverly Hills, CA 90212
Actor

McBee, Cecil
% Inner City Records
MMO Music Group Inc.
423 W. 55th St.
New York, NY 10019
Jazz bassist

McCabe, John
P.O. Box 363
Mackinac Island, MI 49757
Laurel & Hardy expert

McCall's **magazine**
230 Park Ave.
New York, NY 10017
Robert Stein, editor

McCarthy, Eugene Joseph
16 Hickory Hill Rd.
Tappan, NY 10983
*Writer; former Senator (D),
Minnesota, 1958–1970*

McCarthy, Mary Frances
Trinity College
Washington, DC 20017
Nun; retired college president

McCartney, Paul
Waterfall Estate near Peamarch
St. Leonard-on-Sea
Sussex, England
*Singer; songwriter; former member
of the Beatles*

McCasland, Sue
P.O. Box 6581
San Jose, CA 95150
Elvis Presley expert

129

McCauley, R. Paul
201 Brigman Hall
University of Louisville
Louisville, KY 40292
Criminologist; educator

McClory, Robert
Rayburn House Office Bldg.
Washington, DC 20515
*Congressman (R), Illinois,
1963–1983*

McCloskey, Paul N., Jr.
305 Grant Ave.
Palo Alto, CA 94306
*Congressman (R), California,
1967–1969, 1981–1983*

McConnell, Mac
Business Exchange
P.O. Box BX
Studio City, CA 91604
World's foremost barter expert

McCord, A. Ray
P.O. Box 225474
MS 236
Dallas, TX 75265
*Manufacturer; company executive
(Texas Instruments)*

McCormick, William Frederick
2828 Dominique St.
Galveston, TX 77550
*Forensic pathologist;
neuropathologist*

McCracken, Harold
Buffalo Bill Historic Center
Box 1000
Cody, WY 82414
Author; explorer; music director

McDonald, Ronald
McDonald's Plaza
Oakbrook, IL 60521
Clown

McDonald's Corp.
McDonald's Plaza
Oakbrook, IL 60521
Fred Turner, Chairman of Board

McDonnell Douglas Corp.
P.O. Box 516
St. Louis, MO 63166
Sanford N. McDonnell, Chairman

McDowall, Roddy
151 El Camino
Beverly Hills, CA 90212
Actor

McElwaine, Guy
Columbia Pictures
Burbank, CA 91505
Chairman, President

McEnroe, John
U.S. Tennis Assn.
51 E. 42d St.
New York, NY 10017
Prof. tennis player

McEvilly, Thomas Vincent
Department of Geology &
Geophysics
University of California, Berkeley
Berkeley, CA 94720
Seismologist

McFadden, Mary Josephine
264 W. 35th St.
New York, NY 10001
Fashion industry executive

McGhee, George Crews
Farmer's Delight
Middleburg, VA 22117
*Petroleum producer; former
government official*

McGhee, Walter Brownie
APA
120 W. 57th St.
New York, NY 10019
Blues singer; guitarist

McGill, Douglas Brown
Mayo Clinic
200 First St.
Rochester, MN 55905
Gastroenterologist

McGinnis, George S.
Indiana Pacers
Market Square Center
151 N. Delaware
Indianapolis, IN 46204
Prof. basketball player

McGinnis, Thomas Charles
0-100 27th St.
Fair Lawn, NJ 07410
Psychotherapist; clinical hypnotist;
marriage & family therapist

McGinniss, Joe
% Sterling Lord
660 Madison Ave.
New York, NY 10021
Author, Fatal Vision

George McGovern
2029 Connecticut Ave. NW
Washington, D.C. 20008
1972 Democratic nominee for
President; 1984 presidential
candidate; former senator of South
Dakota

McGovern, John Phillip
6969 Brompton St.
Houston, TX 77025
Physician specializing in allergy

McGovern, Maureen Therese
151 El Camino
Beverly Hills, CA 90212
Entertainer

McGrath, William Restore
65 W. Red Oak Ln.
White Plains, NY 10604
Transportation planner

MacGraw, Ali
ICM
8899 Beverly Blvd.
Los Angeles, CA 90048
Actress

McGraw-Hill, Inc.
1221 Avenue of the Americas
New York, NY 10020
Harold W. McGraw, Jr., Chairman

McGuire, Dorothy Hackett
P.O. Box 25940
Los Angeles, CA 90025
Actress

McHugh, John Laurence
150 Strathmore Gate Dr.
Stony Brook, NY 11790
Marine biologist; educator

McKay, Jim
ABC Sports
1330 Avenue of the Americas
New York, NY 10019
TV sports commentator

McKay, John Harvey
Tampa Bay Buccaneers
1 Buccaneer Pl.
Tampa, FL 33607
Football coach

McKee, Edwin Dinwiddie
U.S. Geology Survey
Federal Center
Denver, CO 80225
Geologist

MacKenzie, Stewart
16182 Ballard Ln.
Huntington Beach, CA 92649
Shortwave radio expert

McKeon, Nancy
4550 Via Marina, #201
Marina del Rey, CA 90291
Actress

McKeon, Philip
4550 Via Marina, #201
Marina del Rey, CA 90291
Actor

McKinnon, Clinton Dan
Civil Aeronautics Board
1825 Connecticut Ave. NW
Washington, DC 20428
Chairman

McKuen, Rod
8440 Santa Monica Blvd.
Los Angeles, CA 90069
Poet; composer; author; singer

131

MacLaine, Shirley
9255 Sunset Blvd., #910
Los Angeles, CA 90069
Actress

McLaughlin, Emily
4151 Prospect Ave.
Los Angeles, CA 90028
Actress on General Hospital *since 1963*

McLean, Don
Old Manitou Rd.
Garrison, NY 10524
Singer; songwriter

MacLeod, Gavin
151 El Camino
Beverly Hills, CA 90212
Actor

McMahon, Ed
3000 W. Alameda
Burbank, CA 91523
Spokesperson; MC

McNair, Barbara
1200 Firestone Pkwy.
Akron, OH 44317
Singer; actress

McNally, Terrence
218 W. 10th St.
New York, NY 10014
Playwright

MacNamara, Donald
444 W. 56th St.
New York, NY 10019
Criminologist

McNamara, John Francis
Cincinnati Reds
100 Riverfront Stadium
Cincinnati, OH 45202
Baseball team manager

Macnee, Patrick
222 N. Canon Dr., #204
Beverly Hills, CA 90210
Actor

McNeil, Freeman
New York Jets
598 Madison Ave.
New York, NY 10022
Prof. football player

MacNeil, Robert Breckenridge Ware
WNET/13
356 W. 58th St.
New York, NY 10019
Broadcast journalist; won Emmy Award 1974

McNichol, Kristy
151 El Camino
Beverly Hills, CA 90212
Actress

McRae, Carmen
% Pattack Productions
314 Huntley Dr.
Los Angeles, CA 90048
Jazz singer

MacRae, Gordon
151 El Camino
Beverly Hills, CA 90212
Singer, actor

McRae, Hal
Kansas City Royals
Harry S. Truman Sports Complex
P.O. Box 1969
Kansas City, MO 64141
Prof. baseball player

MacWatters, Virginia
School of Music
Indiana University
Bloomington, IN 47401
Singer; actress

Macy & Co. Inc., R. H.
151 W. 34th St.
New York, NY 10001
Edward S. Finkelstein, Chairman

Maddox, Alva Hugh
P.O. Box 218
Montgomery, AL 36101
State Justice, 1969–present

Maddox, Lester
3000 Charles
Kingman, AZ 86401
Former Governor of Georgia (D),
1967–1971

Madge the Manicurist
Palmolive Co.
300 Park Ave.
New York, NY 10022
Spokeswoman

Madison Square Garden Corp.
Two Penn Plaza
New York, NY 10001
David A. Werblin, Chief Operating
Officer

Magnin, Cyril
59 Harrison St.
San Francisco, CA 94105
Chairman of Board, Joseph Magnin
Co., retail trade executive

Magnin, Edgar Fogel
3663 Wilshire Blvd.
Los Angeles, CA 90010
Rabbi—award for 65 years of service
to LA community

Mailer, Norman
% Rembar
19 W. 44th St.
New York, NY 10036
Author; cofounder Village Voice;
Pulitzer Prize for fiction in 1980

Majors, Lee
Twentieth Century-Fox Television
10201 W. Pico Blvd.
Los Angeles, CA 90064
Actor

Malden, Karl
151 El Camino
Los Angeles, CA 90212
Actor

Male Nurse Assn.
2309 State St.
Saginaw, MI 48602
Judd Wise, President

Malone, Moses
Philadelphia 76ers
Veterans Stadium
P.O. Box 25040
Philadelphia, PA 19147
Prof. basketball player

Manchester, Melissa Toni
ICM
40 W. 57th St.
New York, NY 10019
Singer; songwriter

Mancini, Henry
9200 Sunset Blvd., #823
Los Angeles, CA 90069
Composer

M & M/Mars
High St.
Hackettstown, NJ 07840
Howard Walker, President

Mandrell, Barbara
Box 332
Hendersonville, TN 37075
Performer

Mangione, Charles (Chuck)
1 Marine Midland Plaza, #1635
Rochester, NY 14604
Musician

Manhattan Transfer
ARC
75 Rockefeller Plaza
New York, NY 10019
Singing group

Manilow, Barry
P.O. Box 4095
Beverly Hills, CA 90213
Singer; composer; arranger

Manning, Archie
Houston Oilers
P.O. Box 1516
Houston, TX 77001
Prof. football player

Manoff, Dinah Beth
165 W. 46th St., #914
New York, NY 10036
Actress

133

Manson, Bruce
The Train Museum
P.O. Box 248
Strasburg, PA 17579
Toy train collector

Manson, Charles
California Medical Facility
Vacaville, CA 95688
*Convicted mass murderer; cult
leader*

Mantle, Mickey
5730 Watson Circle
Dallas, TX 75225
Retired baseball player

Marantz Co. Inc.
20525 Nordhoff St.
Chatsworth, CA 91311
Fred C. Tushinsky, President

Marceau, Marcel
Théâtre des Champs Élysées
15 Avenue Montaigne
Paris, France 75008
Actor; pantomimist

March of Dimes
1275 Mamaroneck Ave.
White Plains, NY 10605
Charles L. Massey, President

Marchand, Nancy
9220 Sunset Blvd., #202
Los Angeles, CA 90069
Actress

Marciano, Linda (Lovelace)
120 Enterprise
Secaucus, NJ 07094
Former porno star

Marcus, Stanley
4800 Republic Bank Tower
Dallas, TX 75201
*Retail merchant; marketing
consultant; miniature book publisher*

Margaret Rose, Princess
Kensington Palace
London, N5, England
Sister of Queen Elizabeth II

Margold, Bill
6912 Hollywood Blvd., #308
Hollywood, CA 90028
*Hollywood's top porno agent, actor,
director & writer*

Marin, Richard Anthony (Cheech)
Columbia Pictures
Colgems Sq.
Burbank, CA 91505
*Writer, actor—formed comedy duo
with Tommy Chong*

Marks, Paul Alan
1275 York Ave.
New York, NY 10021
Oncologist; cell biologist

Marriott, Alice Sheets
Marriott Corp.
1 Marriott Dr.
Washington, DC 20058
*Partner, Marriott Corp.; married to
chairman*

Marriott, John Willard
Marriott Corp.
1 Marriott Dr.
Washington, DC 20058
*Chairman & director, Marriott
Corp.*

Marriott, Richard Edwin
Marriott Corp.
1 Marriott Dr.
Washington, DC 20058
Restaurant & theme park executive

Marriott Corp.
1 Marriott Dr.
Washington, DC 20058
John Willard Marriott, Chairman

Marsh, Jean
151 El Camino
Beverly Hills, CA 90212
Actress

Marshall, E. G.
Warner Bros.
75 Rockefeller Plaza
New York, NY 10019
Actor

134

Marshall, Garry
5451 Marathon St.
Los Angeles, CA 90038
TV producer; director; writer

Marshall, Penny
1888 Century Park East, #1400
Los Angeles, CA 90067
Actress

Marshall, Thurgood
U.S. Supreme Court
Washington, DC 20543
Supreme Court Justice, 1967–present

Marshall Figure Salons, Gloria
7425 Old York Rd.
Melrose Park, PA 19026
Sid Craig, Chief Operating Officer

Martin, Billy
New York Yankees
Yankee Stadium
Bronx, NY 10451
Prof. baseball manager

Martin, Dean
9911 W. Pico Blvd., #560
Los Angeles, CA 90035
Singer; actor

Martin, Judith (Miss Manners)
% United Features Syndicate
200 Park Ave.
New York, NY 10017
Expert on etiquette

Martin, Lloyd
4301 Parkwood Ct.
Bakersfield, CA 93309
*Cofounder of foundation for
America's sexually exploited
children*

Martin, Mary
PBS
475 L'Enfant Plaza West, SW
Washington, DC 20024
Actress; singer

Martin, Pamela Sue
P.O. Box 1684
Studio City, CA 91604
Actress

Martin, Quinn
Box 981
Rancho Santa Fe, CA 92067
Television producer

Martin, Steve
7858 Beverly Blvd.
Los Angeles, CA 90048
Comedian

Martin, Tony
132 Lasky Dr.
Beverly Hills, CA 90212
Saxophonist; singer

Marvin, Lee
9255 Sunset Blvd., #610
Los Angeles, CA 90069
Actor

Mary Kay Cosmetics, Inc.
8787 N. Stemmons Fwy.
Dallas, TX 75247
Mary Kay Ash, Chairman

Mason, James
% Maggie Parker
55 Park Ln.
London, W1, England
Actor

Mason, Marsha
8642 Melrose Ave., #200
Los Angeles, CA 90069
Actress

Masters, William Howell
4529 Pershing Pl.
St. Louis, MO 63108
*Physician; educator—codirector
Masters & Johnson, sex therapists*

Mastroianni, Marcello
Via di Porta
San Sebastiano 15
00179 Rome Italy
Actor

Mathers, Jerry
P.O. Box 1605
Canyon Country, CA 91351
Beaver on Leave It to Beaver

135

Mathias, Charles McC., Jr.
Senate Office Bldg.
Washington, DC 20510
U.S. Senator (R), Maryland,
1968–present

Mathis, Johnny
P.O. Box 59278
Los Angeles, CA 90059
Singer

Mattel, Inc.
5150 Rosecrans Ave.
Hawthorne, CA 90250
Arthur S. Spear, Chairman

Matthau, Walter
10100 Santa Monica Blvd., #2200
Los Angeles, CA 90067
Actor

Mature, Victor
Box 706
Rancho Santa Fe, CA 92067
Actor

Maurer, Joan Howard
P.O. Box 654
Culver City, CA 90230
Daughter of former member of
Three Stooges, Moe Howard

Max Factor & Co.
6922 Hollywood Blvd.
Hollywood, CA 90023
Linda Wachner, President

Mays, Willie
51 Mount Vernon Ln.
Atherton, CA 94025
Retired baseball player

Maytag Co.
403 W. 4th Street North
Newton, IA 50208
Daniel J. Krumm, Chairman

Mazel, Judy
151 El Camino
Beverly Hills, CA 90212
Author

Mazursky, Paul
ICM
8899 Beverly Blvd.
Los Angeles, CA 90048
Motion picture writer; director

MCA, Inc.
100 Universal City Plaza
Universal City, CA 91608
Lew R. Wasserman, Chairman

MCI Communications
1133 19th St., NW
Washington, DC 20036
William G. McGowan, Chairman

Meadows, Audrey
% Val Irving Assocs.
342 Madison Ave.
New York, NY 10017
TV actress

Meadows, Jayne
132 Lasky Dr.
Beverly Hills, CA 90212
Actress

Meara, Anne
Janice Morgan Communications
250 W. 57th St.
New York, NY 10019
Comedienne

Mears, Rick Ravon
812 Sesnon St.
Bakersfield, CA 93309
Prof. race car driver

Meat Loaf
83 Riverside Dr.
New York, NY 10024
Rock singer

Medic Alert Donor Program
2323 Colorado
Turlock, CA 95380
Alfred A. Hudder, President

Medical Society for the Study of
Radiesthesia
24 Browning Ave.
Bournemouth, BH5 1NN, England
Dr. M. Harling, Secretary

Meese, Edwin, III
The White House Office
1600 Pennsylvania Ave.
and Executive Office Bldg.
Washington, DC 20500
Counselor to the President,
1981–present

Mehegan, John Francis
72 Morningside Drive South
Westport, CT 06880
Jazz musician

Meier, Richard Louis
7 San Mateo Rd.
Berkeley, CA 94707
Planner; futurist; behavioral scientist

Melcher, John
Senate Office Bldg.
Washington, DC 20510
U.S. Senator (D), Montana,
1977–present

Melnick, Daniel
300 Colgems Sq.
Burbank, CA 91505
Motion picture producer

Men At Work
P.O. Box 289
Abbotsford, Victoria 3067
Australia
Rock group

Mendes, Sergio
Box 118
Hollywood, CA 90028
Musician

Mengers, Sue
ICM
8899 Beverly Blvd.
Los Angeles, CA 90048
Motion picture talent agent

Menninger, Karl Augustus
Menninger Foundation
P.O. Box 829
Topeka, KS 66601
Psychiatrist

Menuhin, Yehudi
19750 Alma Bridge Rd.
Los Gatos, CA 95030
Violinist

Mercouri, Melina
Anagnostropoulon 25
Athens, Greece
Actress

Meredith, Burgess
9255 Sunset Blvd., #1105
Los Angeles, CA 90069
Actor

Meredith, Don
% ABC Public Relations
1330 Avenue of the Americas
New York, NY 10019
Actor; sportscaster; former prof.
football player

Merilan, Charles Preston
University of Missouri
Columbia, MO 65211
Dairy husbandry scientist

Merrell Dow Pharmaceuticals
2140 E. Galbraith Rd.
Cincinnati, OH 45237
Makers of Nicorette—nicotine
chewing gum

Merriam, Daniel Francis
Department of Geology
Syracuse University
Syracuse, NY 13210
Geologist

Merrick, David
246 W. 44th St.
New York, NY 10036
Theatrical producer

Merrill, Dina
% Hesseltine Baker Assocs.
165 W. 46th St.
New York, NY 10036
Actress

Merrill, Gary Franklin
P.O. Box 4509
Portland, ME 04101
Actor

Merrill, Robert
CAMI
165 W. 57th St.
New York, NY 10019
Baritone

Merrill Lynch & Co. Inc.
1 Liberty Plaza
New York, NY 10006
Roger E. Birk, Chairman

Merritt, Doris Honig
Bldg. 1, Rm. 118
National Institutes of Health
Bethesda, MD 20014
Pediatrician; university dean

Meskill, Victor Peter
Dowling College
Office of the President
Oakdale, NY 11769
Educator; college president

Messac, Magali Ernestine Josephine
American Ballet Theater
890 Broadway
New York, NY 10003
Ballerina

Messer, Arnold William
Columbia Pictures
Columbia Plaza East
Burbank, CA 91505
Motion picture company executive

Messer, Thomas M.
1071 Fifth Ave.
New York, NY 10028
Director, Guggenheim Museum

Messick, Dale
1360 N. Ritchie Ct.
Chicago, IL 60610
Cartoonist; creator of the comic strip
Brenda Starr

Mester, Jorge
ICM
40 W. 57th St.
New York, NY 10019
Orchestra conductor

Metcalfe, Burton Denis
10201 W. Pico Blvd.
Los Angeles, CA 90046
Television producer—M*A*S*H

Metzenbaum, Howard M.
Senate Office Bldg.
Washington, DC 20510
U.S. Senator (D), Ohio, 1974,
1977–present

Meyer, Alex Alfred
Amana Refrigeration Inc.
Amana, IA 52203
President

Meyer, Harry M., Jr.
Bur Biologies
FDA
8800 Rockville Pike
Bethesda, MD 20205
Pediatrician—pioneer in developing
German measles vaccine

Michaels, Lorne
Broadway Video
1619 Broadway
New York, NY 10019
TV producer & writer—created
Saturday Night Live

Michener, James A.
Random House
201 E. 50th St.
New York, NY 10022
Author

Midler, Bette
% Atlantic Records
75 Rockefeller Plaza
New York, NY 10019
Singer; entertainer

Mikes of America
P.O. Box 676
Minneapolis, MN 55440
*Mike D. Nelson, President—people
named Mike*

Miles, Joanna
211 S. Beverly Dr., #201
Beverly Hills, CA 90212
Actress

Miles Laboratories, Inc.
1127 Myrtle St.
Elkhart, IN 46515
Theodor H. Heinrichs, Chairman

Milland, Ray
132 Lasky Dr.
Beverly Hills, CA 90212
Motion picture actor; director

Miller, Ann
132 Lasky Dr.
Beverly Hills, CA 90212
Actress; dancer; singer

Miller, Arthur
Tophet Rd.
Roxbury, CT 06783
Playwright

Miller, David Charles, Jr.
American Embassy
36 Laibon Rd.
P.O. Box 9123
Dar es Salaam, Tanzania
Ambassador to Tanzania

Miller, E. Willard
845 Outer Dr.
State College, PA 16801
Geographer

Miller, James C., III
Federal Trade Commission
Pennsylvania Ave. at Sixth St., NW
Washington, DC 20580
Chairman, 1981–present

Miller, Jason
Graham Agency
317 W. 45th St.
New York, NY 10036
Playwright

Miller, Patrick
P.O. Box 725
New Providence, NJ 07974
Expert on model rocketry

Miller, Robert Neil
5700 Logan St.
Denver, CO 80216
Prof. football coach

Miller, Roger Dean
ICM
8899 Beverly Blvd.
Los Angeles, CA 90048
Entertainer

Miller Brewing Co.
3939 W. Highland Blvd.
Milwaukee, WI 53201
John A. Murphy, Chairman

Millett, Katherine Murray
Simon & Schuster
1230 Avenue of the Americas
New York, NY 10020
Feminist leader

Millman, Peter Mackenzie
National Research Council of
Canada
Ottawa, ON K1A OR6
Canada
Astrophysicist

Mills, Donna
9000 Sunset Blvd., #1112
Los Angeles, CA 90069
Actress

Mills, Hayley
22 Grafton St.
London, W1, England
Actress

Milsap, Ronnie
Box 40484
Nashville, TN 37203
Singer

Milton Bradley Co.
111 Maple St.
Springfield, MA 01115
James J. Shea Jr., Chairman

Minnelli, Liza
8642 Melrose Ave., #200
Los Angeles, CA 90069
Singer; actress

Minnelli, Vincente
7950 Sunset Blvd.
Los Angeles, CA 90046
Director

Minnesota Trailbound School of Log Building
3544½ Grand Ave.
Minneapolis, MN 55468
Ron Brodigan, Coordinator

Miss Universe
640 Fifth Ave.
New York, NY 10019
James I. Spiegel, Chief Operating Officer

Mistresses Anonymous
P.O. Box 151
Islip, NY 11751
Melissa Sands, President

Mitchel, Mike
San Antonio Spurs
HemisFair Arena
P.O. Box 530
San Antonio, TX 78298
Prof. basketball player

Mitchell, Arthur
Dance Theater of Harlem
466 W. 152d St.
New York, NY 10031
Dancer; choreographer

Mitchell, John Murray, Jr.
NOAA
8060 13th St.
Silver Spring, MD 20910
Climatologist

Mitchell, Joni
Lookout Management
9120 Sunset Blvd.
Los Angeles, CA 90069
Singer

Mitchell, Lydell Douglas
San Diego Chargers
P.O. Box 20666
San Diego, CA 92120
Prof. football player

Mitchelson, Marvin
1801 Century Park East, #1900
Los Angeles, CA 90067
Famed palimony attorney

Mitchum, Robert
9255 Sunset Blvd., #910
Los Angeles, CA 90069
Actor

Mitterrand, François
Office of the President
Paris, France
President, France—since 1981

Mobil Corp.
150 E. 42d St.
New York, NY 10017
Rawleigh Warner, Jr., Chairman

Modell, Arthur B.
Cleveland Browns
Cleveland Stadium
Cleveland, OH 44114
Owner & president, prof. football team

Moffo, Anna
Carl Byoir & Assocs.
380 Madison Ave.
New York, NY 10017
Opera singer

Molinaro, Al
9172 Sunset Blvd., #2
Los Angeles, CA 90069
Actor

Monagan, Charles A.
Atheneum Publishers
597 Fifth Ave.
New York, NY 10020
Author, Neurotic's Handbook

Mondale, Walter Frederick
3421 Lowell St., NW
Washington, DC 20016
Lawyer; former U.S. Senator (D),
Minnesota, 1964–1977; former Vice
President, 1977–1980; 1984
presidential candidate

Monger, Albert Jackson
3871 Calle Loma Vista
Newbury Park, CA 91320
Retired naval officer, now manager
engineering, Arco Solar Inc.

Montalban, Ricardo
132 Lasky Dr.
Beverly Hills, CA 90212
Actor

Montana, Joe
San Francisco 49ers
711 Nevada St.
Redwood City, CA 94061
Prof. football player

Montgomery, Elizabeth
8642 Melrose Ave.
Los Angeles, CA 90069
Actress

Montgomery, Wilbert
Philadelphia Eagles
Veterans Stadium
Philadelphia, PA 19148
Prof. football player

Montoya, Carlos
345 W. 58th St.
New York, NY 10019
Guitarist

Montt, General Efrain Rios
Office of the President
Guatemala City, Guatemala
Former President, Guatemala, 1982

Monty Python
20 Fitzroy Sq.
London, W1P 6BB, England
Comedy group

Moore, Clayton
4720 Parkolivo
Calabasas, CA 91302
Played The Lone Ranger character

Moore, Dudley Stuart John
ICM
8899 Beverly Blvd.
Los Angeles, CA 90048
Actor

Moore, Gary
430 Park Ave.
New York, NY 10022
Actor; writer; producer

Moore, James Norman
Department of Horticulture
University of Arkansas
Fayetteville, AR 72701
Horticulturist

Moore, John Ashton
903 10th St., SW
Albuquerque, NM 87102
Zoo director—Rio Grande Zoology
Park

Moore, Mary Tyler
9000 Sunset Blvd., #315
Los Angeles, CA 90069
Actress

Moore, Melba
% Hush Productions
231 W. 58th St.
New York, NY 10019
Actress; singer

Moore, Pete
Wetumpka, AL 36092
World's smallest man, 27 inches tall

Moore, Peter Innisfree
Modern Photography
825 Seventh Ave.
New York, NY 10019
Photographer; editor; writer

141

Moore, Roger George
% London Management
235/241 Regent St.
London, W1, England
Actor

Moore, Sara Jane
Women's Federal Prison
P.O. Box W
Alderson, WV 24910
Would-be assassin of Gerald Ford

Morality in Media
475 Riverside Dr.
New York, NY 10027
Rev. Morton A. Hill, S.J., President

Moral Majority
500 Alleghany Ave.
Lynchburg, VA 24501
*Dr. Ronald S. Godwin, Vice
President*

Moran, Erin
5555 Melrose Ave.
Los Angeles, CA 90038
Actress

Morefield, Consul General Richard
5491 Oakleaf Point
San Diego, CA 92124
Freed American hostage from Iran

More for Women
1435 Lexington Ave.
New York, NY 10028
Runett H. Cook, Founder

Moreno, Rita
William Morris Agency
1350 Avenue of the Americas
New York, NY 10019
Actress

Morgan, Alfred Y.
16-16 Whitestone Expwy.
Whitestone, NY 11357
President, White Rock Corp.

Morgan, Harry
P.O. Box 900
Beverly Hills, CA 90213
Actor

Morgan, Joe
Philadelphia Phillies
P.O. Box 7575
Philadelphia, PA 19101
Prof. baseball player

Morgenstern, Dan Michael
Institute of Jazz Studies
Rutgers University
Newark, NJ 07102
Historian of jazz; educator

Moriarty, Michael
STE
888 Seventh Ave.
New York, NY 10019
Actor

Morley, Robert
Fairmans, Wargrave
Berkshire, England
Actor

Morris, Garrett
30 Rockefeller Plaza
New York, NY 10020
Actor; singer

Morse, Robert Alan
132 Lasky Dr.
Beverly Hills, CA 90212
Actor

Morton Salt
110 N. Wacker Dr.
Chicago, IL 60606
W. E. Johnston, Jr., President

Moschitta, John
113 N. Robertson Blvd.
Los Angeles, CA 90048
World's fastest talker

Mosconi, Willie
2027 Oregon Ave.
Philadelphia, PA 19145
*Billiard player—record for highest
billiard run, 526*

Moses, Billy
8642 Melrose Ave., #200
Los Angeles, CA 90069
Actor

142

Mosley, Mark
Washington Redskins
P.O. Box 17247
Dulles International Airport
Washington, DC 20041
Prof. football player

Mota, Manny
Ave. 27 de Febrero, #445
Santo Domingo
Dominican Republic
Prof. baseball player

Mothers Against Drunk Driving
669 Airport Fwy., Suite 310
Hurst, TX 76053
*Philip Roos, Ph.D., Executive
Director*

Mothers-in-Law Club International
720 Adelberg Ln.
Cedarhurst, NY 11516
Sylvia Parker, President

Motorola, Inc.
1303 E. Algonquin Rd.
Schaumburg, IL 60196
Robert W. Galvin, Chairman

Motta, John Richard
Dallas Mavericks
Reunion Arena
777 Sports St.
Dallas, TX 75207
Prof. basketball coach

Mount, Thomas
100 Universal Plaza
Universal City, CA 91608
*Executive vice president in charge of
production at Universal*

Moye, Don
% Rasa Artists
144 W. 27th St.
New York, NY 10001
Jazz musician

Moyers, Bill D.
CBS
524 W. 57th St.
New York, NY 10019
Journalist

Moynihan, Daniel Patrick
Senate Office Bldg.
Washington, DC 20510
*U.S. Senator (D), New York,
1977–present*

Mrs. Smith's Frozen Food Co.
South & Charlotte Sts.
Pottstown, PA 19464
Robert L. Nichols, President

Ms. magazine
370 Lexington Ave.
New York, NY 10017
Patricia Carbine, Editor

Mubarak, Hosni
Office of the President
Cairo, Egypt
President, Egypt—since 1981

Mudd, Richard
1001 Hoyt Ave.
Saginaw, MI 48607
*Lincoln assassination memorabilia
collector*

Mudd, Roger Harrison
4001 Nebraska Ave.
Washington, DC 20016
News broadcaster

Muggeridge, Malcolm
Park Cottage
Robertsbridge
Sussex, England
Editor; writer

Muhleman, Duane Owen
California Institute of Technology
Pasadena, CA 91125
Radio astronomer

Muir, Frank
Stein & Day
Scarborough
Briarcliff Manor, NY 10510
*Author, an irreverent and almost
complete social history of the
bathroom*

143

Muldaur, Maria
599 Edgewood Ave.
Mill Valley, CA 94141
Singer

Mull, Martin
9000 Sunset Blvd., #315
Los Angeles, CA 90069
Actor

Mullavey, Greg
151 El Camino
Beverly Hills, CA 90212
Actor

Mullen, Geril
Le Premier
695 Town Center Dr.
Costa Mesa, CA 92626
*Owner of Le Premier Restaurant,
does not allow tipping*

Mulligan, Richard
% ABC
1330 Avenue of the Americas
New York, NY 10019
Actor

Munoz, Anthony
Cincinnati Bengals
200 Riverfront Stadium
Cincinnati, OH 45202
Prof. football player

Muntz, Earl ("Mad Man")
7700 Densmore Ave.
Van Nuys, CA 91406
Salesman extraordinaire

Muppets
P.O. Box 2495
New York, NY 10001
Show puppets

Murphy, Calvin
Houston Rockets
The Summit
Houston, TX 77046
Prof. basketball player

Murphy, Dale
Atlanta Braves
P.O. Box 4064
Atlanta, GA 30302
Prof. baseball player

Murphy, Daniel J.
Office of the Vice President
Executive Office Building
Washington, DC 20501
*Chief of Staff to Vice President,
1981–present*

Murphy, Eddie
ICM
8899 Beverly Blvd.
Los Angeles, CA 90048
Comedian; actor

Murphy, Patrick Vincent
% Police Foundation
1909 K St., NW
Washington, DC 20006
*Member—International Association
of Chiefs of Police*

Murray, Anne
% Balmur Ltd.
2180 Yonge Street
P.O. Box 18
Toronto, ON M4S 2B9
Canada
Singer

Murray, Arthur
2877 Kalakaua Ave.
Honolulu, HI 66815
Dance teacher

Murray, Bill
1888 Century Park East, #1400
Los Angeles, CA 90067
Comedian; actor

Murray, Donald Patrick
% Film Artists Management
Enterprises
8278 Sunset Blvd.
Los Angeles, CA 90046
Actor

Murray, Eddie
Baltimore Orioles
Memorial Stadium
Baltimore, MD 21218
Prof. baseball player

Musburger, Brent Woody
% CBS Television & Radio
51 W. 52d St.
New York, NY 10019
Sportscaster

Muscular Dystrophy Assn.
810 Seventh Ave.
New York, NY 10019
Robert Ross, Executive Director

Musial, Stan
% Stan Musial & Biggies Inc.
5130 Oakland Ave.
St. Louis, MO 63110
Baseball executive; Hall of Famer

Muskie, Edmund Sixtus
5409 Albia Rd., NW
Washington, DC 20016
*Former Secretary of State,
1980–1981; former Governor of
Maine, 1955–1959; and U.S.
Senator (D), Maine, 1959–1980*

Musser, Tharon
21 Cornelia St.
New York, NY 10014
Theatrical lighting designer

Mutual UFO Network
103 Oldtowne Rd.
Seguin, TX 78155
*Walter H. Andrus, Jr., International
Director*

Myers, Russel
% Chicago Tribune
New York News Syndicate Inc.
220 E. 42d St.
New York, NY 10017
Cartoonist

Myerson, Bess
3 East 71st St.
New York, NY 10021
Columnist; consumer advocate

N

Nabisco Brands, Inc.
Nabisco Brands Plaza
Parsippany, NJ 07054
*Robert M. Schaeberle, Chairman of
Board*

Nabors, Jim
P.O. Box 707
Honokaa, HI 96727
Entertainer

Nader, Ralph
P.O. Box 19367
Washington, DC 20036
Consumer advocate

Nakasone, Yasuhiro
Office of the Prime Minister
Tokyo, Japan
Prime Minister, Japan—since 1982

Namelab
711 Marina Blvd.
San Francisco, CA 94123
*Ira Bachrach, President—company
creates names for new products*

Nash, Graham
ARC
75 Rockefeller Plaza
New York, NY 10019
Singer

Nash, Jay Robert, III
P.O. Box 4327
Chicago, IL 60680
Author; playwright; columnist

Nash, Johnny
% CBS Records
51 W. 52d St.
New York, NY 10019
Singer; songwriter

Nastase, Ilie
U.S. Tennis Assn.
51 E. 42d St.
New York, NY 10017
Prof. tennis player

National Abortion Federation
110 E. 59th St.
New York, NY 10022
*Uta Landy, Ph.D., Executive
Director*

National Abortion Rights Action
League
825 15th St., NW
Washington, DC 20005
*Karen Mulhauser, Executive
Director*

National Anti-Klan Network
P.O. Box 10500
Atlanta, GA 30310
Lyn Wells, Coordinator

National Association for the
Advancement of Aardvarks in
America
947 Perkins Ave.
Waukesha, WI 53186
Biff B. Byrne, President

National Association to Aid Fat
Americans
P.O. Box 43
Bellerose, NY 11426
Lisbeth Fisner, Executive Secretary

National Cable Television Assn.
1724 Massachusetts Ave., NW
Washington, DC 20036
Thomas E. Wheeler, President

National Center for the Prevention
& Treatment of Child Abuse &
Neglect
University of Colorado Medical
Center
1205 Oneida St.
Denver, CO 80220
C. Henry Kempe, M.D., Codirector

National Coalition Against the Death
Penalty
475 Riverside Dr., #1244
New York, NY 10115
Rev. Kathy Young, Chairperson

National Coalition to Prevent
Shoplifting
Atlanta Merchandise Mart
240 Peachtree St., #5-A-5
Atlanta, GA 30303
Judi Rogers, Director

National Enquirer
600 S.E. Coast Ave.
Lantana, FL 33464
Dan Calder, Editor

National Federation of Grandmother
Clubs of America
203 N. Wabash Ave.
Chicago, IL 60601
Jeanne Martin, Office Manager

National Gay Task Force
80 Fifth Ave.
New York, NY 10011
Lucia Valeska, Executive Director

National Geographic Magazine
17th and M Sts., NW
Washington, DC 20036
Gilbert Grosvenor, Editor

National Hospice Organization
1311 A Dolly Madison Blvd.
McLean, VA 22101
*Josefina B. Magno, M.D., Executive
Director*

National Institute of Medical
Herbalists
148 Forest Rd.
Tunbridge Wells
Kent, TN2 5E4, England
Hein Zeylstra, General Secretary

National Kidney Foundation
Two Park Ave.
New York, NY 10016
*Paul S. Archambault, Executive
Director*

National Mental Health Assn.
1800 N. Kent St.
Rosslyn, VA 22209
*Robert B. Herman, Executive
Director*

National Migraine Foundation
5232 N. Western Ave.
Chicago, IL 60625
*Seymour Diamond, Executive
Director*

National Organization for Women (NOW)
425 13th St., NW, Suite 1048
Washington, DC 20004
Judy Goldsmith, President

National Right to Work Committee
8001 Braddock Rd.
Springfield, VA 22160
Reed E. Larson, President

National Socialist White People's Party
2507 N. Franklin Rd.
Arlington, VA 22201
Matt Koehl, Commander—Nazi party

National Socialist White Workers Party
P.O. Box 1981
San Francisco, CA 94101
Allen Vincent, Commander—Nazi party

National Space Institute
600 Maryland Ave., SW
West Wing, Suite 203
Washington, DC 20034
Dr. Mark R. Chartrand, Executive Director

National States Rights Party
P.O. Box 1211
Marietta, GA 30061
J. B. Stoner, National Chairman— white racist political order

National Sudden Infant Death Syndrome Foundation
Two Metro Plaza, #205
8240 Professional Pl.
Landover, MD 20785
Sallyn J. Sohr, Executive Director

National Urban League
500 E. 62d St.
New York, NY 10021
John E. Jacobs, President

National Women's Health Network
224 Seventh St., SE
Washington, DC 20003
Belita Cowen, Executive Director

Natt, Calvin
Portland Trail Blazers
Lloyd Building
700 N.E. Multonomah St., #380
Portland, OR 97232
Prof. basketball player

Neal, Patricia
Gipsey House
Great Messenden
Buckinghamshire, England
Actress

Nebenzahl, Kenneth
333 N. Michigan Ave.
Chicago, IL 60611
Rare book & map dealer

Nederlander, James Morton
1564 Broadway
New York, NY 10036
Theatrical executive

Needham, Hal
3518 W. Cahuenga Blvd., #106
Los Angeles, CA 90068
Director; writer

Negri, Pola
7731 Broadway
San Antonio, TX 79209
Actress

Neill, Noel
Box 1370
Studio City, CA 91604
Actress—Lois Lane of Superman series

Neiman, Leroy
1 West 67th St.
New York, NY 10023
Artist

Nelson, Barry
William Morris Agency
1350 Avenue of the Americas
New York, NY 10019
Actor

Nelson, Edwin Stafford
20910 Mesarica Ave.
Covina, CA 91724
Actor

Nelson, Eric Hilliard (Rick)
9034 Sunset Blvd., #200
Los Angeles, CA 90069
Actor; singer; songwriter

Nelson, Harriet Hilliard
9220 Sunset Blvd., #322
Los Angeles, CA 90069
Actress

Nelson, Larry Gene
% PGA Tour
Sawgrass Ponte
Vedra, FL 32806
Prof. golfer

Nelson, Norton
NYU Medical Center
550 First Ave.
New York, NY 10016
Educator

Nelson, Willie
% Mark Rothbaum
225 Main St.
Danbury, CT 06810
Country musician; songwriter

Nessen, Ronald Harold
1835 K St., NW, #805
Washington, DC 20006
*Public relations executive; former
press secretary to President Gerald
Ford, 1974–1977*

Nettles, Graig
New York Yankees
Yankee Stadium
Bronx, NY 10451
Prof. baseball player

Neurotics Anonymous
P.O. Box 4866
Cleveland Park Station
Washington, DC 20008
Grover Boydston, Chairman

Nevelson, Louise
29 Spring St.
New York, NY 10012
Sculptor

Newhart, Bob
315 S. Beverly Dr.
Beverly Hills, CA 90212
Entertainer; comedian

Newley, Anthony
9255 Sunset Blvd., #1115
Los Angeles, CA 90069
Actor

Newman, Edwin Harold
% NBC
30 Rockefeller Plaza
New York, NY 10020
News commentator

Newman, Paul
9665 Wilshire Blvd., #200
Beverly Hills, CA 90212
Actor; race car driver

Newman, Randy
% Renaissance Management Corp.
433 N. Camden Dr.
Beverly Hills, CA 90210
Singer; songwriter; musician

Newsmaker Interviews
439 S. La Cienega Blvd., #439
Los Angeles, CA 90048
*Arthur Levine, President—
newsletter sent to major radio
stations indicating who is available
for interviews*

***Newsweek* magazine**
444 Madison Ave.
New York, NY 10022
William Broyles, Editor

Newton, Wayne
% Flying Eagle Inc.
4220 Maryland Pkwy.
Bldg. B, Suite 401
Las Vegas, NV 89109
Entertainer; actor; recording artist

Newton-John, Olivia
3575 Cahuenga Boulevard West,
#580
Los Angeles, CA 90068
Singer; actress

New York Daily News
220 E. 42d St.
New York, NY 10017
*Robert M. Hunt, President &
Publisher*

New York Post
210 South St.
New York, NY 10002
Rupert Murdoch, Publisher

New York Times, The
The New York Times Co.
229 W. 43d St.
New York, NY 10036
*Arthur Ochs Sulzberger, Chairman
of Board & Publisher*

Nichols, Mike
ICM
40 W. 57th St.
New York, NY 10019
Stage & film director

Nicholson, Jack
Bresler & Assocs.
190 N. Canon Dr.
Beverly Hills, CA 90210
Actor

Nicklaus, Jack William
321 Northlake Blvd.
North Palm Beach, FL 33403
Prof. golfer

Nicks, Stevie
Penguin Productions
1420 N. Beachwood Dr.
Los Angeles, CA 90028
Musician

Niekro, Joseph Franklin
Houston Astros
Astrodome
P.O. Box 288
Houston, TX 77001
Prof. baseball player

Niekro, Philip Henry (Phil)
Atlanta Braves
P.O. Box 4064
Atlanta, GA 30302
Prof. baseball player

Nielsen, Leslie
10000 Santa Monica Blvd., #305
Los Angeles, CA 90067
Actor

Nielsen, Co., A. C.
Nielsen Plaza
Northbrook, IL 60062
Arthur C. Nielsen, Jr., Chairman

Nike Inc.
3900 S.W. Murray Blvd.
Beaverton, OR 97005
Philip H. Knight, Chairman

Nikolais, Alwin
33 E. 18th St.
New York, NY 10003
Choreographer

Nilsson, Harry
% RCA Records
1133 Avenue of the Americas
New York, NY 10036
Singer; songwriter

Nimoy, Leonard
328A S. Beverly Dr.
Beverly Hills, CA 90212
Actor; director

Nixon, Agnes Eckhardt
% ABC
1330 Avenue of the Americas
New York, NY 10019
TV writer

Nixon, Richard Milhous
26 Federal Plaza
New York, NY 10007
*Former President of U.S.,
1968-1974*

Noel Hume, Ivor
P.O. Box 1711
Williamsburg, VA 23185
Antiquary

Nolan, Richard Charles
Houston Oilers
P.O. Box 1516
Houston, TX 77001
Prof. football coach

Nolte, Nick
Box 1176
North Hollywood, CA 91607
Actor

Noone, Peter
646 N. Robertson Blvd.
Los Angeles, CA 90069
Former leader Herman's Hermits

Norman, Ruth
Unarius Educational Foundation
145 S. Magnolia Ave.
El Cajon, CA 92020
Cosmic visionary & healer

NORML (National Organization for the Reform of Marijuana Laws)
530 Eighth St., SE
Washington, DC 20003
James N. Hall, Executive Director

Norris, Christopher
9105 Carmelita Ave.
Beverly Hills, CA 90210
Actress

North, Jay
P.O. Box 727
Hollywood, CA 90028
Actor—played Dennis the Menace

North American Tiddlywinks Assn.
18802 Nathans Pl.
Gaithersburg, MD 20760
Larry Kahn, Secretary General

Norton, Ken
500 Shatto Pl.
Los Angeles, CA 90020
Prof. boxer

Novak, Kim
635 Madison Ave.
New York, NY 10022
Actress

Novak, William
3 Ashton
Newton, MA 02149
Author, The Great American Man Shortage . . . and Other Roadblocks to Romance

Noxema/Noxell Corp.
P.O. Box 1799
Baltimore, MD 21203
G. Lloyd Bunting, Chairman

Nudist Information Center
P.O. Box 4830
Long Beach, CA 90804
Jan Davis, Founder

Nugent, Nelle
1501 Broadway
New York, NY 10036
Theatrical producer

Nugent, Theodore Anthony
241 E. Saginaw Hwy., #400
East Lansing, MI 48823
Musician

Nunn, Sam
Senate Office Bldg.
Washington, DC 20510
U.S. Senator (D), Georgia, 1973–present

Nureyev, Rudolf Hametovich
% SA Gorlinsky Ltd.
35 Dover St.
London, W1, England
Ballet dancer; director of the Paris Opera Ballet

Nykvist, Sven Vilhem
4 Floragatan
Stockholm 11431
Sweden
Cinematographer

Nyro, Laura
Box 186
Shoreham, NY 11786
Singer

O

Oates, Joyce Carol
Princeton University Creative
Writing Program
185 Nassau St.
Princeton, NJ 08540
Author

Obote, Milton
Office of the President
Kampala, Uganda
President, Uganda—since 1980

O'Brian, Hugh
King Features Syndicate
235 E. 45th St.
New York, NY 10018
Journalist

O'Brien, Lawrence Francis
860 UN Plaza
New York, NY 10017
*Basketball commissioner; former
chairman, Democratic National
Committee*

O'Brien, Margaret
328 S. Beverly Dr., #E
Beverly Hills, CA 90212
Actress

Ocean Spray Cranberries, Inc.
Water St.
Plymouth, MA 02360
Stuart Pedersen, Chairman

O'Connor, Carroll
P.O. Box 49935
Los Angeles, CA 90049
Actor; writer; producer

O'Connor, Donald
Beford Agency
9665 Wilshire Blvd., #200
Beverly Hills, CA 90212
Actor

O'Connor, Sandra Day
U.S. Supreme Court
Washington, DC 20543
*Supreme Court's only woman
Justice, 1981–present*

Ode, Robert
12427 Banyan Dr.
Sun City West, AZ 85375
Freed American hostage from Iran

152

Odell, Joyce
Society for Creative Anachronism
Office of the Registry
P.O. Box 594
Concord, CA 94522
Historic costuming expert

O'Hara, Maureen
Antilles Air Boats Inc.
West Seaplane Ramp
Christiansted
St. Croix, VI 00820
Actress

O'Hare, Madalyn Murray
2210 Hancock Dr.
Austin, TX 78701
*Atheist activist who successfully
waged campaign to ban prayer in
public schools*

O'Keefe, Michael
1888 Century Park East, #1400
Los Angeles, CA 90067
Actor

Olaf V, King
Royal Palace
Oslo, Norway
Ruler of Norway

Oliver, Al
Montreal Expos
P.O. Box 500
Station M
Montreal, Que., H1V 3P2, Canada
Prof. baseball player

Oliver, Edith
The New Yorker magazine
25 W. 43d St.
New York, NY 10036
Theatrical reviewer

Oliver, Susan
139 S. Beverly Dr., #311
Beverly Hills, CA 90212
Actress; director; author

Olivier, Lord Laurence
33 (34) Chancery Ln.
London, Wc2A 1EN,
England
Actor

Olsen, Merlin Jay
2650 Oak Knoll
San Marino, CA 91108
Football player; sports analyst; actor

Olsen, Mrs.
Folger Coffee Co.
301 E. Sixth St.
Cincinnati, OH 45202
Spokeswoman

Olympia Brewing Co.
P.O. Box 947
Olympia, WA 98507
Robert A. Schmidt, Chairman

O'Malley, Peter
Los Angeles Dodgers
Dodger Stadium
1000 Elysian Park Ave.
Los Angeles, CA 90012
Prof. baseball club executive

Onassis, Jacqueline Kennedy
Doubleday & Co.
245 Park Ave.
New York, NY 10017
Former First Lady; editor

O'Neal, Frederick
165 W. 46th St.
New York, NY 10036
Actor; lecturer; director

O'Neal, Ryan
ICM
8899 Beverly Blvd.
Los Angeles, CA 90048
Actor

O'Neal, Tatum
1888 Century Park East, #622
Los Angeles, CA 90067
Actress

O'Neil, Kitty Linn
7017 N. Hayvenhurst Ave., #6
Van Nuys, CA 91406
Stuntwoman—motor sport racer

153

O'Neill, Brian Francis
National Hockey League
960 Sun Life Bldg.
Montreal, PQ H3B 2W2
Canada
Hockey executive

O'Neill, Thomas P. ("Tip")
Room H-204
U.S. Capitol
Washington, DC 20515
*U.S. Congressman (D),
Massachusetts, 1953–present;
Speaker of the House, 1977–present*

Onthank, John Banties
18 Turner Ridge Ct.
Wilton, CT 06897
Candy & soft drink executive

O'Reilly, Terry Joseph
Boston Bruins
150 Causeway St.
Boston, MA 02114
Prof. hockey player

Orfila, Alejandro
Organization of American States
Headquarters
Organization of American States
Bldg.
17th St. & Constitution Ave.
Washington, DC 20006
Argentine diplomat

Orion Pictures Corp.
1875 Century Park East
Los Angeles, CA 90067
Arthur B. Krim, Chairman

Orlando, Tony
151 El Camino
Beverly Hills, CA 90212
Singer

Orr, John Michael
Athletic Department
Iowa State University
Ames, IA 50011
Basketball coach

Orr, Robert Gordon (Bobby)
% Nabisco Brands Inc.
625 Madison Ave.
New York, NY 10022
Former prof. hockey player

Ortho Pharmaceutical Corp.
U.S. Rte. 202
Raritan, NJ 08869
R. N. Wilson, President

Osborne, Kathleen
The White House Office
1600 Pennsylvania Avenue
and Executive Office Bldg.
Washington, DC 20500
*Personal secretary to President
Ronald Reagan*

Osborne, Robert
Hollywood Reporter
6715 Sunset Blvd.
Los Angeles, CA 90028
Entertainment columnist

Oscar Mayer Food Corp.
910 Mayer Ave.
Madison, WI 53704
J. M. Hiegel, President

Osmond, Donald Clark
1420 E. 800 North
Orem, UT 84057
Singer

Osmond, Marie
1420 E. 800 North
Orem, UT 84057
Singer

Osterwald, Bibi (Margaret Virginia)
132 Lasky Dr.
Beverly Hills, CA 90212
Actress

O'Toole, Annette
151 El Camino
Beverly Hills, CA 90212
Actress

154

O'Toole, Peter
% Veerline Ltd.
54 Baker St.
London, WIM 1DJ,
England
Actor

Overeaters Anonymous
2190 W. 190th St.
Torrance, CA 90504
Ralph McIntire, General Manager

Owens, Buck
1900 Avenue of the Stars
Los Angeles, CA 90067
Country music star

Oz, Frank
Henson Assocs.
117 E. 69th St.
New York, NY 10024
Puppeteer

P

Paar, Jack
Doubleday & Co.
245 Park Ave.
New York, NY 10017
Author; former talk show host

Pabst Brewing Co.
1000 N. Market St.
Milwaukee, WI 53201
Thomas N. McGowan, Jr.,
Chairman

Pacino, Al
William Morris Agency
1350 Avenue of the Americas
New York, NY 10019
Actor

Packwood, Robert W.
Senate Office Bldg.
Washington, DC 20510
U.S. Senator (R), Oregon,
1969–present

Page, Alan
Chicago Bears
55 E. Jackson
Chicago, IL 60604
Prof. football player; lawyer

Page, Geraldine
% Stephen Draper Agency
37 W. 57th St.
New York, NY 10019
Actress

Page, Patti
314 Huntley Dr.
Los Angeles, CA 90048
Entertainer

Page, Susie
10065 Foothill Blvd.
Lake View Terrace, CA 91342
Cat expert

Palance, Jack
15301 Ventura Blvd., #345
Sherman Oaks, CA 91403
Actor

Paley, William S.
51 W. 52d St.
New York, NY 10019
Business executive, founder of CBS

Palme, Olaf
Office of the Prime Minister
Stockholm, Sweden
Prime Minister, Sweden—since 1982

Palmer, Arnold
Box 52
Youngstown, PA 15696
Prof. golfer

Palmer, Jim
Baltimore Orioles
Memorial Stadium
Baltimore, MD 21218
Prof. baseball player

Palmer, John
% NBC News
30 Rockefeller Plaza
New York, NY 10020
Television news correspondent

Palmer, Lilli
% Macmillan Inc.
866 Third Ave.
New York, NY 10022
Actress

Palmer, Max
Mimosa Trailer Park
Arnold, MO 63010
*Biggest hand in U.S.A.—11 inches
from tip of middle finger to palm;
ring size 14*

Palmer, Robert
ARC
75 Rockefeller Plaza
New York, NY 10019
Composer; singer

Palmer, Sandra Jean
% Genz 1
W. Camino Real
Boca Raton, FL 33432
Prof. golfer

Pan, Steve Chice-Tung
13 Leighton St.
Natick, MA 01760
Parasitologist

Papandreou, Andreas
Office of the Prime Minister
Athens, Greece
Prime Minister, Greece—since 1981

Papp, Joseph
Public Theater
425 Lafayette St.
New York, NY 10003
Theater producer

Paramount Pictures
One Gulf & Western Plaza
New York, NY 10023
*Michael D. Eisner, Chief Operating
Officer*

Pardo, Dominick George (Don)
30 Rockefeller Plaza
New York, NY 10020
Broadcast announcer

Parents of Punkers
14034 Pioneers Blvd.
Norwalk, CA 90650
Serena Dank, Founder

Paris, Jerry
4151 Prospect Ave.
Los Angeles, CA 90027
Director

Parish, Lance
Detroit Tigers
Tiger Stadium
Detroit, MI 48216
Prof. baseball player

Park, Douglas Bradford
Boston Bruins
150 Causeway St.
Boston, MA 02114
Prof. hockey player

Parker, Alan William
Alan Parker Film Co.
Pinewood Studios
Iver Heath
Buckinghamshire, England
Film director

Parker, David Gene
Pittsburgh Pirates
600 Stadium Circle
Pittsburgh, PA 15212
Prof. baseball player

Parker, Jamison
100 Universal City Plaza
Universal City, CA 91608
Actor

Parker Pen Co.
One Parker Pl.
Janesville, WI 53545
George Parker, Chairman

Parkins, Barbara
151 El Camino
Beverly Hills, CA 90212
Actress

Parks, Bert
8075 W. Third St., #303
Los Angeles, CA 90048
Entertainer

Parrish, Lemar
Washington Redskins
P.O. Box 17247
Dulles International Airport
Washington, DC 20041
Prof. football player

Parsons, Chuck
229 Lake St.
Silver Lake, MN 55381
Expert on Texas outlaws & lawmen

Parsons, Estelle
505 West End Ave.
New York, NY 10024
Actress

Parton, Dolly Rebecca
9255 Sunset Blvd., #1115
Los Angeles, CA 90069
Singer; composer; actress

Paterno, Joseph Vincent
Pennsylvania State University
University Park, PA 16802
Football coach

Patrick, John
Fortuna Mill Estate
Box 2386
St. Thomas, VI 00801
Playwright

Patrick, Ruth (Mrs. Charles Hodge)
Academy of Natural Science
Philadelphia, PA 19103
Limnologist; diatomic taxonomist

Pauken, Thomas W.
ACTION
806 Connecticut Ave., NW
Washington, DC 20525
Director

Paul Masson
P.O. Box 93
Saratoga, CA 95070
*Morris Katz, Executive Vice
President*

Pauley, Jane
NBC
30 Rockefeller Plaza
New York, NY 10020
News host of Today *show*

Pauling, Linus C.
440 Page Mill Rd.
Palo Alto, CA 94306
Peace and Chemistry Nobel laureate

Pavarotti, Luciano
% Herbert Breslin
119 W. 57th St.
New York, NY 10019
Lyric tenor

Paxton, Tom
1234 Summer St., #500
Stamford, CT 06905
Songwriter; entertainer

Payton, Eddie
Detroit Lions
1200 Featherstone Rd.
Box 4200
Pontiac, MD 48057
Prof. football player

Payton, Walter
Chicago Bears
55 E. Jackson
Chicago, IL 60604
Prof. football player

Peace Corps.
806 Connecticut Ave., NW
Washington, DC 20525
Loret Ruppe, Director

Peale, Norman Vincent
1030 Fifth Ave.
New York, NY
Clergyman

Peanut, Mr.
Planters Peanuts
Suffolk, VA 23434
Spokespeanut

Pearl, Minnie
1900 Avenue of the Stars, #300
Los Angeles, CA 90067
Performer

Pearson, Drew
Dallas Cowboys
6116 N. Central Expwy.
Dallas, TX 75206
Prof. football player

Peck, Gregory
P.O. Box 24817
Los Angeles, CA 90024
Actor

Pelé (Edson Arantes Do Nascimento)
75 Rockefeller Plaza
New York, NY 10019
*Soccer player (Athlete of the
Century—1980)*

Pender, Michael
148 Poplar St.
Garden City, NY 11530
Expert on world's fairs

Pendergrass, Teddy
2400 Chestnut St.
Philadelphia, PA 19103
Musician

Pendleton, Clarence M., Jr.
Commission on Civil Rights
1121 Vermont Ave., NW
Washington, DC 20425
Chairman

Penghlis, Thaao
Burbank Studios
Columbia Pictures Television
Burbank, CA 91505
Actor

Penhall, Bruce
2970 Maria St.
Rancho Dominguez, CA 90221
Actor; motorcyclist

Penn, Arthur Hiller
Florin Productions
1860 Broadway
New York, NY 10023
Film, theater director

Penn, Sean
1888 Century Park East, #1400
Los Angeles, CA 90067
Actor

Penney Co., J. C.
1301 Avenue of the Americas
New York, NY 10019
Donald V. Seibert, Chairman

Penthouse **magazine**
909 Third Ave.
New York, NY 10022
Bob Guccione, Editor

People **magazine**
Time-Life Bldg.
New York, NY 10020
Patricia Ryan, Managing Editor

Peppard, George
5555 Melrose Ave.
Los Angeles, CA 90038
Actor

Pepper, Claude
House Office Bldg.
Washington, DC 20515
*U.S. Congressman (D), Florida,
1963–present; U.S. Senator (D),
Florida, 1936–1951*

Pepsico, Inc.
Anderson Hill Rd.
Purchase, NY 10577
Donald M. Kendall, Chairman

Percy, Charles Harting
Senate Office Bldg.
Washington, DC 20510
U.S. Senator (R), Illinois,
1967–present

Perez, Atanasio Rigal (Tony)
Boston Red Sox
24 Yawkey Way
Boston, MA 02215
Prof. baseball player

Pérez de Cuéllar, Javier
United Nations
1 UN Plaza
New York, NY 10017
United Nations Secretary General,
1982–present

Perkins, Anthony
ICM
8899 Beverly Blvd.
Los Angeles, CA 90048
Actor

Perkins, Marlin
52 Aberdeen Pl.
St. Louis, MO 63105
Host of Wild Kingdom

Perrier Co.
Great Water of France
777 W. Putnam Ave.
Greenwich, CT 06830
Ron Davis, President

Perrine, Valerie
9000 Sunset Blvd., #315
Los Angeles, CA 90069
Actress

Perry, Frank
% Frank Perry Films
655 Park Ave.
New York, NY 10021
Motion picture director

Perry, Gaylord
RR 3, Box 565
Williamston, NC 27892
Former prof. baseball player

Perry, Henry
Perry Oceanographic
Wet Submersible Division
100 E. 17th St.
Riviera Beach, FL 33404
Manufactures a $31,500 submarine

Perry, Richard Van
9130 Sunset Blvd.
Los Angeles, CA 90069
Record producer

Perschke, Walter
Numisco Rare Coins Ltd.
1423 W. Fullerton Ave.
Chicago, IL 60614
President

Pescow, Donna Gail
9169 Sunset Blvd.
Los Angeles, CA 90069
Actress

Peters, Bernadette
9000 Sunset Blvd., #315
Los Angeles, CA 90069
Actress

Peters, Henry John
Baltimore Orioles
Memorial Stadium
Baltimore, MD 21218
Baseball club executive

Peters, Roberta
ICM
40 W. 57th St.
New York, NY 10019
Soprano

Peterson, Donald R.
Edon, Inc.
1400 Lake Ridge Ct.
Roswell, GA 30076
President—classic car appraisal
service

Petty, Richard
Rte. #3
Box 621
Randleman, NC 27317
Auto racer

Petty, Tom
Lookout Management
9120 Sunset Blvd.
Los Angeles, CA 90069
Singer

Philip Morris Inc.
120 Park Ave.
New York, NY 10017
George Weissman, Chairman

Phillips, Dail Andres ("Bum")
New Orleans Saints
1500 Poydras St.
New Orleans, LA 70112
Prof. football coach

Phillips, Michelle
Management 3
9744 Wilshire Blvd.
Los Angeles, CA 90212
Singer; actress; former member of Mamas and Papas

Phillips Petroleum Company
Fourth & Keeler
Bartlesville, OK 74003
Wm. C. Douce, Chairman

Phobia Clinic
White Plains Hospital
Davis Ave. at E. Post Rd.
White Plains, NY 10601
Manuel D. Zane, Director

Pierce, Samuel R.
Department of Housing & Urban
Development
451 Seventh St., NW
Washington, DC 20410
Secretary, 1981–present

Piggy, Miss
P.O. Box 2495
New York, NY 10001
Muppet

Pills Anonymous
P.O. Box 473
Ansonia Station
New York, NY 10023
Allen Lipsitz, Public Officer

Pinochet Ugarte, General Augusto
Office of the President
Santiago, Chile
President, Chile—since 1973

Pinter, Harold
% ACTAC
16 Cadogan Ln.
London, SW1, England
Playwright

Piper, Perry
West Liberty, IL 62475
Edsel expert

Pizza Hut, Inc.
9111 E. Douglas
Wichita, KS 67207
Arthur G. Gunther, President

Place, Mary Kay
9744 Wilshire Blvd., #206
Beverly Hills, CA 90212
Actress; singer

Planned Parenthood Federation of America
810 Seventh Ave.
New York, NY 10019
Frederick C. Smith, Chairperson

Plant, Robert Anthony
Swan Song Inc.
444 Madison Ave.
New York, NY 10022
Singer, composer with Led Zeppelin

Playboy Enterprises, Inc.
919 N. Michigan Ave.
Chicago, IL 60611
Hugh M. Hefner, Chairman

Player, Gary Jim
% International Management
Group
One Erieview Plaza
Cleveland, OH 44114
Prof. golfer

Playskool, Inc.
4501 W. Augusta
Chicago, IL 60651
George Volanakis, President

Pleasance, Donald
9200 Sunset Blvd., #431
Los Angeles, CA 90069
Actor

Pleshette, Suzanne
151 El Camino
Beverly Hills, CA 90212
Actress

Plimpton, George Ames
541 E. 72d St.
New York, NY 10021
Author; editor

Plummer, Christopher
ICM
8899 Beverly Blvd.
Los Angeles, CA 90048
Actor

Plunkett, Jim
Los Angeles Raiders
332 Center St.
El Segundo, CA 90245
Prof. football player

Pointer Sisters
RCA
6363 W. Sunset Blvd.
Los Angeles, CA 90028
Singing group

Poitier, Sidney
% Verdon Productions
9350 Wilshire Blvd.
Beverly Hills, CA 90212
Actor

Polaroid Corp.
549 Technology Sq.
Cambridge, MA 02139
Edwin H. Land, Chairman

Police, The
Frontier Booking International
1776 Broadway
New York, NY 10019
Rock group

Pollack, Reginald Murray
205 River Bend Rd.
Great Falls, VA 22066
Painter

Pollack, Sydney
Mirage Enterprises
4000 Warner Blvd.
Burbank, CA 91505
Film director

Popsicle Industries Inc.
110 Highway 4
P.O. Box 200
Englewood, NJ 07631
James D. Cockman, President

Porter, Daryl
St. Louis Cardinals
Busch Memorial Stadium
250 Stadium Plaza
St. Louis, MO 63102
Prof. baseball player

Potsmokers Anonymous
316 E. Third St.
New York, NY 10009
Perry Izenton, Associate Director

Potvin, Denis Charles
David Cogan Management Co.
Empire State Bldg.
New York, NY 10001
*Prof. hockey player, New York
Islanders*

Powell, Jane
7060 Hollywood Blvd., #610
Los Angeles, CA 90028
Actress; singer

Powell, Lewis, Jr.
U.S. Supreme Court
Washington, DC 20543
Supreme Court Justice, 1972–present

Powers, Stephanie
151 El Camino
Beverly Hills, CA 90212
Actress

Premenstrual Syndrome Action
P.O. Box 9326
Madison, WI 53715
Virginia Cassara, Director

162

Preminger, Otto
Sigma Productions Inc.
129 E. 64th St.
New York, NY 10021
*Motion picture & stage producer &
director*

Pressler, Larry
Senate Office Bldg.
Washington, DC 20510
*U.S. Senator (R), South Dakota,
1979–present*

Preston, Billy
% De Passe-Jones Management
6255 Sunset Blvd.
Los Angeles, CA 90028
Musician; songwriter; singer

Preston, Robert
% John Springer Assocs.
667 Madison Ave.
New York, NY 10021
Actor

Previn, André
% Harrison/Parrott Ltd.
12 Penzance Pl.
London, W11, England
Composer; conductor

Price, Ray
% Ray Price Enterprises
P.O. Box 30384
Dallas, TX 75230
Singer

Price, Vincent
9169 Sunset Blvd.
Los Angeles, CA 90069
Actor

Pride, Charley
% Chardon, Inc.
5924 Royal Ln., Suite 104
Dallas, TX 75230
Singer

Prince
P.O. Box 10118
Minneapolis, MN 55401
Rock singer

Prince, Harold S.
1270 Avenue of the Americas
New York, NY 10020
Theatrical producer

Principal, Victoria
3970 Overland Ave.
Culver City, CA 90230
Actress

Pritikin, Nathan
P.O. Box 5335
Santa Barbara, CA 93108
Nutritionist; author

Procrastinators Club of America
1111 Broad-Locust Bldg.
Philadelphia, PA 19102
Les Waas, President

Procter & Gamble
301 E. Sixth St.
Cincinnati, OH 45202
*Owen B. Butler, Chairman—makers
of Ivory, Head & Shoulders, Scope,
Sure, Charmin*

Project Concern International
3550 Afton Rd.
San Diego, CA 92123
*Robert C. Crowk, Executive
Director—provides care to
population of host country*

Prowse, Juliet
151 El Camino
Beverly Hills, CA 90212
Actress; dancer

Proxmire, William
Senate Office Bldg.
Washington, DC 20510
*U.S. Senator (D), Wisconsin,
1957–present*

Pruitt, Gregory Donald
Cleveland Browns
Cleveland Stadium
Cleveland, OH 44114
Prof. football player

Pryor, Richard
Columbia Pictures
Columbia Plaza
Burbank, CA 91505
Comedian; actor

Puck, Wolfgang
Spago Restaurant
8795 Sunset Blvd.
Los Angeles, CA 90069
Owner; former chef at Ma Maison Restaurant

Puns Corps. (Association for the Improvement of Government Jargon)
Box 2364
3108 Dashiell Rd.
Falls Church, VA 22042
Robert L. Birch, Coordinator

Puzo, Mario
G. P. Putnam's Sons
200 Madison Ave.
New York, NY 10016
Author

Pyle, Denver
7060 Hollywood Blvd., #610
Los Angeles, CA 90028
Actor

Q

Quaid, Dennis William
222 N. Canon Dr., #204
Beverly Hills, CA 90212
Actor

Quaker Oats Co., The
Merchandise Mart Plaza
Chicago, IL 60654
Robert D. Stuart, Jr., Chairman of Board

Queen
46 Pembridge Rd.

London, W11 3HN, England
Rock group

Quinn, Anthony
Vigna San Antonio
Cecchi Di Roma, Italy
Actor

Quintero, Jose Benjamin
% Society of Stage Directors and
Choreographers
1501 Broadway
New York, NY 10036
Theatrical director

R

Rabb, Ellis
5000 Poplar Ave., #10
Memphis, TN 38117
Actor; director; writer

Rabbitt, Eddie
9229 Sunset Blvd., 9th Fl.
Los Angeles, CA 90069
Singer; songwriter

Rabe, David William
% Bohan & Neuwald Agency
905 West End Ave.
New York, NY 10025
Playwright

Rabe, William
Lake Superior State College
Sault Ste. Marie, MI 49783
Expert on stone skipping

Radio Free Europe/Radio Liberty
1201 Connecticut Ave., NW
Washington, DC 20036
Glenn Ferguson, President

Radner, Gilda
9200 Sunset Blvd., Suite 428
Los Angeles, CA 90069
Comedienne; actress

Rae, Charlotte
3000 W. Alameda Ave.
Burbank, CA 91505
Actress

Rafelson, Bob
% Wolff
1400 N. Fuller Ave.
Hollywood, CA 90046
Film director

Raffin, Deborah
967 N. La Cienega Blvd.
Los Angeles, CA 90069
Actress

Rafkin, Alan
% ABC Press Relations
1330 Avenue of the Americas
New York, NY 10019
Television director

Ragu Foods Inc.
33 Benedict Pl.
Greenwich, CT 06830
George F. Goebeler, President

Raines, Tim
Montreal Expos
P.O. Box 500
Station M
Montreal, PQ H1V 3P2
Canada
Prof. baseball player

Rainier III, Prince
Royal Palace
Monaco-Ville, Monaco
Chief of State, Monaco—since 1949

Raitt, Bonnie
% Dick Waterman
1588 Crossroads of the World
Hollywood, CA 90028
Singer; musician

Ralston Purina Co.
Checkerboard Sq.
St. Louis, MO 63164
*W. P. Stiritz, Chairman of Board,
President*

Ramada Inns, Inc.
3838 E. Van Buren
Phoenix, AZ 85008
Richard Snell, Chairman of Board

Ramirez, Raul
U.S. Tennis Assn.
51 E. 42d St.
New York, NY 10017
Prof. tennis player

Randall, Tony
9200 Sunset Blvd., #909
Los Angeles, CA 90069
Actor

Randolph, Jennings
Senate Office Bldg.
Washington, DC 20510
*U.S. Senator (D), West Virginia,
1958–present*

Randolph, Joyce
295 Central Park West
New York, NY 10024
Trixie Norton on Honeymooners

Ransohoff, Martin
Columbia Pictures
300 Colgems Sq.
Burbank, CA 91505
Motion picture producer

Rape Crisis Center
P.O. Box 21005
Washington, DC 20009
Loretta J. Ross, Director

Rashad, Ahmad
Minnesota Vikings
9520 Viking Dr.
Eden Prairie, MN 55344
Prof. football player

Rather, Dan
CBS News
524 W. 57th St.
New York, NY 10019
Network news anchorman

Rawls, Lou
CBS Records
51 W. 52d St.
New York, NY 10019
Singer

Rayburn, Gene
% Goodson-Todman Productions
375 Park Ave.
New York, NY 10020
TV game show host

Raye, Martha
Ruth Webb
7500 Devista Dr.
Los Angeles, CA 90046
Actress

Raymond, Gene
9570 Wilshire Blvd.
Beverly Hills, CA 90212
Actor; producer; director; composer

RCA Corp.
30 Rockefeller Plaza
New York, NY 10020
*Thorton F. Bradshaw, Chairman of
Board*

Reader's Digest
Pleasantville, NY 10570
Edward T. Thompson, Editor

Reagan, Nancy Davis
The White House
1600 Pennsylvania Ave.
Washington, DC 20500
First Lady

Reagan, Ronald
The White House
1600 Pennsylvania Ave.
Washington, DC 20500
President of United States,
1980–present

Reasoner, Harry
CBS News
524 W. 57th St.
New York, NY 10019
TV news reporter

Rebozo, Charles ("Bebe")
490 Bay Ln.
Key Biscayne, FL 33149
Banker; friend of former President
Richard Nixon

Reddy, Helen
10350 Santa Monica Blvd., #210
Los Angeles, CA 90025
Singer

Redenbacher, Orville
Hunt-Wesson
1645 W. Valencia Dr.
Fullerton, CA 92634
Popcorn expert

Redford, Robert
Sundance
Provo, UT 84601
Actor; director

Redgrave, Lynn
Box 1207
Topanga, CA 90290
Actress

Redgrave, Vanessa
1 Ravenscourt Rd.
London, W6, England
Actress; political activist

Redheads International, Inc.
23101 Moulton Pkwy., #110
Laguna Hills, CA 92653
Stephen Douglas, President—
organization for people with red hair

Reed, Arthur
1753 69th Ave.
Oakland, CA 94621
Oldest man in America—123

Reed, Donald A.
Count Dracula Society
334 W. 54th St.
Los Angeles, CA 90037
Dracula expert

Reed, Donna
9255 Sunset Blvd., #910
Los Angeles, CA 90069
Actress

Reed, Jerry
% Jerry Reed Enterprises
1107 18th Avenue South
Nashville, TN 37212
Musician; composer; singer

Reed, Oliver
189 Regent St., #505A
Triumph House
London, W1R 7Hf, England
Actor

Reed, Rex
New York Post
210 South St.
New York, NY 10002
Movie critic; author

Reeve, Christopher
120 S. El Camino Dr., #104
Los Angeles, CA 90212
Actor

Regan, Donald T.
Department of the Treasury
15th St. & Pennsylvania Ave.
Washington, DC 20220
Secretary, 1981–present

168

Regine
502 Park Ave.
New York, NY 10022
Disco owner

Rehnquist, William
U.S. Supreme Court
Washington, DC 20543
Supreme Court Justice, 1971–present

Reiche, Frank P.
Federal Election Commission
1325 K St., NW
Washington, DC 20005
Chairman

Reiner, Carl
141 El Camino Dr., #205
Beverly Hills, CA 90212
Actor; writer

Reiner, Rob
1888 Century Park East, #1400
Los Angeles, CA 90067
Actor; writer

Reinking, Ann
% Hesse/Hine/Baker
119 W. 57th St.
New York, NY 10019
Actress; dancer

Remick, Lee
ICM
8899 Beverly Blvd.
Los Angeles, CA 90048
Actress

Rene Guyon Society
256 S. Robertson Blvd.
Beverly Hills, CA 90211
*Tim O'Hara, spokesperson—
organization for sexual freedom;
seeks amendment of the statutory
welfare law*

Renick, Ralph Apperson
316 N. Miami Ave.
Miami, FL 33130
Journalist

Resolve, Inc.
P.O. Box 474
Belmont, MA 02178
*Barbara Eck Manning, Executive
Director—fertility*

Rettig, Tommy
9409 Kester Ave.
Panorama City, CA 91402
*Child actor, played Timmy on
Lassie series*

Revill, Lynette H.
P.O. Box 275
Cheswick, PA 15024
Private investigator

Revlon, Inc.
767 Fifth Ave.
New York, NY 10022
*Michel C. Bergerac, Chairman of
Board*

Rey, Anthony Maurice
% Resorts International Casino
Hotel
Boardwalk and North Carolina
Ave.
Atlantic City, NJ 08401
Hotel executive

Rey, Fernando
Orense 62
Madrid 20, Spain
Actor

Reynolds, Burt
8730 Sunset Blvd., #201
Los Angeles, CA 90069
Actor

Reynolds, Debbie
6514 Lankershim Blvd.
North Hollywood, CA 91606
Actress

Reynolds, Jack
San Francisco 49ers
711 Nevada St.
Redwood City, CA 94061
Prof. football player

Reynolds Aluminum
6601 Broad St. Rd.
Richmond, VA 23233
Dietrich E. Reimann, Chief
Operating Officer

Ricardo, Don
64 Hillside Terr.
Pasadena, CA 91105
Vintage auto expert

Rice, Jim
Boston Red Sox
24 Yawkey Way
Boston, MA 02215
Prof. baseball player

Rich, Buddy
Willard Alexander
660 Madison Ave.
New York, NY 10002
Drummer

Richards, Keith
Rolling Stones
75 Rockefeller Plaza
New York, NY 10019
Rock musician; songwriter

Richards, Dr. Renee
1605 Union St.
San Francisco, CA 94123
Former prof. tennis player

Richardson, Harold Beland
San Francisco Giants
Candlestick Park
San Francisco, CA 94124
Baseball club executive

Richie, Lionel
1112 N. Sherbourne Dr.
Los Angeles, CA 90069
Singer; songwriter; producer

Richman, Roger
Roger Richman Productions
8823 Cynthia St.
Los Angeles, CA 90069
Agent for dead celebrities' estates

Rickles, Don
8966 Sunset Blvd.
Los Angeles, CA 90069
Comedian; actor

Rickover, Admiral Hyman
Department of Energy
Washington, DC 20545
Retired naval officer

Ride, Sally
400 Maryland Ave., SW
Washington, DC 20546
First U.S. female astronaut in space

Rigby McCoy, Cathy
P.O. Box 387
Blue Jay, CA 92317
Former Olympic gymnast

Riggins, John
Washington Redskins
P.O. Box 17247
Dulles International Airport
Washington, DC 20041
Prof. football player

Riggs, Rollin A. & Bruce Jacobsen
3423 Yale Station
New Haven, CT 06520
Authors of The Rites of Spring, *a*
students' guide to spring break in
Florida

Riley, Jeannie C.
Brentwood, TN 37027
Singer

Ringling Bros. & Barnum & Bailey
Circus World Inc.
P.O. Box 800
Orlando, FL 32801
James G. Murphy, President

Ringwald, Molly
120 El Camino Dr., #104
Beverly Hills, CA 90212
Actress

Ripley, S. Dillon
Smithsonian Institution
1000 Jefferson Dr., SW
Washington, DC 20560
Secretary

170

Ritt, Martin
9255 Sunset Blvd., #910
Los Angeles, CA 90069
Director; actor

Ritter, John
11777 San Vicente Blvd., #600
Los Angeles, CA 90049
Actor

Ritz Bros.
Harry: Box 42861
Las Vegas, NV 89104

Jimmy: 13839 Archwood St.
Van Nuys, CA 91405
Entertainers

Rivera, Chita
151 El Camino
Beverly Hills, CA 90212
Entertainer

Rivera, Geraldo
1330 Avenue of the Americas
New York, NY 10019
Broadcast journalist

Rivers, Joan
9255 Sunset Blvd., #1115
Los Angeles, CA 90069
Comedienne

Rivers, Mickey
Texas Rangers
Arlington Stadium
P.O. Box 1111
Arlington, TX 76010
Prof. baseball player

Rizzuto, Philip Francis
New York Yankees
Yankee Stadium
Bronx, NY 10451
Sportscaster

Robards, Jason Nelson, Jr.
% STE
888 Seventh Ave.
New York, NY 10019
Actor

Robb, Charles S.
State Capitol
Richmond, VA 23219
*Governor of Virginia (D),
1981–present*

Robb, Lynda Johnson
611 Chain Bridge Rd.
McLean, VA 22101
*Wife of Governor Charles S. Robb;
daughter of former President
Lyndon Johnson*

Robbins, Harold
Pocket Books
1230 Avenue of the Americas
New York, NY 10020
Author

Robbins, Jerome
New York City Ballet
New York State Theater
Lincoln Center Plaza
New York, NY 10023
Choreographer; director

Roberts, Eric
151 El Camino
Beverly Hills, CA 90212
Actor

Roberts, Pernell
% Morgan Stanley & Co.
1251 Avenue of the Americas
New York, NY 10020
Actor

Roberts, Tanya
1446 Belfast Dr.
Los Angeles, CA 90069
Actress

Roberts, Walter Orr
1829 Bluebell Ave.
Boulder, CO 80302
Solar astronomer

Robertson, Cliff
ICM
8899 Beverly Blvd.
Los Angeles, CA 90048
Actor; writer; director

171

Robertson, Dale
Box 226
Yukon, OK 73099
Actor

Robertson, Isiah
Buffalo Bills
1 Bills Dr.
Orchard Park, NY 14127
Prof. football player

Robinson, Chris
4151 Prospect Ave.
Los Angeles, CA 90027
Actor

Robinson, Frank
San Francisco Giants
Candlestick Park
San Francisco, CA 92124
Prof. baseball coach

Robinson, Len ("Truck")
Phoenix Suns
P.O. Box 1369
Phoenix, AZ 85001
Prof. basketball player

Robinson, Max
190 N. State
Chicago, IL 60601
Television news broadcaster

Robinson, Smokey
William Morris Agency
1350 Avenue of the Americas
New York, NY 10019
Singer; composer

Rockefeller, David
30 Rockefeller Plaza
New York, NY 10020
Banker

Rockefeller, Mrs. Happy
Pocantico Hills
North Tarrytown, NY 10591
Widow of Nelson Rockefeller

Rockefeller, John Davison, IV
% State Capitol
Charleston, WV 25305
*Governor of West Virginia (D),
1977–present*

Rockette Alumnae Assn.
47 Kensington Terr.
Maplewood, NJ 07040
Emma Bisnod, President

Rockwell, Ronald James, Jr.
6282 Coachlite Way
Cincinnati, OH 45243
Laser and electro-optics

Rockwell International Corp.
600 Grant St.
Pittsburgh, PA 15219
*Robert Anderson, Chairman of
Board*

Rodgers, Robert Leroy
Milwaukee Brewers
Milwaukee County Stadium
Milwaukee, WI 53214
Prof. baseball team manager

Rodgers, William Henry
32 Parks Dr.
Sherborn, MA 01770
Runner

Rodino, Peter W., Jr.
House Office Bldg.
Washington, DC 20515
*U.S. Congressman (D), New Jersey,
1949–present*

Rogers, Ginger
18745 Highway 62
Eagle Point, OR 97525
Dancer; actress

Rogers, Kenneth Ray
Ken Kragen & Co.
1112 N. Shebourne Dr.
Los Angeles, CA 90069
Entertainer

Rogers, Roy
% Art Rush Inc.
10221 Riverside Dr.
North Hollywood, CA 91602
Motion picture actor

Rogers, Stephen
Syracuse Newspapers Ltd.
Clinton Sq., Box 4915
Syracuse, NY 13221
Newspaper publisher

Rogers, Tristan
% Baker and Winokur
9533 Brighton Way
Beverly Hills, CA 90210
Actress

Rogers, Wayne
151 El Camino
Beverly Hills, CA 90212
Actor

Rogers, Will, Jr.
Tubac, AZ 85640
Entertainer

Rollins, Howard E.
7139 Beverly Blvd., #1
Los Angeles, CA 90036
Actor

Romero-Barcelo, Carlos
State Capitol
San Juan, Puerto Rico 00902
Governor of Puerto Rico

Romper Room Entertainment Inc.
200 E. Joppa Rd., #400
Towson, MD 21204
John H. Claster, President

Ronstadt, Linda
644 N. Doheny Dr.
Los Angeles, CA 90069
Singer

Ronzoni Macaroni
50-02 Northern Blvd.
Long Island City, NY 11101
Emanuele Ronzoni, Jr., Chairman

Rooney, Andrew Aitken
CBS
51 W. 52d St.
New York, NY 10019
Television commentator; writer

Rooney, Arthur Joseph
940 N. Lincoln Ave.
Pittsburgh, PA 15233
*Prof. football club executive—
Pittsburgh Steelers*

Rooney, Mickey
7500 Devista Dr.
Los Angeles, CA 90046
Actor

Roosevelt, Selma
The White House Office
1600 Pennsylvania Ave.
& Executive Office Bldg.
Washington, DC 20500
Chief of Protocol, 1980–present

Rorer, William Herbert, III
500 Virginia Dr.
Fort Washington, PA 19034
*Pharmaceutical company executive
(Rorer Co.)*

Rose, Beatrice
233 Mira Flores Dr.
Palm Beach, FL 33480
Artist

Rose, Miles
120 W. 78th St., #3D
New York, NY 10024
Investment broker

Rose, Pete
Philadelphia Phillies
P.O. Box 7575
Philadelphia, PA 19101
Prof. baseball player

Rose Marie
% J. Robert Prete Management Co.
449 S. Beverly Dr.
Beverly Hills, CA 90212
Actress

Rosenberg, Robert Michael
Dunkin' Donuts Inc.
P.O. Box 317
Randolph, MA 02368
*Fast-food franchise company
executive*

Roskelley, John
1223 Skipworth Rd.
Spokane, WA 99206
Mountaineer

Ross, Diana
151 El Camino
Beverly Hills, CA 90212
Singer; actress; entertainer

Ross, Katharine
1888 Century Park East, #1400
Los Angeles, CA 90067
Actress

Ross, Marion
Marion Ross Enterprises Inc.
% Barbara Best
511 N. San Vicente Blvd.
Los Angeles, CA 90048
Actress

Rossner, Judith
% Julian Bach Agency
747 Third Ave.
New York, NY 10017
Novelist

Rostenkowski, Dan
House Office Bldg.
Washington, DC 20515
U.S. Congressman (D), Illinois, 1961–present

Roundtree, Richard
7033 Sunset Blvd., #320
Los Angeles, CA 90028
Actor

Rourke, Mickey
400 S. Beverly Dr., #216
Los Angeles, CA 90212
Actor

Rowles, Polly
J.M.B.
400 Madison Ave., 20th Fl.
New York, NY 10017
Famous underwear inspector for Hanes

Royal Crown Companies Inc.
41 Perimeter Center East, NE
Atlanta, GA 30346
William T. Young, Chairman of Board

Rozelle, Pete
National Football League
410 Park Ave.
New York, NY 10022
Prof. football commissioner

R2D2
P.O. Box 2009
San Rafael, CA 94912
Robot, Star Wars

R2-32
Cottonwood Police Station
Cottonwood, AZ 86326
Police robot

Rubbermaid, Inc.
1147 Akron Rd.
Wooster, OH 44691
Stanley C. Gault, Chairman of Board

Rubik, Erno
Rubik's International Game magazine
Editorial Office
Budapest, H-1906
P.O.B. 223
Hungary
Invented Rubik's Cube

Rudie, Evelyn
1211 Fourth St.
Santa Monica, CA 90401
Actress, played Eloise

Ruff, Howard
P.O. Box 31
Springville, UT 84663
Financial analyst

Rugee, Dr. Daniel
The White House Office
1600 Pennsylania Ave.
& Executive Office Building
Washington, DC 20500
Physician to President Ronald Reagan

174

Ruland, Jeff
Washington Bullets
1 Harry S. Truman Dr.
Landover, MD 20786
Prof. basketball player

Rusk, Dean
1 Lafayette Square
620 Hill St.
Athens, GA 30601
Former Secretary of State,
1961–1969

Russell, Jane
Box 590
Sedona, AZ 86336
Actress

Russell, Kurt
151 El Camino
Beverly Hills, CA 90212
Actor

Russell Stover Candies, Inc.
1004 Baltimore Ave.
Kansas City, MO 64105
Louis L. Ward, Chairman of Board

Ryan, Nolan
Houston Astros
Astrodome
P.O. Box 288
Houston, TX 77001
Prof. baseball player

Rydell, Mark
7950 Sunset Blvd.
Los Angeles, CA 90046
Director

S

Safe Return Amnesty Committee
175 Fifth Ave., #1010
New York, NY 10010
Ensign Tod, Director

Sagan, Carl
Random House
201 E. 50th St.
New York, NY 10022
Author

Sager, Carole Bayer
151 El Camino
Beverly Hills, CA 90212
Lyricist

Sager, Marcel
EFO Society
(Errors, Freaks & Oddities)
John Notchner, Secretary
P.O. Box 1125
Falls Church, VA 22041
Stamp collector

St. John, Jill
ICM
8899 Beverly Blvd.
Los Angeles, CA 90048
Actress

St. Laurent, Yves
15 Columbus Circle
New York, NY 10023
or
55 Rue de Babylone
75008 Paris, France
Owner of perfumery; fashion designer

Sainte-Marie, Buffy
RR #1, Box 368
Kapaa, Kauai, HI 96746
Singer

Sakharov, Vladimir
Ballantine Books
201 E. 50th St.
New York, NY 10019
Former KGB agent

Sakowitz, Robert Tobias
1111 Main St.
P.O. Box 1387
Houston, TX 77001
Retail apparel, specialty stores executive

Salazar, Alberto
Athletics West
3968 W. 13th Ave.
Eugene, OR 97402
Marathon runner

176

Saldana, Theresa
967 N. La Cienega Blvd.
Los Angeles, CA 90069
Actress; founder and President of
Victims for Victims organization

Salinger, Pierre
248 Rue de Rivoli
75001 Paris, France
Journalist

Salk, Dr. Jonas
2444 Ellentown Rd.
La Jolla, CA 92037
Developed polio vaccine

Salvation Army
120 W. 14th St.
New York, NY 10011
Ernest W. Holz, National
Commander

Sambo's Restaurants, Inc.
6400 Cindy Ln.
Carpinteria, CA 93013
Robert K. Luckey, Chairman of
Board

Samrin, Heng
Office of the President
Phnom Penh, Kampuchea
President—since 1979 (formerly
Cambodia)

Sam the Sham
3667 Tetwiler Ave.
Memphis, TN 38122
Musician

Sanders, James C.
Small Business Administration
1441 L Street, NW
Washington, DC 20416
Administrator

Sanford, Isabel
100 Universal City Plaza
Universal City, CA 91608
Actress

Sanka
Maxwell House
250 North St.
White Plains, NY 10625
S. B. Morris, General Manager

Santana, Carlos
% Bill Graham Productions
201 11th St.
San Francisco, CA 94103
Rock musician

Sant'Angelo, Giorgio
Giorgio Sant'Angelo Designs Inc.
20 W. 57th St.
New York, NY 10019
Fashion designer

Sara Lee, Kitchens of
500 Waukegan Rd.
Deerfield, IL 60015
P. Frederick Kahn, Senior Vice
President

Sarbanes, Paul S.
Senate Office Bldg.
Washington, DC 20510
U.S. Senator (D), Maryland,
1977–present

Sardi, Vincent, Jr.
234 W. 44th St.
New York, NY 10036
Restaurant executive, owner Sardi's
Restaurant

Sarnoff, Dorothy
Speech Dynamics Inc.
111 W. 57th St.
New York, NY 10019
Speech teacher

Sassoon, Vidal
2049 Century Park East
Los Angeles, CA 90067
Hairstylist

Savalas, Telly Aristoteles
4348 Van Nuys Blvd., Suite 207
Sherman Oaks, CA 91403
Actor

Savard, Serge
Montreal Canadiens
2313 W. St. Catherine St.
Montreal, PQ H3H 1N2
Canada
Prof. hockey player

Sawyer, John
J. Sawyer Co.
8050 Hosbrook Ct.
Cincinnati, OH 45236
*Football team executive; part owner
of the Cincinnati Bengals*

Sax, Steve
Los Angeles Dodgers
Dodger Stadium
1000 Elysian Park Ave.
Los Angeles, CA 90012
Prof. baseball player

Sayers, Gale
624 Buch Rd.
Northbrook, IL 60062
*Educator; retired prof. football
player*

Scalia, Jack
8642 Melrose Ave.
Los Angeles, CA 90069
Former model; actor

Scarborough, Charles Bishop, III
% NBC News
30 Rockefeller Plaza
New York, NY 10020
Broadcast journalist; author

Scavullo, Francesco
212 E. 63d St.
New York, NY 10021
Fashion photographer

Schallert, William Joseph
1801 Avenue of the Stars, #911
Los Angeles, CA 90067
Actor

Scheer, Carl
Denver Nuggets
McNichols Sports Arena
1635 Clay St.
Denver, CO 80204
Prof. basketball team executive

Scheider, Roy
120 E. 56th St., #600
New York, NY 10022
Actor

Scheie, Harold Glendon
Scheie Eye Institute
51 W. 39th St.
Philadelphia, PA 19104
Ophthalmologist

Schell, Maximilian
2 Kepler Strasse
Munich 27, West Germany
Actor

Schick, Inc.
33 Riverside Ave.
Westport, CT 06880
James W. Hart, Chairman of Board

Schifrin, Lalo Boris
BMI
320 W. 57th St.
New York, NY 10019
Composer

Schlafly, Phyllis Stewart
68 Fairmont
Alton, IL 62002
Author; lawyer; antifeminist activist

Schlichter, Art
Baltimore Colts
P.O. Box 2000
Owings Mills, MD 21117
Prof. football player

Schlickau, George Hans
Rte. 2
Haven, KS 67543
Cattle breeder

Schlitz Brewing Co., Jos.
One Stroh Dr.
Detroit, MI 48226
*Roger Fridholm, Chief Operating
Officer*

Schmeling, Max
2115 Hallenstedt
Hamburg, West Germany
*Former heavyweight boxing
champion*

Schmidt, Helmut
SPD-Parteivorstand
D-5300 Bonn 1
West Germany
*Former German Chancellor,
1974–1982*

Schmidt, Michael Jack
Philadelphia Phillies
P.O. Box 7575
Philadelphia, PA 19101
Prof. baseball player

Schmitt, Harrison H.
P.O. Box 8261
Albuquerque, NM 87198
*Apollo 17 moonwalker; former U.S.
Senator*

Schoen, L. S. Samuel
U-Haul International
Phoenix, AZ
Founder & president of U-Haul

Schrader, Paul
% Columbia Pictures
Colgems Square
Burbank, CA 91505
Film writer; director

Schroeder, Patricia
House Office Bldg.
Washington, DC 20515
*U.S. Congresswoman (D),
Colorado, 1973–present*

Schulz, Charles
1 Snoopy Pl.
Santa Rosa, CA 95401
Cartoonist, Peanuts

Schwalb, Fernando
Office of the Prime Minister
Lima, Peru
Prime Minister, Peru—since 1982

Schwarzenegger, Arnold
P.O. Box 1234
Santa Monica, CA 90406
Body builder; actor

Schwebel, Stephen M.
United Nations
1 UN Plaza
New York, NY 10017
*United States Representative on
International Court of Justice,
1981–present*

Scorsese, Martin
190 N. Canon Dr., #202
Beverly Hills, CA 90210
Film director; writer

Scott, Colonel Charles
Office of Public Affairs
Department of the Army
Fort McPherson, GA 30330
Freed American hostage from Iran

Scott, David R.
858 W. Jackson St., #202
Lancaster, CA 93534
Former astronaut

Scott, George C.
8966 Sunset Blvd.
Los Angeles, CA 90069
Actor; director

Scott, Willard
NBC
30 Rockefeller Plaza, #789
New York, NY 10020
Radio, TV performer

Scott Paper Co.
Scott Plaza
Philadelphia, PA 19113
*Charles D. Dickey, Jr., Chairman of
Board*

Scrooge
1447 Westwood Rd.
Charlottesville, VA 22901
*Chuck Langham, Executive
Director—Society to Curtail
Ridiculous, Outrageous and
Ostentatious Gift Exchange*

Sculatti, Gene
Warner Bros.
75 Rockefeller Plaza
New York, NY 10019
Editor, Catalog of Cool

179

Scully, Vin
NBC
30 Rockefeller Plaza
New York, NY 10020
Sports broadcaster

Seaga, Edward
State Offices
Kingston, Jamaica
Prime Minister, Jamaica—since 1983

Seals & Crofts
811 San Fernando Rd., #202
San Fernando, CA 91340
Musicians; songwriters

Sears, Ernest Robert
2009 Nob Hill
Columbia, MO 65201
Geneticist

Sears, Roebuck & Co.
Sears Tower
Chicago, IL 60684
Edward R. Telling, Chairman of
Board

Seaver, Tom
New York Mets
William A. Shea Stadium
Roosevelt Ave. & 126th St.
Flushing, NY 11368
Prof. baseball player

Sedaka, Neil
1370 Avenue of the Americas
New York, NY 10019
Singer, songwriter

Seeger, Pete
% Harold Leventhal
250 W. 57th St.
New York, NY 10107
Folk singer; composer

Segal, Erich
119 W. 57th St., #1106
New York, NY 10019
Author; wrote Love Story; *educator*

Segal, George
151 El Camino
Beverly Hills, CA 90212
Actor

Seger, Bob
% Punch Enterprises
567 Purdy St.
Birmingham, MI 48009
Musician

Segovia, Andres
ICM
40 W. 57th St.
New York, NY 10019
Guitarist

Selle, Ronald
17706 Dogwood Ln.
Hazel Crest, IL 60429
Sued Bee Gees for plagiarism

Selleck, Robert W.
1745 N. Kolmar Ave.
Chicago, IL 60639
President & Chief Executive Officer,
Pepsi-Cola

Selleck, Tom
9056 Santa Monica Blvd., #201
Los Angeles, CA 90069
Actor; sex symbol

Selman, Leroy
Tampa Bay Buccaneers
1 Buccaneer Place
Tampa, FL 33607
Prof. football player

Sevareid, Arnold Eric
2020 M St., NW
Washington, DC 20036
Broadcaster; author

Seven-Up Co.
121 S. Meramec Ave.
St. Louis, MO 63105
Edward W. Frantel, President

Severinsen, Carl ("Doc")
% NBC
Tonight Show
3000 W. Alameda Ave.
Burbank, CA 91523
Conductor; musician

Sexual Assault Services
Washington County Human
Services Inc.
7066 Stillwater Boulevard North
Oakdale, MN 55119
Cheryl Champion, Coordinator

Seymour, Jane
16 Berners St.
London, W1, England
Actress

Shackelford, Ted
5160 Genesta Ave.
Encino, CA 91316
Actor

Shad, John, Sr.
Securities & Exchange Commission
500 N. Capitol St., NW
Washington, DC 20549
Chairman

Shakespeare, Frank
Board for International
Broadcasting
Department of State Building
Washington, DC 20451
Chairman

Shakey's Pizza
Shakey's Inc.
3600 First International Bldg.
Dallas, TX 75202
Louis A. Cappello, President

Shaklee, Forrest Clell
Shaklee Corp.
444 Market St.
San Francisco, CA 94111
Nutritional researcher

Shal, Morton Lyon
% Harcourt Brace Jovanovich Inc.
757 Third Ave.
New York, NY 10017
Comedian

Shalit, Gene
15 E. 48th St., #903
New York, NY 10017
Critic

Shamir, Yitzhak
Office of the Prime Minister
Jerusalem, Israel
Prime Minister, Israel—since 1983

Sha Na Na
P.O. Box 92326
Milwaukee, WI 53202
TV rock group

Shane, Joseph Lawrence
Scott Paper Co.
Scott Plaza
Philadelphia, PA 19113
Chief Financial Officer

Shankar, Ravi
6 Pavlova
Little Gibbs Rd.
Bombay, India
Musician

Shapiro, Max
Great American Sports Camps
5764 Paradise Dr., #7
Corte Madera, CA 94925
Fulfills baseball fantasies

Sharif, Omar
147-149 Wardour St.
London, W1V 3TB, England
Actor

Sharkey, Jack
Box 242, Pleasant St.
Epping, NH 03042
Former prof. boxer

Shasta Beverages
26901 Industrial Blvd.
Haywood, CA 94545
Andrew F. Weidener, President

Shatner, William
1888 Century Park East, #622
Los Angeles, CA 90067
Actor

Shaw, Artie
2127 W. Palos Ct.
Newbury Park, CA 91320
Musician; writer

181

Shaw, Carole
Big Beautiful Woman
3518 W. Cahuenga Blvd.
Los Angeles, CA 90068
Editor—magazine geared toward large-sized women

Shaw, Irwin
Box 39
Klosters, Switzerland
Author

Shayne, Alan
Warner Bros.
4000 Warner Blvd.
Burbank, CA 91522
President of programming

Shea, John
ICM
40 W. 57th St.
New York, NY 10019
Actor

Shearing, George Albert
8919 N. La Crosse Ave.
Skokie, IL 60077
Pianist; composer

Sheehy, Gail Henion
% William Morrow & Co.
105 Madison Ave.
New York, NY 10016
Author

Sheen, Martin
1888 Century Park East, Suite 1616
Los Angeles, CA 90067
Actor

Sheffield, William
State Capitol
Juneau, AK 99801
Governor of Alaska (D), 1983–present

Sheldon, Neal
3790 A Silver Star Rd.
Orlando, FL 32808
Founder of "execumatch" dating service for the wealthy

Sheldon, Sidney
Warner Books
75 Rockefeller Plaza
New York, NY 10019
Author

Shell, Arthur
Los Angeles Raiders
332 Center St.
El Segundo, CA 90245
Prof. football player

Shell Oil Co.
P.O. Box 2463
Houston, TX 77001
L. C. Van Wachem, Chairman of Board

Shelton, Lonnie
Seattle Supersonics
419 Occidental South
Seattle, WA 98104
Prof. basketball player

Shelton, Reid Leroy
% Gage Group Inc.
1650 Broadway
New York, NY 10019
Actor

Shepard, Alan
3344 Chevy Chase St., #200
Houston, TX 77019
Former astronaut

Shepard, Sam
% Magic Theatre, Bldg. D.
Fort Mason Center
San Francisco, CA 94123
Playwright; actor

Shepherd, Cybill
15301 Ventura Blvd., #345
Sherman Oaks, CA 91403
Model; actress

Sherman, Robert Bernard
999 N. Doheny Dr., #403
Los Angeles, CA 90069
Songwriter; Academy Award winner for Mary Poppins

Shields, Brooke
P.O. Box B
Haworth, NJ 07641
Actress; cover girl; student

182

Shields, Robert
ICM
8899 Beverly Blvd.
Los Angeles, CA 90048
Mime; artist

Shimada, Yoko
1 Samon Cho
Shinjuku-Ku
Tokyo, Japan
Actress

Shire, David Lee
% Plant, Cohen & Co.
9777 Wilshire Blvd.
Beverly Hills, CA 90212
Composer

Shire, Talia Rose
1888 Century Park East, #1400
Los Angeles, CA 90067
Actress

Shock Society
Medical College of Georgia
Augusta, GA 30913
*Dr. Sherwood M. Reichard,
President*

Shoemaker, Willie
1900 Avenue of the Stars, #2820
Century City, CA 90067
Jockey

Shoen, Leonard Samuel
Regency Towers, Suite 22A
3111 Bel Air Dr.
Las Vegas, NV 89109
President & founder of U-Haul

Shoplifters Anonymous
Professional Bldg., #300
202 Concord Rd.
Aston, PA 19014
Lawrence A. Conner, President

Shore, Dinah
% Henry Jaffe Enterprises
5800 Sunset Blvd.
Los Angeles, CA 90028
Singer; TV talk show hostess

Short, Bobby
% Betty Lee Hunt Assocs.
1501 Broadway
New York, NY 10036
Entertainer; author

Shorter, Frank C.
% NBC Sports
30 Rockefeller Plaza
New York, NY 10020
Sportscaster; lawyer

Shriver, Eunice Mary Kennedy
% Joseph P. Kennedy, Jr.,
Foundation
1701 K St., NW
Washington, DC 20006
Civic worker

Shriver, Nellie
Vegetarian Information Service
Box 5888
Bethesda, MD 20814
*Coordinator, American vegetarians'
organization that plans to boycott
McDonald's until they put veggie
burgers on the menu*

Shriver, Sargent
600 New Hampshire Ave., NW
Washington, DC 20006
*1972 vice presidential candidate;
1976 presidential candidate*

Shula, Don
330 Biscayne Blvd.
Miami, FL 33132
*Prof. football coach, Miami
Dolphins*

Shultz, George P.
Department of State
2201 C St., NW
Washington, DC 20520
Secretary, 1983–present

Sickman, Rodney V.
RR #3, Box 527
Washington, MO 63090
Freed American hostage from Iran

Sidney, Sylvia
% John Springer
667 Madison Ave.
New York, NY 10021
Actress

Siegel, Morris J.
1780 55th St.
Boulder, CO 80301
Founder, Celestial Seasonings Herb Tea Co.

Sigmund Freud Archives
300 Central Park West
New York, NY 10024
K. R. Eissler, Secretary

Signoret, Simone
15 Place Dauphine
Isle de la Cite
75001 Paris, France
Actress

Sikorsky, Albert
P.O. Box 3906
Baltimore, MD 21222
Expert on clowns & clowning

Silkma, Jack
Seattle SuperSonics
419 Occidental South
Seattle, WA 98104
Prof. basketball player

Sills, Beverly
145 E. 52d St., #804
New York, NY 10022
Director, New York City Opera Co.

Silverman, Fred
% Metro-Goldwyn-Mayer Film Co.
10202 W. Washington Blvd.
Culver City, CA 90230
Broadcasting executive

Silvers, Phil
132 Lasky Dr.
Beverly Hills, CA 90212
Actor

Simmons, Jean
% Morgan Maree
6363 Wilshire Blvd.
Los Angeles, CA 90048
Actress

Simmons, Richard
9306 Santa Monica Blvd.
Los Angeles, CA 90067
Fitness guru

Simmons, Ted
Milwaukee Brewers
Milwaukee County Stadium
Milwaukee, WI 53214
Prof. baseball player

Simon, Carly
Arlyne Rothberg Inc.
145 Central Park West
New York, NY 10023
Singer; composer

Simon, John Ivan
New York magazine
755 Second Ave.
New York, NY 10017
Film & drama critic

Simon, Neil
% Eugene O'Neill Theatre
230 W. 49th St.
New York, NY 10019
Playwright

Simon, Paul
% Ian Hoblyn
498 West End Ave.
New York, NY 10024
Musician; composer

Simon & Schuster
1230 Avenue of the Americas
New York, NY 10020
Richard E. Snyder, Chief Operating Officer

Simplicity Pattern Co. Inc.
200 Madison Ave.
New York, NY 10016
Graham Ferguson Lacey, Chairman of Board

Simpson, O. J.
11661 San Vicente Blvd., #600
Brentwood, CA 90049
Former prof. football player; actor

Sims, Buty
Detroit Lions
1200 Featherstone Rd.
Box 4200
Pontiac, MI 48057
Prof. football player

184

Sims, Naomi Ruth
Naomi Sims Collection
48 E. 21st St.
New York, NY 10010
*Wig company executive; former
model*

Sinatra, Frank
8966 Sunset Blvd.
Los Angeles, CA 90069
Singer; actor; entertainer

Singer Co., The
P.O. Box 10151
Stamford, CT 06904
Joseph B. Flavin, Chairman

Singleton, Ken
Baltimore Orioles
Memorial Stadium
Baltimore, MD 21218
Prof. baseball player

Sipe, Brian
Cleveland Browns
Cleveland Stadium
Cleveland, OH 44114
Prof. football player

Sirhan, Sirhan
Soledad State Prison
Soledad, CA 93960
*Convicted assassin of Robert F.
Kennedy*

Skelton, Red
P.O. Box 136
Anza, CA 92306
Comedian

Skinner, Burrhus Frederic
13 Old Dee Rd.
Cambridge, MA 02138
Psychologist; educator

Sklar, Richard
1330 Avenue of the Americas
New York, NY 10019
*Vice president, programming, ABC
Radio, New York*

Skywalker, Luke
Lucasfilm
P.O. Box 8669
Universal City, CA 91608
Jedi Knight

Slade, Bernard Newbound
650 Park Ave.
New York, NY 10021
Playwright

Slesinger, Patricia
415 N. Camden Dr.
Beverly Hills, CA 90210
Author, Goldbook Catalog of
World's Finest Goods

Slick, Grace Wing
44 Montgomery St.
San Francisco, CA 94104
Rock singer, Jefferson Starship

Sloane, Martin
% United Features Syndicate
200 Park Ave.
New York, NY 10017
Expert on coupons

Smith, Alexis
ICM
40 W. 57th St.
New York, NY 10019
Actress

Smith, Beth
150 N. Wacker Dr.
Chicago, IL 60606
Founder, Nanny, Inc.

Smith, Buffalo Bob
3900 N. Ocean Dr.
Lauderdale-by-the-Sea, FL 33308
Former host of Howdy Doody

Smith, Carleton
Two S. First National Plaza, Suite
3000
Chicago, IL 60603
Art authority

Smith, Cecil Howard
Los Angeles Times
Times-Mirror Sq.
Los Angeles, CA 90053
TV critic

Smith, Dick
209 Murray Ave.
Larchmont, NY 10538
*Founded makeup department at
NBC*

185

Smith, Jaclyn
ICM
8899 Beverly Blvd.
Los Angeles, CA 90048
Actress

Smith, Kate
9255 Sunset Blvd., #1115
Los Angeles, CA 90069
Singer

Smith, Liz
New York Daily News
220 E. 42d St.
New York, NY 10017
Entertainment columnist

Smith, Maggie
% Fraser & Dunlop
91 Regent St.
London, W1R 8RU, England
Actress

Smith, Rex
65 W. 55th St., #306
New York, NY 10019
Actor

Smith, Robyn Caroline
% Jockeys' Guild
555 Fifth Ave., #1501
New York, NY 10017
Jockey

Smith, Stanley Roger
888 17th St., NW, #1200
Washington, DC 20006
Prof. tennis player

Smith, Willi Donnell
62 W. 39th St.
New York, NY 10018
Fashion designer

Smith, William French
Department of Justice
Constitution Ave. & 10th St., NW
Washington, DC 20530
*Former attorney General of U.S.,
1981–84*

Smothers, Dick
260 S. Beverly Dr.
Beverly Hills, CA 90212
Actor; singer; comedian

Smothers, Tom
260 S. Beverly Dr.
Beverly Hills, CA 90212
Actor; singer; comedian

Smucker Co., J. M.
Strawberry Ln.
P.O. Box 280
Orrville, OH 44667
*Paul H. Smucker, Chairman of
Board*

Smyth, Reginald
Whitegates
Caledonian Rd.
Hartrepool, Cleveland, England
*Cartoonist—created Andy Capp
character*

Snead, Samuel Jackson
% Uni-Managers International
10880 Wilshire Blvd.
Los Angeles, CA 90024
Prof. golfer

Snider, Edward Malcolm
Philadelphia Flyers
The Spectrum
Pattison Pl.
Philadelphia, PA 19148
Chairman of Board, hockey club

Snodgress, Carrie
9157 Sunset Blvd., #206
Los Angeles, CA 90069
Actress

Snow, Hank
P.O. Box 1084
Nashville, TN 37202
Country music entertainer

Snow, Phoebe
% Columbia Records
51 W. 52d St.
New York, NY 10019
Musician; composer

186

Snyder, Tom
% ABC
Seven Lincoln Sq.
New York, NY 10023
TV journalist

Socialist Labor Party of America
P.O. Box 50218
Palo Alto, CA 94303
Robert Bills, National Secretary

Society of Dirty Old Men
Box 18202
Indianapolis, IN 46218
L. Robert Quarles II, Vice-President

Solar Building Institute
P.O. 5506
Atlanta, GA 30307
Jeffrey Tiller, President

Soldati, Dennis
97-40 62d Dr., #8-E
Rego Park, NY 11374
Juggling expert

Solo, Han
Lucasfilm
P.O. Box 8669
Universal City, CA 91608
Pilot in Star Wars

Solzhenitsyn, Aleksandr
% Harper & Row, Inc.
10 E. 53d St.
New York, NY 10022
Soviet writer

Somers, Suzanne
927 N. La Cienega Blvd.
Los Angeles, CA 90069
Actress

Sommer, Elke
ICM
8899 Beverly Blvd., #402A
Los Angeles, CA 90048
Actress

Sons of the Whiskey Rebellion
2618 Buhl Bldg., #261B
Detroit, MI 48226
John H. Norris, Adjutant

Sony Corporation of America
9 W. 57th St.
New York, NY 10019
Kazuo Iwama, Chairman of Board

Sothern, Ann
132 Lasky Dr.
Beverly Hills, CA 90212
Actress

Soul, David
151 El Camino
Beverly Hills, CA 90212
Actor

Spacek, Sissy
1888 Century Park East, #1400
Los Angeles, CA 90067
Actress

Spanjaard, Barry
26409 Bentgrass Way
Canyon Country, CA 91351
*Only known American-born
survivor of the Nazi death camps*

Spano, Vincent
P.O. Box 674
Old Chelsea Station
New York, NY 10013
Actor

Speakes, Larry M.
The White House Office
1600 Pennsylvania Ave.
& Executive Office Bldg.
Washington, DC 20500
Acting press secretary, 1981–present

Special Olympics
1701 K St., NW, #203
Washington, DC 20006
Eunice Kennedy Shriver, President

Special Recreation, Inc.
362 Koser Ave.
Iowa City, IA 52240
*John. A. Nesbitt, Ed.D.,
President—Equal opportunity for
disabled persons in recreation*

Speck, Richard
Stateville Correctional Center
C01065, S016
P.O. Box 112
Joliet, IL 60434
Mass murderer

Spector, Phil
% Warner-Spector Records
P.O. Box 69529
Los Angeles, CA 90069
Record producer

Spelling, Aaron
10201 W. Pico Blvd.
Los Angeles, CA 90064
Writer; producer

Sperber, Philip
Armour Bldg.
30 Normandy Heights Rd.
Convent Station, NJ 07961
*Chairman of The Negotiating
Group, firm that manages business
negotiation*

Spielberg, Steven
4000 Warner Blvd., Bldg. 102
Burbank, CA 91505
Motion picture director

Spillane, Mickey
% New American Library
1633 Broadway
New York, NY 10019
Author

Spock, Benjamin McLane
P.O. Box N
Rogers, AR 72756
Physician; author; political activist

Springer, John Shipman
667 Madison Ave.
New York, NY 10021
Public relations company executive

Springfield, Rick
7 W. 66th St.
New York, NY 10023
Singer; actor

Springsteen, Bruce
% Premier Talent Agency
3 E. 54th St.
New York, NY 10022
Singer; songwriter; guitarist

Squibb Corp.
40 W. 57th St.
New York, NY 10019
*Richard M. Furlaud, Chairman of
Board*

Stabler, Kenneth Michael
New Orleans Saints
1500 Poydras St.
New Orleans, LA 70112
Prof. football player

Stack, Robert
409 N. Camden Dr., #202
Beverly Hills, CA 90212
Actor

Stahl, Lesley
CBS News
51 W. 52d St.
New York, NY 10019
TV journalist

Stallone, Sylvester
9665 Wilshire Blvd., #200
Beverly Hills, CA 90212
Actor; director

Stamos, John
6430 Sunset Blvd., #1203
Los Angeles, CA 90028
Actor

Standard Oil Co. (AMOCO)
P.O. Box 5910-A
Chicago, IL 60680
*John E. Swearington, Chairman of
Board*

**Standard Oil of California
(Chevron)**
225 Bush St.
San Francisco, CA 94104
G. M. Keller, Chairman of Board

Stander, Lionel
% ABC Entertainment
1330 Avenue of the Americas
New York, NY 10019
Actor

Stanley Tools & Hardware
The Stanley Works
195 Lake St.
New Britain, CT 06052
D. W. Davis, Chairman of Board

Stanwyck, Barbara
% A. Morgan Maree & Assocs.
6363 Wilshire Blvd.
Los Angeles, CA 90048
Actress

Stapleton, Jean
9220 Sunset Blvd., #202
Los Angeles, CA 90069
Actress

Stapleton, Maureen
ICM
40 W. 57th St.
New York, NY 10019
Actress

Stargell, Wilver Dornell
Pittsburgh Pirates
600 Stadium Circle
Pittsburgh, PA 15212
Retired prof. baseball player

Stark, Koo
% Wilbur Stark
3712 Barham Blvd., Suite #230
Los Angeles, CA 90068
*Actress; occasional date of
England's Prince Andrew*

Starr, Ringo
Bruce Grakal
1427 Seventh St.
Santa Monica, CA 90401
*Musician; actor; former member of
the Beatles*

Staub, Rusty
New York Mets
William A. Shea Stadium
Roosevelt Ave. & 126th St.
Flushing, NY 11368
Prof. baseball player

Staubach, Roger Thomas
6116 N. Central Expwy.
Dallas, TX 75206
*Former football player; real-estate
executive*

Steib, Dave
Toronto Blue Jays
Box 7777
Adelaide St. P.O.
Toronto, ON M5C 2K7
Canada
Prof. baseball player

Steiger, Janet D.
Postal Rate Commission
2000 L Street, NW
Washington, DC 20268
Chairperson

Steiger, Rod
1888 Century Park East, #1400
Los Angeles, CA 90067
Actor

Steinberg, David
151 El Camino
Beverly Hills, CA 90212
Comedian; author; actor

Steinbrenner, George Michael, III
512 Florida Ave.
Tampa, FL 33601
*Principal owner, New York
Yankees; shipbuilding executive*

Steinem, Gloria
% Ms. magazine
370 Lexington Ave.
New York, NY 10017
Feminist writer

Stennis, John
Senate Office Bldg.
Washington, DC 20510
*U.S. Senator (D), Mississippi,
1947–present*

Steorts, Nancy H.
Consumer Product Safety
Commission
1111 18th St., NW
Washington, DC 20207
Chairperson

Stephenson, Jan
PGA
100 Avenue of Champions
Palm Beach Gardens, FL 33410
Prof. golfer

Sterling, Chandler Winfield
830 Forest Ct.
Oconomowoc, WI 53066
Bishop

Stern, Isaac
ICM
40 W. 57th St.
New York, NY 10019
Violinist

Stern, Leonard Norman
700 S. Fourth St.
Harrison, NJ 07029
*President, Hartz Mountain
Industries*

Stevens, Andrew
10100 Santa Monica Blvd., #224
Los Angeles, CA 90067
Actor; producer

Stevens, Cat
BKM Inc.
9076 St. Ives Dr.
Los Angeles, CA 90069
Singer; musician; composer

Stevens, Connie
151 El Camino
Beverly Hills, CA 90212
Actress

Stevens, John Paul
U.S. Supreme Court
Washington, DC 20543
Supreme Court Justice, 1975–present

Stewart, Al
3300 Warner Blvd.
Burbank, CA 91505
Musician

Stewart, James
P.O. Box 90
Beverly Hills, CA 90213
Actor

Stewart, Linda
1523A N. La Brea Ave., #117
Hollywood, CA 90028
Expert on Star Wars, The Empire
Strikes Back, Return of the Jedi

Stewart, Rod
151 El Camino
Beverly Hills, CA 90212
Singer

Stigwood, Robert
Robert Stigwood Organization
1775 Broadway
New York, NY 10019
Entertainment company executive

Stiller, Jerry
Janice Morgan Communications
250 W. 57th St.
New York, NY 10019
Comedian

Stockman, David A.
Office of Management & Budget
Executive Office Bldg.
Washington, DC 20503
Director, 1981–present

Stockton, David Knapp
Keystone Ranch Golf Club
Box 38
Keystone, CO 80435
Prof. golfer

Stockton, Dick
300 E. 56th St.
New York, NY 10022
CBS sports broadcaster

Stone, Irving
% Doubleday & Co.
245 Park Ave.
New York, NY 10017
Author

Stoppard, Tom
% Kenneth Ewing Fraser & Dunlop
Ltd.
91 Regent St.
London, WC1 4AE, England
Playwright

Storm, Gale
9056 Santa Monica Blvd., #203
Los Angeles, CA 90069
Actress

Storm, Michael
65 W. 66th St.
New York, NY 10023
Actor

Stouffer Corp.
29800 Bainbridge Rd.
Solon, OH 44139
*D. E. Guerrant, Chairman of Board
& President*

Strasberg, Susan
% Arco Embassy Pictures
6601 Romaine St.
Los Angeles, CA 90038
Actress

Strasser, Robin
65 W. 66th St.
New York, NY 10023
Actress

Strauss, Jack
% Henri Bollinger
9200 Sunset Blvd., #601
Los Angeles, CA 90069
World champion poker player

Strauss, Peter
132 S. Rodeo Dr.
Beverly Hills, CA 90212
Actor

Streep, Meryl
ICM
40 W. 57th St.
New York, NY 10019
Actress

Streisand, Barbra
9255 Sunset Blvd., #318
Los Angeles, CA 90069
Actress; singer

Strock, Don
Miami Dolphins
3550 Biscayne Blvd.
Miami, FL 33137
Prof. football player

Stroh Brewery Co.
One Stroh Dr.
Detroit, MI 48226
Peter Stroh, Chairman of Board

Struthers, Sally Anne
% Segal-Goldman
9348 Santa Monica Blvd.
Beverly Hills, CA 90210
Actress

Stublen, Kenny
New Orleans Saints
1500 Poydras St.
New Orleans, LA 70112
Prof. football player

Studds, Gerry E.
1511 Longworth House Office
Building
Washington, DC 20515
*U.S. Congressman (D),
Massachusetts, 1973–present who
was reprimanded for having sexual
relations with a congressional page*

Styne, Jule
237 W. 51st St.
New York, NY 10019
Composer; producer

Subaru of America, Inc.
7040 Central Hwy.
Pennsauken, NJ 08109
*Sherman E. Rose, Chairman of
Board*

Sullivan, Susan
3970 Overland Ave.
Culver City, CA 90230
Actress

Sullivan, William Hallisey, Jr.
New England Patriots
Schaefer Stadium
Foxboro, MA 02035
Owner & president of football club

Summer, Anita
619 Oakwood Ct.
Westbury, NY 11590
Syndicated entertainment columnist

Summer, Donna
% Munao Management
1224 N. Vine St.
Los Angeles, CA 90038
Singer; actress; songwriter

191

Sunde, Rob
WCBS Radio
51 W. 52d St.
New York, NY 10019
Expert on oenology (study &
appreciation of wine)

Susskind, David Howard
Susskind Co.
1350 Avenue of the Americas
New York, NY 10019
Television, movie & theater
producer

Sutherland, Donald
McNicol Pictures
760 N. La Cienega Blvd., #300
Los Angeles, CA 90069
Actor

Sutter, Bruce
St. Louis Cardinals
Busch Memorial Stadium
250 Stadium Plaza
St. Louis, MO 63102
Prof. baseball player

Sutton, Don
Milwaukee Brewers
Milwaukee County Stadium
Milwaukee, WI 53214
Prof. baseball player

Suzy
% Milton Fenster Assocs.
540 Madison Ave.
New York, NY 10022
Society columnist

Swados, Elizabeth
Public Theater
425 Lafayette St.
New York, NY 10003
Writer; composer; director

Swit, Loretta
9145 Sunset Blvd., 2d Fl.
Los Angeles, CA 90069
Actress

T

T, Mr.
3000 W. Alameda Ave.
Burbank, CA 91523
Actor

Taco Bell
17381 Red Hill Ave.
Irvine, CA 92714
Charles L. Boppell, President

Talese, Gay
109 E. 61st St.
New York, NY 10021
Writer

Talking Heads
Gary Kurfist
1775 Broadway
New York, NY 10019
Rock group

Tampax, Inc.
5 Dakota Dr.
Lake Success, NY 11042
E. Russell Sprague, Chairman of Board

Tandy, Jessica
63-23 Carlton St.
Rego Park, NY 11374
Actress

Tarkenton, Francis Asbury
Tarkenton & Assocs.
3340 Peachtree Rd., NE
Atlanta, GA 30326
Former prof. football player; sports commentator

Tastykake, Inc.
2801 W. Hunting Park Ave.
Philadelphia, PA 19129
Phillip J. Baur, Jr., Chief Operating Officer

Tattoo Club of America
36 Mill Hill Rd.
Woodstock, NY 12498
Spider Webb, President

Tayback, Vic
7800 Beverly Blvd.
Los Angeles, CA 90036
Actor

Taylor, Elizabeth
9255 W. Sunset Blvd., #505
Los Angeles, CA 90069
Actress

Taylor, James Vernon
% Peter Asher Management
644 N. Doheny Dr.
Los Angeles, CA 90069
Musician

193

Taylor, Lawrence
New York Giants
Giants Stadium
East Rutherford, NJ 07073
Prof. football player

Taylor, Marvin
20811 Briarwood
Sonora, CA 95370
Runs museum devoted to UFOs

Taylor, Paul
% Yesselman
550 Broadway
New York, NY 10012
Choreographer

Technicolor, Inc.
2049 Century Park, #2400
Los Angeles, CA 90067
*Morton Kamerman, Chairman of
Board*

Telephone Companies

**American Telephone & Telegraph
Co. (AT&T)**
195 Broadway
New York, NY 10007
Charles L. Brown, Chairman

Bell Telephone Co. of Nevada
645 E. Plumb Ln.
Reno, NV 89505
Donald E. Guinn, President

**Chesapeake & Potomac Telephone
Co., The**
2055 L St., NW
Washington, DC 20036
Samuel E. Bonsack, President

Illinois Bell Telephone Co.
225 W. Randolph St.
Chicago, IL 60606
William L. Weiss, President

Indiana Bell Telephone Co., Inc.
2040 N. Meridian St.
Indianapolis, IN 46204
Philip A. Campbell, President

Michigan Bell Telephone Co.
444 Michigan Ave.
Detroit, MI 48226
David K. Easlick, President

**Mountain States Telephone &
Telegraph Co., The**
931 14th St.
Denver, CO 80202
Robert K. Timothy, President

**New England Telephone &
Telegraph Co.**
185 Franklin St.
Boston, MA 02107
William C. Mercer, President

New Jersey Bell Telephone Co.
540 Broad St.
Newark, NJ 07101
Rocco J. Marano, President

New York Telephone Co.
1095 Avenue of the Americas
New York, NY 10036
Delbert C. Staley, President

Northwestern Bell Telephone Co.
1314 Douglas on-the-Mall
Omaha, NE 68102
Jack A. MacAllister, President

Ohio Bell Telephone Co., The
100 Erieview Plaza
Cleveland, OH 44114
William E. MacDonald, President

**Pacific Northwest Bell Telephone
Co.**
1600 Bell Plaza
Seattle, WA 98191
Andrew V. Smith, President

**Pacific Telephone & Telegraph Co.,
The**
140 New Montgomery St.
San Francisco, CA 94105
Donald E. Guinn, President

South Central Bell Telephone Co.
P.O. Box 771, Headquarters Bldg.
Birmingham, AL 35201
Wallace R. Bunn, President

**Southern Bell Telephone &
Telegraph Co.**
Southern Bell Center
675 W. Peachtree St., NE
Atlanta, GA 30301
John L. Clendenin, President

Southwestern Bell Telephone Co.
1010 Pine St.
St. Louis, MO 63101
Zane E. Barnes, President

Templeton, Gary
San Diego Padres
P.O. Box 2000
San Diego, CA 92120
Prof. baseball player

Temptations
Star Direction
605 N. Oakhurst Dr.
Beverly Hills, CA 90210
Singing group

Tennant, Veronica
National Ballet of Canada
157 King Street East
Toronto, ON M5C 1G9
Canada
Ballerina

Teresa, Mother
Mission of Charity
Calcutta, India
Missionary, Nobel Prize winner

Terkel, Studs Louis
500 N. Michigan Ave.
Chicago, IL 60611
Interviewer; author

Terrail, Patrick
8368 Melrose Ave.
Los Angeles, CA 90069
Restaurateur, owner of Ma Maison

Tesich, Steve
ICM
40 W. 57th St.
New York, NY 10019
Author

Texaco Inc.
2000 Westchester Ave.
White Plains, NY 10650
*John K. McKinley, Chairman of
Board*

Tharp, Twyla
% Twyla Tharp Dance Foundation
38 Walker St.
New York, NY 10013
Dancer; choreographer

Thatcher, Margaret
Office of the Prime Minister
London, England
*Prime Minister, England—since
1979*

Theismann, Joe
Washington Redskins
P.O. Box 17247
Dulles International Airport
Washington, DC 20041
Prof. football player

Theus, Reggie
Chicago Bulls
333 N. Michigan Ave.
Chicago, IL 60601
Prof. basketball player

Thomas, B. J.
% Ram International
P.O. Box 76436
Atlanta, GA 30328
Singer

Thomas, Danny
1801 Avenue of the Stars
Los Angeles, CA 90067
Entertainer; TV producer

Thomas, Gorman
Cleveland Indians
Cleveland Stadium
Cleveland, OH 44114
Prof. baseball player

Thomas, Isaiah
Detroit Pistons
Pontiac Silverdome
1200 Featherstone
Pontiac, MI 48057
Prof. basketball player

Thomas, Marlo
P.O. Box 663
Beverly Hills, CA 90213
Actress; feminist

Thomas, Richard
9000 Sunset Blvd., #315
Los Angeles, CA 90069
Actor

Thomas, Walter
31 Warren St.
New York, NY 10007
Author, The Nuclear War Fun
Book

Thomlinson, Ralph
Department of Sociology
California State University
Los Angeles, CA 90032
Demographer; educator

Thom McAn Shoe Co.
67 Millbrook St.
Worcester, MA 01606
J. Richard Nedder, President

Thompson, Bradbury
Jones Park
Riverside, CT 06878
*Designer—designed 45 U.S postage
stamps*

Thompson, David O'Neal
1630 Wetton St., #225
Denver, CO 80202
*Prof. basketball player, Denver
Nuggets*

Thompson, James R.
State Capitol
Springfield, IL 62706
*Governor of Illinois (R),
1977–present*

Thompson, Jason
Pittsburgh Pirates
600 Stadium Circle
Pittsburgh, PA 15212
Prof. baseball player

Thompson, Michael
Portland Trail Blazers
Lloyd Building
700 Multnomah St. N.E.
Portland, OR 97232
Prof. basketball player

Thompson, Sada Carolyn
9220 Sunset Blvd., #202
Los Angeles, CA 90069
Actress

Thornburgh, Richard L.
State Capitol
Harrisburg, PA 17101
*Governor of Pennsylvania (R),
1979–present*

Thornton, Andie
Cleveland Indians
Cleveland Stadium
Cleveland, OH 44114
Prof. baseball player

3M Company
3M Center
St. Paul, MN 55144
Lewis W. Lehr, Chairman of Board

Thurmond, Strom
Senate Office Bldg.
Washington, DC 20510
*U.S. Senator (R), South Carolina,
1955–present*

Tiegs, Cheryl
Nina Blanchard
1717 N. Highland Ave., #901
Los Angeles, CA 90028
Model; spokeswoman

Tierney, Gene
9644 Heather Rd.
Beverly Hills, CA 90210
Actress

Tillis, Mel
% Sawgrass Music Publishers
1722 West End Ave.
Nashville, TN 37203
Musician; songwriter

Time, Inc.
1270 Avenue of the Americas
New York, NY 10020
Ralph Davidson, Chairman of Board

Time magazine
1271 Avenue of the Americas
New York, NY 10020
Henry Anatole Grunwald, Editor in Chief

Timex Corp.
1579 Straits Turnpike
Middlebury, CT 06762
Fred Olsen, Chairman of Board

Tinker, Grant
3000 W. Alameda Ave.
Burbank, CA 91523
Chairman of Board, Chief Executive Officer, NBC

Tippers International
P.O. Box 2351
Oshkosh, WI 54903
John E. Schein, President

Toby, Jackson
Department of Sociology
Murray Hall
Rutgers University
New Brunswick, NJ 08903
Educator; sociologist

Todd, Kenneth
Department of Veterinary Medicine
University of Illinois
1101 W. Peabody
Urbana, IL 61801
Parasitologist

Todd, Richard
New York Jets
598 Madison Ave.
New York, NY 10022
Prof. football player

Tombaugh, Clyde W.
P.O. Box 306
Mesilla Park, NM 88047
Discovered Pluto in 1930

Tomlin, Lily
P.O. Box 27700
Los Angeles, CA 90027
Comedienne; actress

Tonka Toy Corp.
4144 Shoreline Blvd.
Spring Park, MN 55384
Stephen C. Shank, President

Tony the Tiger
Kellogg Co.
235 Porter
Battle Creek, MI 49016
Spokesman for Sugar Frosted Flakes

Tootsie Roll Industries
7401 S. Cicero Ave.
Chicago, IL 60629
Melvin J. Gordon, Chairman of Board

Torme, Melvin Howard
3518 W. Cahuenga Blvd., #206
Los Angeles, CA 90068
Singer

Torn, Rip
9200 Sunset Blvd., #1210
Los Angeles, CA 90069
Actor; director

Torre, Joseph Paul
Atlanta Braves
P.O. Box 4064
Atlanta, GA 30302
Prof. baseball manager

Torrey, William Arthur
New York Islanders
Nassau Coliseum
Uniondale, NY 11553
President & general manager

Toto
CBS Records
51 W. 52d St.
New York, NY 10019
Rock group

Tough Love
Community Service Foundation
P.O. Box 70
Sellersville, PA 18960
Phyllis & David York,
Administrators—organization that
promotes firm but loving treatment
of problem kids

Tower, John G.
Senate Office Bldg.
Washington, DC 20510
Former U.S. Senator (R), Texas

Townsend, Peter
% Premier Talent
3 E. 54th St.
New York, NY 10022
Musician; composer; singer

Trans World Airlines
605 Third Ave.
New York, NY 10016
C. E. Meyer, Jr., President

Travanti, Daniel J.
9220 Sunset Blvd., #202
Los Angeles, CA 90069
Actor

Travis, Merle Robert
38 E. Music Circle, #300
Nashville, TN 37203
Country music singer; songwriter

Travolta, John
1888 Century Park East, #1400
Los Angeles, CA 90067
Actor

Trevino, Lee Buck
8515 Greenville Ave., Suite S-207
Dallas, TX 75243
Prof. golfer

Triangle Laundry
805 N. 45th St.
Omaha, NE 68132
Singles laundry

Trigere, Pauline
550 Seventh Ave.
New York, NY 10018
Dress designer

Trimble, Bjo
Megamart
P.O. Box 1248
Inglewood, CA 90308
Star Trek expert

Tripucka, Kelly
Detroit Pistons
Pontiac Silverdome
1200 Featherstone
Pontiac, MI 48057
Prof. basketball player

Trottier, Bryan John
% International Sports
Management
488 Madison Ave.
New York, NY 10022
*Prof. hockey player, New York
Islanders*

Trudeau, Garry B.
% Universal Press Syndicate
4400 Johnson Dr.
Fairway, KS 66205
Cartoonist, created Doonesbury

Trudeau, Pierre
Office of the Prime Minister
Ottawa, Canada
*Prime Minister, Canada, 1968–1979,
1980–present*

Truffaut, François
5 Rue Robert-Estienne
75008 Paris, France
Film director

Trumbull, Douglas
% Entertainment Effects Group
13335 Maxella Ave.
Venice, CA 90291
*Creator of special effects; film
director*

T.S.H.I.R.T.S
1716 Main St., #300
Venice, CA 90291
*John Munro-Hall, President—The
Society Handling the Interchange of
Remarkable T-Shirts*

Tucker, Tanya
MCA
70 Universal City Plaza
Universal City, CA 91510
Singer

Tune, Tommy
Marvin Shulman Inc.
890 Broadway
New York, NY 10003
Musical theater director; performer; choreographer

Turner, Ike
% Bolic Sound Recording Studio
1310 N. La Brea Ave.
Inglewood, CA 90302
Musician

Turner, Janine
967 N. La Cienega Blvd.
Los Angeles, CA 90069
Actress

Turner, Kathleen
222 N. Canon Dr., #204
Beverly Hills, CA 90210
Actress

Turner, Lana
P.O. Box 69187
Los Angeles, CA 90069
Actress

Turner, Robert Edwin (Ted)
1050 Techwood Dr.
Atlanta, GA 30318
Broadcasting executive; sports executive

Turner, Tina
151 El Camino
Beverly Hills, CA 90212
Singer

Turrentine, Stanley William
% Associated Booking Corp.
1955 Broadway
New York, NY 10023
Musician

Tuttle, Lyle
30 Seventh St.
San Francisco, CA 94103
Tattoo artist to stars

T.V. Guide
100 Matsonford Rd.
Radnor, PA 19087
R. C. Smith, Editor

Twentieth Century-Fox Film Corp.
10201 W. Pico Blvd.
Los Angeles, CA 90064
Alan J. Hirschfield, Chairman of Board

Twitty, Conway
P.O. Box 23470
Nashville, TN 37202
Country & western entertainer

Tyson, Cicely
1888 Century Park East, #622
Los Angeles, CA 90067
Actress

U

Ubell, Earl
CBS News
524 W. 57th St.
New York, NY 10019
TV science editor

Udall, Morris K.
House Office Bldg.
Washington, DC 20515
U.S. Congressman (D), Arizona,
1961–present

Uggams, Leslie
ICM
8899 Beverly Blvd.
Los Angeles, CA 90048
Entertainer

Ulene, Arthur Lawrence
2401 W. Olive St.
Burbank, CA 91506
Physician, specializing gynecology

Ullmann, Liv
% Robert Lantz
114 E. 55th St.
New York, NY 10022
Actress

Uncle Ben's, Inc.
13000 Westheimer
Houston, TX 77077
T. G. Armstrong, President

Unger, Garry Douglas
Calgary Flames
P.O. Box 1540
Station M
Calgary, AB T2P 3B9
Canada
Prof. hockey player

Union Carbide Corp.
Old Ridgebury Rd.
Danbury, CT 06817
Warren M. Anderson, Chairman

Uniroyal Tire Co.
World Headquarters
Middlebury, CT 06749
Sheldon R. Salzman, President

Unitas, John Constantine
6354 York Rd.
Baltimore, MD 21212
Former prof. football player

United Airlines, Inc.
P.O. Box 66100
Chicago, IL 60666
Richard J. Ferris, Chairman

United Artists Communications
172 Golden Gate Ave.
San Francisco, CA 94102
Marshall Naify, Chairman of Board

United Auto Workers
8000 E. Jefferson Ave.
Detroit, MI 48214
Odessa Komer, Director

United Cerebral Palsy
66 E. 34th St.
New York, NY 10016
Earl H. Cunerd, Executive Director

**United Parcel Service of America
Inc.**
Greenwich Office Park 5
Greenwich, CT 06830
*George C. Lamb, Chairman of
Board*

United States Olympic Committee
1750 E. Boulder St.
Colorado Springs, CO 80909
F. Don Miller, Executive Director

Unser, Al
7625 W. Central Ave.
Albuquerque, NM 87105
Prof. auto racer

Unser, Bobby
7700 W. Central Ave.
Albuquerque, NM 87105
Prof. race car driver

Upchurch, Rick
Denver Broncos
5700 Logan St.
Denver, CO 80216
Prof. football player

Updike, John Hoyer
Georgetown, MA 01833
Writer

Upjohn Co.
7000 Portage Rd.
Kalamazoo, MI 49001
Dr. W. N. Hubbard, Jr., President

Urich, Robert
409 N. Camden Dr., #202
Beverly Hills, CA 90210
Actor

Uris, Leon
% Doubleday & Co.
245 Park Ave.
New York, NY
Author

Ustinov, Peter Alexander
197/149 Wardone St.
London, W1, England
Actor; producer

Utility Commissions

Alabama Public Service Commission
State Office Bldg.
Montgomery, AL 36130
Bill Joe Camp, President

Alaska Public Utilities Commission
Department of Commerce &
Economic Development
338 Denali St.
Anchorage, AK 99501
Carolyn S. Guess, Commissioner

**Arizona Division of Utilities
Corporation Commission**
1210 W. Washington St.
Phoenix, AZ 85007
Neill T. Dimmick, Director

**Arkansas Public Service
Commission**
Department of Commerce
400 Union Station
Little Rock, AR 72201
Nathan M. Norton, Jr., Chairman

California Public Utilities Comm.
350 McAllister St.
San Francisco, CA 94102
John E. Bryson, President

**Colorado Public Utilities
Commission**
Department of Regulatory Agencies
State Services Bldg., 5th Fl.
Denver, CO 80203
Harry Galligan, Chairman

201

Connecticut Public Utilities Control Authority
Department of Public Utility Control
165 Capitol Ave., Rm. 573
Hartford, CT 06115
Thomas H. Fitzpatrick, Chairman

Delaware Public Utilities Control
Department of Administrative Service
1560 S. Du Pont Hwy.
Dover, DE 19901
Robert J. Kennedy, Director

District of Columbia Public Service Commission
Room 204
Cafritz Building
1625 I St., NW
Washington, DC 20006
William Stratton, President

Florida Public Service Commission
101 E. Gaines St.
Tallahassee, FL 32301
David L. Swafford, Executive Director

Georgia Public Service Commission
244 Washington St., Rm. 162
Atlanta, GA 30334
Ford B. Spinks, Chairman

Guam Public Utilities Commission
173 W. Aspinall Ave.
Agana, Guam 96910
Galo E. Camacho, Chairman

Hawaii Public Utilities Commission
Department of Budget & Finance
1164 Bishop St., #911
Honolulu, HI 96813
Albert Q. Y. Tom, Chairman

Idaho Public Utilities Commission
472 W. Washington St.
Boise, ID 83720
Conley Ward, Chairman

Illinois Commerce Commission
527 E. Capitol
Springfield, IL 62701
Michael V. Hasten, Chairman

Indiana Public Service Commission
State Office Bldg., Rm. 901
Indianapolis, IN 46204
Larry Wallace, Chairman

Iowa Commerce Commission
Lucas Bldg.
Des Moines, IA 50319
Andrew Varley, Chairman

Kansas Corporation Commission
State Office Bldg.
Topeka, KS 66612
Richard C. Loux, Chairman

Kentucky Public Service Commission
730 Schenkel Ln.
P.O. Box 615
Frankfort, KY 40061
Marlin Volz, Chairman

Louisiana Public Service Commission
1630 One American Pl.
Baton Rouge, LA 70825
Ed Kennon, Chairman

Maine Public Utilities Commission
State House, Station #18
Augusta, ME 04333
Ralph Gelder, Chairman

Maryland Utility Consumer Advisory Board
Public Service Commission
American Bldg.
231 E. Baltimore St.
Baltimore, MD 21202
Thomas J. Hatem, Chairman

Massachusetts Department of Public Utilities
Executive Office of Consumer Affairs
100 Cambridge St.
Boston, MA 02202
Doris Pote, Chairperson

Michigan Public Service Commission
Department of Commerce
6545 Mercantile Way
Lansing, MI 48909
Daniel J. Demlow, Chairman

Minnesota Public Service Commission
Department of Public Service
160 E. Kellogg Blvd.
St. Paul, MN 55101
Randall Young, Executive Secretary

Mississippi Public Service Commission
1900 Sillirs Bldg.
Jackson, MS 39201
E. W. Robinson, Executive Secretary

Missouri Public Service Commission
Jefferson Bldg.
P.O. Box 360
Jefferson City, MO 65102
Charles J. Fraas, Jr., Chairman

Montana Public Service Commission
1227 11th Ave.
Helena, MT 59620
Gordon Bollinger, Chairman

Nebraska Public Service Commission
301 Centennial Mall South
Lincoln, NE 68509
Terrence L. Kubicek, Executive Secretary

Nevada Public Service Commission
505 E. King St., #304
Carson City, NV 89710
Roger C. Bos, Chairman

New Hampshire Public Utilities Commission
Eight Old Suncook St.
Concord, NH 03301
Michael Love, Chairman

New Jersey Board of Public Utilities
101 Commerce St.
Newark, NJ 07102
George H. Barbour, President

New Mexico Public Service Commission
Bataan Memorial Bldg.
Santa Fe, NM 87503
Richard P. Montoya, Chairman

New York Public Service Commission
Empire State Plaza
Agency Bldg. 3
Albany, NY 12223
Paul L. Gioia, Chairman

North Carolina Utilities Commission
Department of Commerce
430 N. Salisbury St.
Raleigh, NC 27611
Robert Koger, Chairman

North Dakota Public Service Commission
State Capitol, 12th Fl.
Bismark, ND 58505
Richard Elkin, President

North Mariana Islands Public Works
Saipan, CM 96950
Pedro Sasamoto, Director

Ohio Public Utilities Commission
375 S. High St.
Columbus, OH 43215
William S. Newcomb, Jr., Chairman

Oklahoma Corporation Commission
Jim Thorpe Bldg.
Oklahoma City, OK 73105
Hamp Baker, Chairman

Oregon Public Utility Commission
Labor & Industries Bldg.
Salem, OR 97310
John Lobdell, Commissioner

Pennsylvania Public Utilities Commission
North Office Bldg., #104
Harrisburg, PA 17120
Susan M. Shanaman, Chairperson

Puerto Rico Public Service Commission
P.O. Box S-952
Old San Juan, PR 00902
Luis Berrios Amadeo, President

203

Rhode Island Public Utility
Commission
Department of Business Regulation
100 Orange St.
Providence, RI 02903
Edward F. Burke, Chairman

South Carolina Public Service
Commission
111 Doctor Circle
Columbia, SC 29203
Rudolph Mitchell, Chairman

South Dakota Public Utilities
Commission
Department of Commerce
Capitol Bldg., 1st Fl.
Pierre, SD 57501
*Patricia de Hueck, Executive
Secretary*

Tennessee Public Service
Commission
Cordell Hull Bldg., RM C1-100
Nashville, TN 37219
Frank Cochran, Chairman

Texas Public Utilities Commission
7800 Shoal Creek Blvd.
Austin, TX 78757
John E. Cunningham, Director

Utah Public Service Commission
Department of Business Regulation
330 E. Fourth South
Salt Lake City, UT 84111
Milly O. Bernard, Chairman

Vermont Public Service Board
State Office Bldg.
Montpelier, VT 05602
Louise McCarren, Chairperson

Virginia State Corporation
Commission
Jefferson Bldg.
Richmond, VA 23219
*Thomas P. Harwood, Jr.,
Commissioner*

Virgin Islands Department of Public
Works
P.O. Box H
Christiansted
St. Croix, VI 00820
Arnold Golden, Commissioner

Washington Utilities &
Transportation Commission
Highways-Licenses Bldg.
Olympia, WA 98504
Robert W. Bratton, Chairman

West Virginia Public Service
Commission
State Capitol, Rm. E 228
Charleston, WV 25305
E. Dandridge McDonald, Chairman

Wisconsin Public Service
Commission
468 Hill Farms State Office Bldg.
Madison, WI 53702
Stanley York, Chairman

Wyoming Public Service
Commission
Capitol Hill Bldg.
Cheyenne, WY 82001
John R. Smythe, Commissioner

V

Vaccaro, Brenda
ICM
8899 Beverly Blvd.
Los Angeles, CA 90048
Actress

Vachon, Rogatien Rosaire
Boston Bruins
150 Causeway
Boston, MA 02114
Prof. hockey player

Valavanis, William
412 Pinnacle Rd.
Rochester, NY 14623
Bonsai expert

Valenti, Jack Joseph
1600 I St., NW
Washington, DC 20006
Director, American Film Institute;
President, Motion Picture
Association

Valenzuela, Fernando
Los Angeles Dodgers
Dodger Stadium
1000 Elysian Park Ave.
Los Angeles, CA 90012
Prof. baseball pitcher

Valium Anonymous
Box 404
Altoona, IA 50009
Leland F. Ahern, President

Vallee, Rudy
Meikejohn Assocs.
9250 Wilshire Blvd.
Beverly Hills, CA 90212
Singer

Valli, Frankie
Private Stock Records
40 W. 57th St.
New York, NY 10023
Singer

Vampire Research Center
P.O. Box 252
Elmhurst, NY 11373
Stephen Kaplan, Founder &
Director

Van Ark, Joan
3970 Overland Ave.
Culver City, CA 90230
Actress

Van Buren, Abigail
132 Lasky Dr.
Beverly Hills, CA 90212
Columnist; writer

Vanderbilt, Gloria Morgan
% Murjani USA
498 Seventh Ave.
New York, NY 10018
Artist; actress; fashion designer

Van Devere, Trish
222 N. Canon Dr.
Beverly Hills, CA 90210
Actress

Vandeweghe, Kiki
9665 Wilshire Blvd., #200
Beverly Hills, CA 90212
Denver Nuggets basketball star; financial wizard

Van Gilder, Jack
1925 Walnut, SW
Seattle, WA 98116
Kit building & flying expert

Van Halen
P.O. Box 2128
North Hollywood, CA 91602
Rock group

Van Patten, Dick Vincent
NEW Co.
151 N. San Vicente Blvd.
Beverly Hills, CA 90211
Actor

Van Pelt, Brad
New York Giants
Giants Stadium
East Rutherford, NJ 07073
Prof. football player

Vaughan, Sarah Lois
9200 Sunset Blvd., #823
Los Angeles, CA 90069
Singer

Vaughn, Robert (Francis)
ICM
8899 Beverly Blvd.
Los Angeles, CA 90048
Actor

Velasquez, Jorge Luis, Jr.
P.O. Box 90
Jamaica, NY 11417
Jockey

Verber, Richard William
724 W. Cornelia
Chicago, IL 60657
Chess master

Vereen, Ben
151 El Camino
Beverly Hills, CA 90212
Actor; singer

Vicks Health Care Division
Ten Westport Rd.
Wilton, CT 06897
H. Smith Richardson, Jr., Chairman of Board

Victims for Victims
1800 S. Robertson
Bldg. 6, Suite 400
Los Angeles, CA 90035
Theresa Saldana, President & Founder

Vidal, Gore
Random House
201 E. 50th St.
New York, NY 10022
Writer

Vidor, King Wallis
Willow Creek Ranch
Rte. 1
Paso Robles, CA 93446
Motion picture director & producer

Vigoda, Abe
132 Lasky Dr.
Beverly Hills, CA 90212
Actor

Viljoen, Marais
Office of the President
Cape Town, South Africa
President, South Africa—since 1979

Villapiano, Philip James (Phil)
Buffalo Bills
1 Bills Dr.
Orchard Park, NY 14127
Prof. football player

206

Villechaize, Herve
P.O. Box 1305
Burbank, CA 91507
Actor

Villella, Edward Joseph
% Prodigal Productions Inc.
129 W. 69th St.
New York, NY 10023
Ballet dancer; choreographer

Vincent, Allen
National Socialist White Workers
Party
P.O. Box 1981
San Francisco, CA 94101
Commander, Nazi party

Vincent, Jan-Michael
ICM
8899 Beverly Blvd.
Los Angeles, CA 90048
Actor

Vinton, Bobby (Stanley Robert)
P.O. Box 49690
Los Angeles, CA 90049
Entertainer

Vogue magazine
350 Madison Ave.
New York, NY 10017
Lorraine Davis, Managing Editor

Voight, Jon
8642 Melrose Ave.
Los Angeles, CA 90069
Actor

Volcker, Paul A.
Federal Reserve System
20th St. & Constitution Ave., NW
Washington, DC 20551
Chairman

Volkswagen of America
27621 Parkview Blvd.
Warren, MI 48092
James W. McLernon, President

Volvo North America Corp.
Rockleigh Industrial Park
Rockleigh, NJ 07647
Pehr Gyllenhannar, Chairman

Von Furstenberg, Diane Simone Michelle
530 Seventh Ave.
New York, NY 10018
Fashion designer

Von Rase, Donald
4229 Beverly Rd.
Madison, WI 53711
Agent for the common person

Von Sydow, Max Carl Adolf
9169 Sunset Blvd.
Los Angeles, CA 90069
Actor

Vorhauer, Bruce W., Ph.D.
% Debra Gayor
149 Fifth Ave.
New York, NY 10010
Inventor of new contraceptive sponge

Vreeland, Diana
New York Metropolitan Museum of
Art
Fifth Ave. & 82d St.
New York, NY 10028
Design consultant

Vuitton, Henry-Louis
78 Bis-Avenue Marceau
7500 Paris, France
Designer

W

Wagner, Doris
8917 Aden Rd.
Harvard, IL 60033
Foster mother of 978 children

Wagner, Lindsay
9255 Sunset Blvd., #411
Los Angeles, CA 90069
Actress

Wagner, Richard
Cincinnati Reds
100 Riverfront Stadium
Cincinnati, OH 45202
Baseball executive

Wagner, Robert
151 El Camino
Beverly Hills, CA 90212
Actor

Wakeman, Rick
Beldock Levine & Hoffman
565 Fifth Ave.
New York, NY 10017
Rock musician

Walken, Christopher
853 Seventh Ave., #9A
New York, NY 10019
Actor

Walker, Charles D.
P.O. Box 516
St. Louis, MO 63166
*America's first private citizen in
space*

Walker, Nancy
9200 W. Sunset Blvd., #1009
Los Angeles, CA 90069
Actress

Walking Association
4113 Lee Hwy.
Arlington, VA 22207
*Robert B. Sleight, Executive
Director—people with interest in
walking*

Wallace, George Corley
P.O. Box 17222
Montgomery, AL 36104
*Governor of Alabama (D),
1963–1967, 1971–1979,
1983–present*

Wallach, Eli
90 Riverside Dr.
New York, NY 10024
Actor

208

Wall Street Journal, The
Dow Jones and Co. Inc.
22 Cortlandt St.
New York, NY 10007
Warren H. Philips, Chairman &
Chief Executive Officer

Walston, Ray
9000 Sunset Blvd., #315
Los Angeles, CA 90069
Actor

Walt Disney Productions
500 S. Buena Vista St.
Burbank, CA 91521
E. Cardon Walker, Chairman

Walter, Jessica
222 N. Canon Dr., #200
Beverly Hills, CA 90210
Actress

Walters, Barbara
ABC News
1330 Avenue of the Americas
New York, NY 10019
TV journalist

Walters, Harry N.
Veterans Administration
Vermont Ave. & H St.
Washington, DC 20420
Administrator of veterans' affairs

Walther, Roger
The Hot Line
207 S. Broadway, #B-3
Los Angeles, CA 90012
Owner of telephone fantasy service
for homosexuals

Walton, William Theodore (Bill)
San Diego Clippers
San Diego Sports Arena
3500 Sports Arena Blvd.
San Diego, CA 92110
Prof. basketball player

Waitz, Greta
Suomen Urheiluliitto
Box 25202
B. F. 00251
Helsinki 25, Finland
Marathon runner

Wambaugh, Joseph
P.O. Box 46-B
Balboa Island, CA 92662
Author

Wang Computers
Wang Laboratories Inc.
One Industrial Ave.
Lowell, MA 01851
Dr. An Wang, Chairman of Board

Ward, Bill
Box 75
Grahamsville, NY 12740
Erotic artist

Ward, Jim
Gauntlet
8720 Santa Monica Blvd.
Los Angeles, CA 90069
Owner of jewelry store for exotic
piercings

Ward, Rachel
7319 Beverly Blvd., #1
Los Angeles, CA 90036
Actress

Warhol, Andy
19 E. 32d St.
New York, NY 10016
Artist; filmmaker

Warner, John William
U.S. Senate
Washington, DC 20510
U.S. Senator (R), Virginia,
1979–present; former husband of
Elizabeth Taylor

Warner Bros. Inc.
4000 Warner Blvd.
Burbank, CA 91505
Robert Daly, Chief Operating
Officer

Warner Communications Inc.
75 Rockefeller Plaza
New York, NY 10019
Steven J. Ross, Chairman of Board

Warner-Lambert Co.
201 Tabor Rd.
Morris Plains, NJ 07950
Ward S. Hagen, Chairman—makers
of Listerine, Rolaids, Trident, etc.

Warren, Lesley Ann
1888 Century Park East, #1400
Los Angeles, CA 90067
Actress

Warrick, Ruth
101 W. 67th St.
New York, NY 10023
Actress, Phoebe Tyler on All My
Children

Warwick, Dionne
Arista Records
6 W. 57th St.
New York, NY 10019
Singer

Washington Post
1150 15th St., NW
Washington, DC 20071
Benjamin Bradlee, Executive Editor

Washington Post Co.
1150 15th St., NW
Washington, DC 20071
Katharine Graham, Chairman of
Board

Wasserman, Lew R.
MCA Inc.
100 Universal City Plaza
Universal City, CA 91608
Business executive

Watt, James G.
Department of the Interior
18th & C Sts., NW
Washington, DC 20240
Former secretary, 1981–1983

Wayne, Patrick
15301 Ventura Blvd, #345
Sherman Oaks, CA 91403
Actor; son of John Wayne

Weathers, Carl
9255 Sunset Blvd., #610
Los Angeles, CA 90069
Actor

Weaver, Sigourney
ICM
8899 Beverly Blvd.
Los Angeles, CA 90048
Actress

Webber, Thomas Raymond
128 Fir St.
New Lenox, IL 60451
Paine Webber Jackson & Curtis,
1981–present, commodity exchange
executive

Weicker, Lowell P., Jr.
Senate Office Bldg.
Washington, DC 20510
U.S. Senator (R), Connecticut,
1971–present

Weinberger, Caspar W.
Department of Defense
The Pentagon
Washington, DC 20301
Secretary, 1981–present

Weisbord, Sam
151 El Camino
Beverly Hills, CA 90212
Theatrical agency, Chief Executive
(William Morris)

Weiskopf, Thomas Daniel
Paradise Valley, AZ 85253
Prof. golfer

Weitz, John
600 Madison Ave.
New York, NY 10022
Fashion designer

Welch, Raquel
146 Central Park West
New York, NY 10023
Actress

Welch Foods Inc.
2 S. Portage St.
Westfield, NY 14787
T. C. Whitney, President

Weld, Tuesday
% Viderman Oberman & Aosoos.
103 W. Pico Blvd.
Los Angeles, CA 90015
Actress

Welk, Lawrence
12735 Ventura Blvd., #28
Studio City, CA 91604
Orchestra leader

Weller, Peter
151 El Camino
Beverly Hills, CA 90212
Actor

Welles, Orson
% Weissberger & Harris
120 E. 56th St.
New York, NY 10022
Actor; radio & theatrical producer

We Love Lucy Fan Club
Box 480216
Los Angeles, CA 90048
Thomas J. Watson, President

West, Dottie
Capitol Records
Hollywood & Vine
Hollywood, CA 90028
Singer

Western Electric Co. Inc.
222 Broadway
New York, NY 10038
Donald E. Procknow, President

Westheimer, Dr. Ruth
WYNY
Rm. 252
30 Rockefeller Plaza
New York, NY 10020
Radio talk show sex therapist

Westinghouse Electric Corp.
Westinghouse Bldg.
Pittsburgh, PA 15222
R. E. Kirby, Chairman of Board

Westmore, Michael George
3830 Sunswept Dr.
Studio City, CA 91604
Makeup artist

Westmoreland, William
P.O. Box 1059
Charleston, SC 29402
General, head of American forces in Vietnam

Westphal, Paul
Seattle SuperSonics
419 Occidental South
Seattle, WA 98104
Prof. basketball player

Wexler, Arnie
58 Kier St.
Sayreville, NJ 08872
Vice President, national council on compulsive gambling

Whelchel, Lisa
967 N. La Cienega Blvd.
Los Angeles, CA 90069
Actress

Whirlpool Corp.
Administrative Center
Benton Harbor, MI 49022
John H. Platts, Chairman of Board

White, Betty
% Andrews & Robb Agents
Box 727
Hollywood, CA 90028
Actress

White, Byron
U.S. Supreme Court
Washington, DC 20543
Supreme Court Justice, 1962–present

White, Danny
Dallas Cowboys
6116 N. Central Expwy.
Dallas, TX 75206
Prof. football player

White, Mark
State Capitol
Austin, TX 78701
Governor of Texas (D), 1983–present

White, Rodney
5646 Frederick St.
Omaha, NE 68106
Hairiest man in America

Wiesenthal, Simon
Mestrozigasse 5
Vienna 19 Austria
Nazi hunter

Wilkins, Dominique
Atlanta Hawks
100 Techwood Dr., NW
Atlanta, GA 30303
Prof. basketball player

William, Prince
Kensington Palace
London, W8, England
Prince of England; first child of Charles & Diana

Williams, Andy
816 N. LaCienega Blvd.
Los Angeles, CA 90069
Singer

Williams, Billy Dee
8966 Sunset Blvd.
Los Angeles, CA 90069
Actor

Williams, Buck
New Jersey Nets
185 E. Union Ave.
East Rutherford, NJ 07073
Prof. basketball player

Williams, Darnell
101 W. 67th St.
New York, NY 10023
Actor

Williams, Doug
Tampa Bay Buccaneers
1 Buccaneer Pl.
Tampa, FL 33607
Prof. football player

Williams, Gus
Seattle SuperSonics
419 Occidental South
Seattle, WA 98104
Prof. basketball player

Williams, Hank, Jr.
P.O. Box 790
Cullman, AL 35055
Country music singer

Williams, John
Responsible Dating Service
C.P. Box 219
Manhattan Beach, CA 90266
President—dating club for people with herpes

Williams, Paul
151 El Camino
Beverly Hills, CA 90212
Actor

Williams, Ray
Kansas City Kings
1800 Genessee
Kansas City, MO 64102
Prof. basketball player

Williams, Robin
3920 Sunny Oak Rd.
Sherman Oaks, CA 91403
Actor; comedian

Williams, Sly
New York Knicks
Madison Square Garden Center
4 Pennsylvania Plaza
New York, NY 10001
Prof. basketball player

Williams, Treat
151 El Camino
Beverly Hills, CA 90212
Actor

Willis, Stanley
6211 Stewart Rd.
Cincinnati, OH 45227
Handcuffs & restraints collector

Wilson, Brian Douglas
2910 Lincoln Blvd.
Santa Monica, CA 90405
Recording artist; composer; record producer

Wilson, Carl Dean
% Jerry Schilling Management
8860 Evanview Dr.
Los Angeles, CA 90069
Singer

Wilson, Flip
William Morris Agency
1350 Avenue of the Americas
New York, NY 10019
Comedian

Wilson, Mary
741 S. Adam
Glendale, CA 91205
Original member of the Supremes

Wilson, Nancy
181 S. Sycamore Ave., 101
Los Angeles, CA 90036
Singer

Wilson, Pete
Senate Office Bldg.
Washington, DC 20510
U.S. Senator (R), California,
1983–present

Wilson, Peter Cecil
Chateau de Clarary
06810 Auribeau sur Siagne
France
Auctioneer

Wilson, Tom
Field Newspaper Syndicate
401 N. Wabash Ave.
Chicago, IL 60611
Cartoonist, Ziggy

Wilson, Willy
Kansas City Royals
Harry S. Truman Sports Complex
P.O. Box 1969
Kansas City, MO 64141
Prof. baseball player

Wilson Sporting Goods Co.
2223 West St.
River Grove, IL 60171
Robert H. Beeby, President

Winfield, Dave
New York Yankees
Yankee Stadium
Bronx, NY 10451
Prof. baseball player

Winger, Debra
1888 Century Park East, #1400
Los Angeles, CA 90067
Actress

Winkler, Henry
Box 1764
Studio City, CA 91604
Actor

Winkler, Irwin
10125 W. Washington Blvd.
Culver City, CA 90230
Motion picture producer

Winnebago Corp.
1233 Midway Rd.
Minasha, WI 54952
George Mader, Chief Operating
Officer

Winnebago Industries
Junctions 9 and 69
Forest City, IA 50436
John K. Hanson, Chairman of
Board

Winslow, Kellen
San Diego Chargers
9449 Friars Rd.
San Diego, CA 92120
Prof. football player

Winsten, Archer
New York Post
210 South St.
New York, NY 10002
Movie critic

Winters, Jonathan
George Spota
11151 Ophir Dr.
Los Angeles, CA 90024
Actor

213

Winters, Shelley
ICM
8899 Beverly Blvd.
Los Angeles, CA 90048
Motion picture actress

Wishingrad, Barbara
Wishgarden
P.O. Box 1304
Boulder, CO 80306
Herbalist specializing in pre- and postnatal care

Witt, Paul Junger
1438 N. Gower St.
Hollywood, CA 90028
TV producer

Wolfe, Sidney
Health Research Group
2000 P St., NW
Washington, DC 20036
Author, Stopping Valium

Wolffe, Julian
33 Riverside Dr., #14C
New York, NY 10023
Sherlock Holmes expert

Wolfman Jack (Robert Smith)
% Far West Communications
1680 Vine St., #900
Hollywood, CA 90028
Disc jockey

Women's Equal Rights Legal Defense and Education Fund
6380 Wilshire Blvd., #1404
Los Angeles, CA 90040
Gloria Allred, President

Wonder, Stevie
9000 Sunset Blvd., #617
Los Angeles, CA 90069
Musician

Wood, Mabel
3950 Chambers Rd.
RD 3
Horseheads, NY 14845
Cobweb painting expert

Wood, Ronald
Rolling Stones Records
75 Rockefeller Plaza
New York, NY 10019
Musician

Woodhouse, Barbara
Pillar Productions
8375 Fountain Ave., #308
Los Angeles, CA 90069
Dog trainer

Woodley, David
Miami Dolphins
3550 Biscayne Blvd.
Miami, FL 33137
Prof. football player

Woods, Philip Wells (Phil)
Box 278
Delaware Water Gap, PA 18327
Jazz musician

Woods, Robert
65 W. 66th St.
New York, NY 10023
Actor

Woodward, Joanne
9665 Wilshire Blvd., #200
Beverly Hills, CA 90212
Actress

Woolworth Co., F. W.
233 Broadway
New York, NY 10007
E. F. Gibbons, Chairman of Board

Wopat, Tom
120 El Camino Dr., #104
Beverly Hills, CA 90212
Actor

World Jai-Alai
3500 N.W. 37th Ave.
Miami, FL 33142
Richard P. Donovan, President

World Trade Centers Assn.
One World Trade Center, 63W
New York, NY 10048
Guy F. Tozzoli, President

Wouk, Herman
BSW Literary Agency
3255 N St., NW
Washington, DC 20007
Author

Wray, Fay
2160 Century Park East
Los Angeles, CA 90067
Actress, King Kong's girlfriend

Wright, James C., Jr.
House Office Bldg.
Washington, DC 20515
*U.S. Congressman (D), Texas,
1955–present*

W. Wrigley, Co.
410 N. Michigan Ave.
Chicago, IL 60611
William Wrigley, President

Wurlitzer Co.
403 E. Gurler Rd.
DeKalb, IL 60115
A. D. Arsen, Chairman of Board

Wyatt, Jane
151 El Camino
Beverly Hills, CA 90212
Actress

Wyeth, Andrew
Chadds Ford, PA 19317
Artist

Wyman, Jane
3970 Overland Ave.
Culver City, CA 90230
Actress

Wynette, Tammy
Jim Halsey Co. Inc.
Corporate Pl., PH
5800 E. Skelly Dr.
Tulsa, OK 74135
Singer

X

Xerox Corporation
P.O. Box 1600
Stamford, CT 06904
C. Peter McColough, Chairman of Board

Xiaoping, Deng
Office of the Chairman
Peking, China
Chairman, Communist party's advisory commission—since 1977

Y

Yablans, Frank
10201 W. Pico Blvd.
Los Angeles, CA 90064
Motion picture company executive

Yarborough, William Caleb
National Association of Stock Car
Racing
1801 Volusia Ave.
Daytona Beach, FL 32014
Prof. stock car racer

Yary, Anthony Ronald
Minnesota Vikings
9520 Viking Dr.
Eden Prairie, MN 55344
Prof. football player

Yastremski, Carl
Boston Red Sox
24 Yawkey Way
Boston, MA 02215
Former prof. baseball player

Yates, Peter
ICM
8899 Beverly Blvd.
Los Angeles, CA 90048
Film director

York, Michael (Michael York-Johnson)
Actors Equity
165 W. 46th St.
New York, NY 10036
Actor

York, Susannah
ICM
40 W. 57th St.
New York, NY 10019
Actress

Young, George Bernard, Sr.
New York Giants
Giants Stadium
East Rutherford, NJ 07073
Prof. football executive

Young, Martin D.
8421 N.W. Fourth Pl.
Gainesville, FL 32601
Parasitologist

Young, Robert
1901 Avenue of the Stars, #840
Los Angeles, CA 90067
Actor

Youngblood, Herbert Jackson, III
7282 Emerson St.
Westminster, CA 92683
Prof. athlete

Youngblood, Jack
Los Angeles Rams
2327 W. Lincoln Ave.
Anaheim, CA 92801
Prof. football player

Youngman, Henny
151 El Camino
Beverly Hills, CA 90212
Comedian

Young Men's Christian Assn. of the U.S. (YMCA)
101 N. Wacker Dr.
Chicago, IL 60606
Solon B. Cousins, Executive Director

Young Women's Christian Assn. of the U.S.A. (YWCA-USA)
135 W. 50th St.
New York, NY 10022
Sara-Alyce P. Wright, Executive Director

Yount, Robin
Milwaukee Brewers
Milwaukee County Stadium
Milwaukee, WI 53214
Prof. baseball player

Z

Zanuck, Richard Darryl
P.O. Box 900
Beverly Hills, CA 90213
Motion picture executive

Zapata, Carmen
6107 Ethel Ave.
Van Nuys, CA 91401
Actress; producer

Zappa, Frank
% Pumpko Industries Ltd.
7720 Sunset Blvd.
Los Angeles, CA 90046
Musician; composer

Zeffirelli, Franco
7950 Sunset Blvd.
Los Angeles, CA 90046
Theater & film director

Zeiller, Warren
910 Catalonia Ave.
Coral Gables, FL 33134
Aquarium executive

Zeman, Jacklyn
9441 Wilshire Blvd., #620-D
Beverly Hills, CA 90212
Actress

Zenith Radio Corp.
1000 Milwaukee Ave.
Glenview, IL 60025
Joseph S. Wright, Chairman of Board

Zero Population Growth
1346 Connecticut Ave., NW
Washington, DC 20036
Carole L. Baker, Executive Director

Zevon, Warren
% Asylum Records
962 N. La Cienega Blvd.
Los Angeles, CA 90069
Singer; songwriter

Zicree, Marc
% Bantam Books
666 Fifth Ave.
New York, NY 10019
Twilight Zone expert

Zimbalist, Efrem, Jr.
120 El Camino Dr., #104
Beverly Hills, CA 90212
Actor; producer

Zimbalist, Stephanie
409 N. Camden Dr., Suite 202
Beverly Hills, CA 90210
Actress

Zindel, Paul
% Harper & Row Inc.
10 E. 53d St.
New York, NY 10022
Author

Zisk, Richard Walter
Seattle Mariners
419 Second Ave.
Seattle, WA 98104
Prof. baseball player

Zmed, Adrian
Columbia Pictures Television
Columbia Plaza
Burbank, CA 91505
Actor

Zorn, Jim
Seattle Seahawks
5305 Lake Washington Blvd.
Kirkland, WA 98033
Prof. football player